Practical Employment Law

PRACTICAL EMPLOYMENT LAW

A Guide For Human Resource Managers

PAUL LEWIS

Copyright © Paul Lewis, 1992

The right of Paul Lewis to be identified as author of this work has been asserted in accordance with the Copyright, Designs and Patents Act 1988.

First published 1992

Blackwell Publishers
108 Cowley Road
Oxford OX4 1JF
UK

238 Main Street, Suite 501
Cambridge, Massachusetts 02142
USA

British Library Cataloguing in Publication Data
A CIP catalogue record for this book is available from the British Library.

Library of Congress Cataloging-in-Publication Data
A CIP catalogue record for this book is available from the Library of Congress.

ISBN 0–631–186794

Typeset in 11 on 13pt Plantin
by Hope Services (Abingdon) Ltd.
Printed in Great Britain by
T. J. Press Ltd, Padstow, Cornwall

This book is printed on acid-free paper

To Lew, Mina, Mary, Sarah and James

Contents

List of Figures

List of Tables

List of Statutes

List of Statutory Instruments

List of Cases

HRM: an Overview

The policies and practices which have become known as human resource management (HRM) originated in the United States some forty years ago and were initially closely associated with the two giant multinationals of IBM and Hewlett Packard. From the outset, corporations such as these offered their employees positive benefits such as good pay, single status terms and conditions and a guarantee of employment security in return for an involvement in, and commitment to the goals of the organization. This organizational commitment was, and is, at practical odds with trade-union membership and activity and, in its emphasis upon the individual employee, diluted the essential collectivism of trade unions.

This cocktail of valuable benefits to employees in return for their commitment in a context of non-unionism still remains characteristic of the IBM/Hewlett Packard 'model'. Yet not surprisingly such 'tight ships' are rare and, in the case of IBM, it has recently stumbled into serious financial difficulties requiring a significant retreat from its traditional polity of avoiding compulsory redundancies. Nor does the tight ship seem necessary. Japanese multinationals, for example, (and not only in Japan) also offer some measure of employment security in the context of HRM style policies, but with a demonstrated ability to accommodate a range of approaches to trade-union representation without any weakening of individual employee commitment.

This catholicity of HRM experience is largely explained by cultural diversity. Managerial strategists, as anybody else, need to adapt their ambitions to the constraints of what already exists. Even in the United States, management and unions seem perfectly capable of recognizing each other's legitimacy while negotiating comprehensive agreements which incorporate HRM practices. The best example of this is the experience of General Motors and the United Automobile Workers.

What really matters to the practitioner is what works, and a package of traditional policies and practices allied to the more innovative reforms associated with HRM may be more viable than a grand design.

This series is therefore mainly concerned with HRM in its much wider, looser form than the precise expression characteristic of the early US innovators and their current imitators. This covers a much wider range of experience. There will also be a pronounced emphasis on practical implementation, although each author will be encouraged to offer some vision of whole woods, even forests, as well as descriptions of individual trees.

One final comment is in order. The series is not intended to promote the principles and practices of HRM as a panacea for the ills of modern economies and societies. As any other organizational innovation, it imposes costs as well as benefits and employees have responsibilities as well as rights. It deserves attention and interest because it is there, it is widespread, and it is still growing. But private and public sector organizations, especially large ones, can endanger the wider society as well as enhance it. Their policies and practices require close scrutiny and the application of a cool scepticism if we are to avoid the all too common approach of uncritical applause. This is the spirit of this series.

Professor Brian Towers, Series Editor
Department of Human Resource Management
Strathclyde Business School

Foreword

The publishing of books on employment law seems to be the only economic activity characterized by continuous growth. Hence another text on the same theme needs careful justification.

Paul Lewis's book is among the early contributions to this new human resource management series. As such it is written in the context of HRM, in particular, how HRM can contribute towards a strategic management approach, i.e. the setting and achieving of organizational goals to which employees are committed in return for tangible rights and benefits.

At the same time, as human resource management has developed over the past twenty years, so has employment law burgeoned. Much of this law reflects the increasing emphasis upon protecting individual employees and enhancing their rights against employers by means of legislation. However, throughout the eighties and into the nineties rights, while remaining as a structure, have been increasingly rolled back in their implementation. This process has been even more evident in terms of collective rights, especially in respect of the limits imposed upon trade-union action. Furthermore, membership in the European Community is increasingly influencing and altering employment law of which the most obvious recent examples are equal value legislation, transfer of undertakings and health and safety at work.

Human resource professionals are therefore required to have a comprehensive overview and, on occasion, detailed knowledge of employment law. This requirement is best achieved in the context of a human resource management framework.

In this volume, after an introduction to the legal system, Paul Lewis guides the reader through the HRM function from recruitment, through employment and termination, explaining the legal background and implications at every stage and including guidance and advice for handling a case at industrial tribunal. Additional chapters are also included on collective labour law. Where detail is required, the comprehensive index provides easy, quick access.

The substantive merit of the book lies in its authoritative, up-to-date, practical and well-written exposition of current employment law. Its originality lies in its organization of the legal material in an HRM framework. Managers are not lawyers and they need to know employment law in a managerial context. Paul Lewis's book offers them such an opportunity.

Brian Towers

Preface

Practical Employment Law is about the legal aspects of human resource management. It takes each major function of human resource management, examines the legal context within which it takes place, and considers the possible legal implications of different types of action. The aim is to provide guidance for human resource professionals in order to help them avoid making decisions which might bring them into conflict with the law. An attempt is also made to show how the law may be of positive use to human resource managers in meeting the objectives of their organizations.

It is assumed that management will want to take a strategic approach to the use of human resources. As part of this, they will want to consider how best they can meet their legal obligations and under what circumstances, if any, they would wish to invoke the arguments or procedures of the law. This principle directs the approach adopted by *Practical Employment Law* – it hopes to perform a protective function (enabling managers to stay within the law) as well as a strategic one (allowing productive use of the law in order to meet organizational objectives).

A second principle is that an integrated approach is taken by human resource managers, so that all personnel matters are viewed as part of the overall function of effective human resource management. The comprehensive structure of *Practical Employment Law* reflects the application of this principle. Third, it is assumed that human resource managers wish to integrate the individual employee into the organization on a basis of commitment. Guidance is offered on how employment law might contribute to this process. Finally, an organic and devolved (rather than a bureaucratic and centralized) business structure is seen as part of human resource management. In this context *Practical Employment Law* points to situations where law can be used to instigate or adjust to change, and seeks to assist line management with devolved human resource management duties.

It seems certain that there will continue to be a substantial volume of employment law; indeed, the amount is likely to increase. A good knowledge of employment law is therefore an important – perhaps an increasingly important – part of the manager's kit. *Practical Employment Law* seeks to help provide this knowledge.

It also seeks to provide some indication of possible future changes in legislation. In July 1991 the government issued a green paper *Industrial Relations in the 1990s*, which contained proposals relating to industrial action, collective agreements and trades union membership, elections and finance. These proposals are mentioned at appropriate points in the text, as are aspects of the recent white paper, *People, Jobs and Opportunity* (Cm 1810, February 1992).

I wish to thank a number of people who read part or all of the early typescript and made helpful comments. Many improvements were made to the text as a result of their kindness, expertise and patience. All of these people acted in a personal rather than an official capacity, and none of them are responsible for any faults which remain. That responsibility rests solely with the author.

My thanks are due to: John Briggs, Her Majesty's Principal Inspector of Factories, based in Newcastle upon Tyne, and to Brian King, Accident Prevention Manager at the Teesside Works of British Steel plc; to Harold Tavroges, solicitor, and part-time chairman of industrial tribunals in Newcastle upon Tyne; to Sue Ward, pensions consultant, Newcastle upon Tyne, and to the staff at the Northern Regional Office of ACAS in Newcastle upon Tyne.

The editor of the *Successful HRM* series, Brian Towers, Professor of Industrial Relations at the University of Strathclyde, drew on his wealth of editorial experience to provide advice which helped to shape and focus this work. He also read and made useful comments about the text. I am greatly indebted to him. I am also indebted to the staff of Blackwell for compiling the index, and to the Controller of Her Majesty's Stationery Office for granting me permission to reproduce the Department of Employment's form for the advance notification of redundancies (see below, pp. 212–15), and the Redundancy Payments Ready Reckoner (see below, p. 204). Finally, I wish to thank Maureen Parkin for providing a first-class typescript and ensuring the smooth-running of the production timetable.

I have attempted to state the law as at 1 August 1991, although later developments have been included where this has proved possible. The law is that relating to England and Wales. Much of the legislation applies to Scotland, and has been enacted separately in Northern Ireland. Nevertheless, legislation in both countries differs from that in England and Wales to some degree and there are also differences in legal systems. Therefore, *Practical Employment Law* should not be seen as authoritative in relation to Scotland and Northern Ireland. No attempt has been made to deal with employment law in the Channel Islands and the Isle of Man.

Paul Lewis
Jesmond
Newcastle upon Tyne

List of Abbreviations

AC	Appeal Cases Reports
ACAS	Advisory, Conciliation and Arbitration Service
AIDS	Acquired Immune Deficiency Syndrome
All ER	All England Reports
anor	another (in the names of legal cases)
APEX	Association of Professional, Executive, Clerical and Computer Staffs
ASLEF	Associated Society of Locomotive Engineers and Firemen
AVC	Additional voluntary contribution
BS	British Standard
c	Chapter (in relation to statutes)
CA	Court of Appeal
CAC	Central Arbitration Committee
CBI	Confederation of British Industry
CC	County court
Ch	Chancery Division Reports
Cm	Command (numbers on official papers)
CO	Certification Officer
COIT	Central Office of Industrial Tribunals
COP	Code of practice
COSHH	Control of Substances Hazardous to Health
CRE	Commission for Racial Equality
CS	Court of Session
dB(A)	Decibels (adjusted)
DE	Department of Employment
DHSS	Department of Health and Social Security
DP	Data protection
DPA	Data Protection Act 1984

DPR	Data Protection Registrar
DSS	Department of Social Security
EA	Employment Act (various)
EAT	Employment Appeal Tribunal
EC	European Community
ECHR	European Court of Human Rights
ECJ	European Court of Justice
EDT	Effective date of termination (of employment)
EEC	European Economic Community
EO	Equal opportunities
EOC	Equal Opportunities Commission
EPA	Employment Protection Act 1975
EP(C)A	Employment Protection (Consolidation) Act 1978
EqPA	Equal Pay Act 1970
ETO	Economic, technical or organizational reason (for dismissal arising out of the transfer of an undertaking)
EWC	Expected week of confinement
FA	Factories Act 1961
FSAVC	Free standing additional voluntary contribution
FTC	Fixed-term contract
FTLR	Financial Times Law Reports
GB	Great Britain
GLR	Guardian Law Reports
GOQ	Genuine occupational qualification (RRA and SDA)
GP	General Practitioner
Green Paper	Industrial Relations in the 1990s, Cm 1602, HMSO, 1991
HC	House of Commons
High Ct	High Court
HL	House of Lords
HMSO	Her Majesty's Stationery Office
HRM	Human resource management
HSC	Health and Safety Commission
HSE	Health and Safety Executive
HSWA	Health and Safety at Work etc. Act 1974
ICR	Industrial Cases Reports
ICTA	Income and Corporation Taxes Act 1988
IDS	Incomes Data Services
IRLIB	Industrial Relations Legal Information Bulletin
IRLR	Industrial Relations Law Reports
IT	Industrial tribunal

ITR	Industrial Tribunal Reports
KB	King's Bench Division Reports
MATSA	Managerial, Administrative and Technical Staffs Association (part of the General, Municipal, Boilermakers and Allied Trades Union)
MEL	Maximum exposure level
MSF	Manufacturing, Science and Finance Union
NAPO	National Association of Probation Officers
NATFHE	National Association of Teachers in Further and Higher Education
NGA	National Graphical Association (1982)
NHS	National Health Service
NI	National Insurance
NIRC	National Industrial Relations Court
NRA	Normal retiring age
NUGSAT	National Union of Gold, Silver and Allied Trades
NUM	National Union of Mineworkers
NUR	National Union of Railwaymen
NUS	National Union of Seamen
NUTGW	National Union of Tailors and Garment Workers
OES	Occupational exposure standard
OPAS	Occupational Pensions Advisory Service
OPB	Occupational Pensions Board
ors	Others (in the names of legal cases)
OSRPA	Offices, Shops and Railway Premises Act 1963
PAYE	Pay as you earn (taxation)
PHA	Pre-hearing assessment (by an industrial tribunal)
POEU	Post Office Engineering Union
PPE	Personal protective equipment
QB	Queen's Bench Division Reports
R	Regina (in the names of legal cases)
RIDDOR	Reporting of Injuries, Diseases and Dangerous Occurrences Regulations 1985
ROIT	Regional Office of Industrial Tribunals
RP	Redundancy payment
RRA	Race Relations Act 1976
s	Section (of a statute)
SD	Sex discrimination
SDA	Sex Discrimination Act (1975, 1986)
SEA	Single European Act 1986
Ss	Sections (of a statute)

SERPS	State Earnings-Related Pension Scheme
SI	Statutory instrument
SMP	Statutory Maternity Pay
SOGAT	Society of Graphical and Allied Trades (1982)
SOSR	Some other substantial reason (for dismissal)
SR	Safety representative
SSA	Social Security Act (various)
SSAT	Social Security Appeals Tribunal
SSHBA	Social Security and Housing Benefit Act 1982
SSP	Statutory Sick Pay
SSPA	Statutory Sick Pay Act 1991
TGWU	Transport and General Workers' Union
TLR	Times Law Reports
TUA	Trade Union Act (1913, 1984)
TUC	Trades Union Congress
TULRA	Trade Union and Labour Relations Act 1974
UK	United Kingdom
UMA	Union membership agreement ('Closed Shop')
USDAW	Union of Shop, Distributive and Allied Workers
VDU	Visual display unit
WLR	Weekly Law Reports

1

The Legal System

Introduction

This chapter deals with the main sources and types of law. It describes the system of courts, and the personnel of the law. All this general legal context is important because employment law is not a completely separate branch of the law. Employment law involves general legal principles (for example, of contract) and cases may be heard in mainstream legal institutions (such as the High Court).

Employment law does, however, have some of its own specialist institutions. Foremost among these are industrial tribunals and the Advisory, Conciliation and Arbitration Service (ACAS), but there are other institutions too. This chapter describes the various specialist employment law bodies.

Sources of Law

Common law

The body of common law contains concepts and principles determined by judges through the process of deciding cases. The central legal relationship in the employment field – the contract of employment – is a common law concept. There is no Act of Parliament which says that the relationship between an employee and an employer is governed by a contract of employment. Yet it is because judges have ruled so. Case law, therefore, can be the source of major legal concepts.

It is also very important in the interpretation of the laws passed by Parliament. For example, Parliament has laid down that employee misconduct is a fair reason for dismissal, but the Act – the

Employment Protection (Consolidation) Act 1978 – does not say in detail how an employer's actions are to be judged if he or she does dismiss. Therefore the courts have established the detailed rules through case law, in this instance in *British Home Stores* v. *Burchell.*

The judges are active, therefore, both in the creation and the interpretation of law.

Statute law

The path to statute law

Statute law is derived from Parliament. It comprises Acts of Parliament, regulations and orders made under such Acts and delegated legislation, for example, bye-laws made by local government under powers given to them by Parliament.

The first step towards the making of statute law is often the issuing of a consultation document by the appropriate government department. In the employment field this is normally the Department of Employment. Consultation documents contain a date by which any interested person or organization can send in their comments. The right to comment is available to individuals as well as to those who hold positions, who may comment on behalf of their organizations. The government may or may not be influenced by these comments.

The next step is likely to be a white paper, setting out the government's proposals. Later this will be converted into a draft Act of Parliament – a bill – which will be presented to and debated by, and probably amended by, Parliament. Not only does the whole of each of the Houses of Parliament debate the bill, but also each establishes a committee to go through it in detail. The amended bill then comes back to the whole house for voting. Once passed by Parliament, the bill must receive the Royal Assent before it becomes an Act of Parliament. This does not mean it will become operational immediately. Its operation may be delayed, or different parts may start to operate at different times.

Different types of statute

Many minor and often uncontroversial legal changes need to be made and it would be cumbersome, slow and expensive if all changes required amending legislation which had to follow the full Parliamentary process. For example, the government may wish to increase the limits for redundancy pay so that they keep up with inflation. It would be a nonsense if this required a bill to be laid before Parliament, a

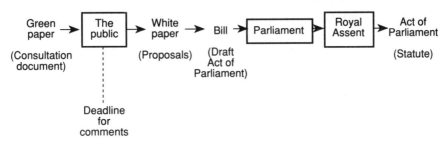

Figure 1.1 The path to statute law

committee to be established and debate and possibly amendment. Statutory instruments are a way around this problem.

Where law is expected to need extension, or change is anticipated, an Act can give the Minister power to issue orders or regulations to give effect to such changes. For example, the limit on redundancy pay is specified, but alongside it is a right for the Minister to vary it by order. Another type of statutory instrument is a set of regulations.

These are often used where an Act lays down only general provisions, but where detailed law is required for particular circumstances. A good example is the Health and Safety at Work etc. Act 1974. This lays down very general duties, for example, in section 2. Regulations issued under the Act then cover specific circumstances such as the control of substances hazardous to health.

Both orders and regulations have the full force of law and are of the same status as the Act under which they are made. Both must have Parliamentary approval using either the negative or the positive procedure. Under the former a statutory instrument will be approved unless a majority vote against it within a specified period. Under the latter, a majority vote in favour will be required if it is to become law. In neither case is there scope for amendment – the instrument is voted upon in its entirety as originally presented to Parliament. However, there may be debate.

European Community law

There is statute and case law deriving from the European Community (EC).[1] Articles of EC Treaties have direct application, as do regulations made under those articles and decisions of the European Court of Justice. Where the EC issues directives, Member States must pass their own legislation in order to comply. The Sex

Discrimination Act of 1986, Equal Pay Amendment Regulations 1983 and Transfer of Undertakings Regulations 1981 are examples of employment law enacted in Britain in order to meet EC requirements. Where a directive is not implemented by a Member State, or not fully implemented, complaints may be taken on the basis of the directive itself against organizations made responsible by the State and given special powers for providing a public service under the control of the State (*Foster and ors* v. *British Gas plc*). Moreover, where the article of a treaty is sufficiently precise, as in the case of article 119 of the Treaty of Rome, which deals with equal pay, the article itself may be used as the basis for a complaint (*Secretary of State for Scotland and Greater Glasgow Health Board* v. *Wright and Hannah*). Where there is a conflict, EC law overrides UK law.

The European law-making process is understandably more distant and complex than that of domestic Parliaments. The primary decision–making institution of the EC is the Council of Ministers which is made up of representatives of the governments of the 12 Member States. There are 76 votes in the Council, the maximum held by any one country being ten (UK, Germany, France and Italy). The executive of the EC is the Commission, which comprises full-time salaried Commissioners and their staff. The 17 Commissioners are drawn from all 12 member countries – two each from the United Kingdom, Germany, France, Italy and Spain and one each from the others. The Commission proposes legislation which is then considered by the Council of Ministers. Through the Commission, the Council consults the European Parliament.[2] This is a body elected by the voters in each country. There are 518 members, 81 of whom come from the United Kingdom. The Parliament is in fact consulted a second time (under what is called the co-operation procedure) after the Council has reached a common position, that is, an agreement in principle. The Parliament may reject, amend or accept the Council's position. In cases of rejection, the Council will need a unanimous vote in favour if it is to go against the Parliament's expressed wishes. Where the Council's position is amended, the proposal is reviewed by the Commission before being returned to the Council.

Most of the provisions of the Single European Act 1986 (operative July 1987) use this procedure and are subject to qualified majority voting (that is, 54 or more votes) in the Council. One of the exceptions, however, is the area relating to the rights and interests of employed persons, which includes the Community Charter of Fundamental Social Rights (the Social Charter). Provisions relating to technical standards are not an exception and are likely to result in a number of changes in the health and safety field. Moreover, the general improvement of health and safety at work is emphasized as an EC objective and is subject to qualified majority voting (see chapter 5).

Figure 1.2 sets out the EC legislative process in simplified form. It can be seen that the European Court of Justice (ECJ), based in Luxembourg, is the vehicle by which EC law is interpreted and enforced. The ECJ should not be confused with the European Court of Human Rights (ECHR) set up under the European Charter of Human Rights 1950 by the wider, 21-country Council of Europe. Alleged breaches of human rights are filtered by a European Commission of Human Rights and cases which have merit are then heard by the Court which sits in Strasbourg. The decisions of the European Court of Human Rights are persuasive, but are not legally binding.

The EC has recently embarked upon a 'Social Action Programme'. This is derived from the Community Charter of Fundamental Social Rights for Workers (the 'Social Charter'). The main legislative device for implementing the programme is the directive, which requires Member States to enact their own legislation within a given time period. Below is a list of the directives proposed by the Commission:

- Atypical workers, that is, part time and temporary workers. (A directive relating to the health and safety of temporary workers has already been adopted – see below, p. 138.)
- Working time.
- Collective redundancies.
- Information, consultation and participation (European Works Councils).
- Protection of workers posted to another EC country.
- Travel conditions for the disabled.
- Health and safety (ten directives have been proposed here; see below, pp. 138–9).
- Protection of young people.

These proposals may be subject to change or even rejection, and new proposals may be added. Matters concerned with the terms and conditions of employment of workers are subject to unanimous voting. However, the Social Policy Protocol agreed at Maastricht will allow some employment matters to be subject to qualified majority voting, although the UK will not be bound by EC decisions arrived at through this procedure (see p. 7). Issues concerning health and safety at work are already subject to qualified majority voting (see below, pp. 135–6).

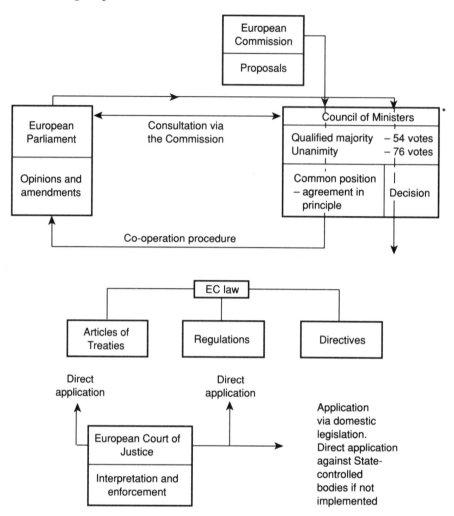

* The number of votes held by each of the 12 Member States is as follows:

United Kingdom	10	Greece	5
Germany	10	Netherlands	5
France	10	Portugal	5
Italy	10	Denmark	3
Spain	8	Ireland	3
Belgium	5	Luxembourg	2
			76

Figure 1.2 Simplified description of the EC legislative process

A Proof of Employment Relationship Directive has already been adopted (by the Council of Ministers) – see below, p. 54 – and a directive on the protection of pregnant women at work could be adopted soon.

The scope and method of EC decision-making are likely to alter as a result of the Treaty agreed at Maastricht in December 1991 and the protocols attached to it. It seems likely that EC influence will increase in areas such as economic and monetary policy and that there will be greater inter-governmental co-operation among Member States over matters such as foreign policy, defence, immigration and crime prevention. Provision is made for the wider use of qualified majority voting and the European Parliament will have a right of veto in certain areas (such as the free movement of workers). The ECJ may impose fines on Member States not complying with its judgments or failing to implement EC law.

The EC Member States agreed to a Social Policy Protocol being annexed to the Maastricht Treaty. This Protocol allows the 11 Member States apart from the UK to use a procedure for implementing the Social Charter through qualified majority voting, from 1 January 1993. The procedure will apply to matters of equal treatment, working conditions and information and consultation of the workforce. The UK will not be bound by decisions made through the use of this procedure and unanimity will still be required in relation to terms and conditions of employment more generally, with the exception of health and safety at work as already noted. Bodies representing management and labour are being encouraged to negotiate agreements which might meet the EC's requirements as well as taking into account the traditions of each Member State.

Types of Law

Criminal law

The criminal law is concerned with preventing breaches of society's rules and with punishing offenders. Those responsible for such breaches commit crimes – such as theft, murder, drunken driving and so on – and an agent of the State will prosecute them if there is sufficient evidence. In most cases that agent is the Crown Prosecution Service, although in very serious cases it may be the Director of Public Prosecutions. In the Health and Safety at work field the Health and Safety Inspector is responsible for prosecution. The test of proof in criminal law is that the case is established beyond all reasonable doubt. This is a strict test of proof reflecting the fact that guilt has associated with it a stigma, possible financial penalty (a fine)[3] or loss of liberty (a custodial sentence), although probation, community service and so on are increasingly common forms of punishment. Criminal cases are normally dealt with in the magistrates' courts, although more serious or contested cases may or must (depending upon their nature) then be sent to the Crown Court for trial.

Civil law

Meaning of civil law

The civil law is concerned with settling disputes between private parties, for example, between individuals, between individuals and organizations and between organizations. Thus, a dispute between a householder and his or her neighbour about nuisance created by the neighbour's noise would be a civil matter. So would a dispute between two individuals over a debt; between a worker and an employer over wages due; between a customer and a shop over a faulty product; or between a retail firm and one of its suppliers over late delivery. A person or organization wishing to pursue a civil claim – the plaintiff – has to establish, on the balance of probabilities, that they have suffered some loss as a result of the defendant's unlawful act, and show the extent of that loss in a claim for damages. Sometimes an order (or injunction) may be sought to stop the unlawful act (for example, an employer wanting to stop a strike, a householder wanting to stop a neighbour's noise).

Categories of civil law

There are three categories of civil law – contract, trust and tort. A contract exists where two or more parties agree to make an exchange, but it need not in every case be in writing. There must be consideration – something provided by one party in exchange for what is received from the other. In most cases this is money, such as wages for work or money for consumer items. Contracts are entered into after an offer is made by one party and accepted by another. Where there is a contract, a breach by one party may give rise to a legitimate claim for damages for breach of contract by the other. The law of trusts operates in areas where a person is charged with looking after someone else's money. A failure to properly discharge such a role can lead to claims for damages for breach of trust. This would be possible, for instance, in relation to pension fund trustees. A tort is simply a civil wrong (as opposed to a criminal wrong, that is, a crime). There are a variety of different torts, largely the product of judicial creation. Examples are:

- Nuisance
- Defamation – libel and slander
- Negligence
- Trespass – person, land, property
- Inducing a breach of contract
- Breach of statutory duty

Whereas a claim for damages for breach of contract can be pursued only where a contract exists, the law of torts applies generally, although different rules apply to different torts. Unions do much work, for example, in assisting members' claims for damages where an employer has been negligent. Here the rules are that there has to be, first, a duty of care, second, a breach of that duty and third, a loss suffered as a result. The duty of care can be established by reference to the contract of employment, and indeed statute law also lays down

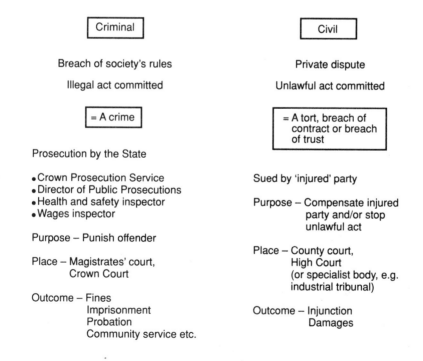

Figure 1.3 Comparison of criminal and civil law cases

such a duty (in the Health and Safety at Work etc. Act 1974). By failing in his or her duty of care the employer has committed a tort – the tort of negligence. As is noted later, unions commit torts when they engage in industrial action.

Relationship between criminal and civil law

In general there is little relationship between the two systems. As already noted, they have different standards of proof. Moreover, cases take place in different courts and the atmosphere as well as the outcome is different. However an important factor is that one event can give rise to both criminal and civil proceedings. If, for example, in the workplace a hole is left uncovered without being cordoned off and without any warning signs and a worker falls into it, injures their back and is off work and loses money, that worker may pursue a civil case to claim damages for losses occuring because of the employer's negligence. At the same time the factory inspector may feel that the employer's behaviour constitutes a crime – a failure to perform the duties laid down in the Health and Safety at Work etc. Act 1974, and may decide to prosecute. The civil case will be heard in the county court or High Court, the criminal case probably in the magistrates' court. The criminal system tends to be less slow than the civil system so these cases will be heard at different times as well as in different places. The civil court will decide whether there has been negligence, and if so what damages are appropriate. The criminal case will decide if the employer is in breach of the Health and Safety at Work etc. Act 1974. Similarly with a car accident there may be civil and criminal cases arising from one event, and the plaintiff in the civil case is not always kept informed about developments in the criminal case. Occasionally, where damages are a relatively minor matter, they may be simply added on to the criminal case. For example, a publican who was fiddling the brewery was prosecuted for fraud. The magistrates also dealt with a small compensation claim by the brewery as well as judging the criminal matter.

It is, perhaps, the civil law which is more likely to impinge upon the work of the human resource manager, particularly through unfair dismissal and other protective legislation. However, the criminal law plays a significant role in relation to health and safety at work and may be relevant to other types of employment situation. For example, picketing may give rise to various criminal offences. Similarly, it is a crime to pay less than the minimum wage in those industries where this is determined by law. In view of the current debate about pay policy, it is perhaps worth noting that there were two periods in the 1960s when a breach of government pay policy constituted a crime.

The System of Courts in England and Wales

The system is divided broadly into criminal and civil sections, although in practice there is a degree of overlap. The jurisdiction of the different courts is set out briefly below: (the specialist employment law bodies are described on pp. 16–26).

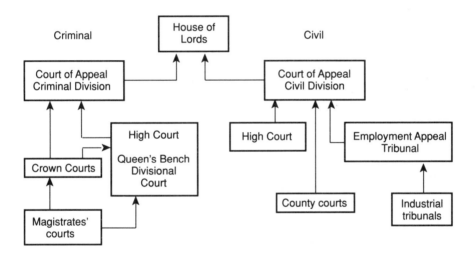

Figure 1.4 The courts system in simplified form

Magistrates' courts

These deal with the vast majority of criminal cases. Proceedings are either summary – dealt with in the magistrates' court – or committal, where the magistrates conduct a preliminary enquiry before committing the accused for trial in the Crown Court. In practice, there are now very few preliminary inquiries; in most committals there is no inquiry at all. There is a hearing only if the defence requests it. The summary procedure is used for less serious cases, such as minor theft, drunkenness in a public place and many road traffic offences, while committal is used for more serious offences. The magistrates also have responsibility for some civil matters, for instance, maintenance orders and certain other aspects of family law, and licensing.

Crown Courts

Crown Courts hear appeals on questions of fact from summary cases in the magistrates' courts and deal with indictable offences, that is, where the offence is more serious and the charges are set out in detail. Except on appeal, a jury is present if the defendant pleads not guilty. Magistrates often sit with judges in the Crown Court. Some cases are sent by the magistrates to the Crown Court for sentencing because of the limited sentencing powers in the magistrates' courts.

County courts

These have a wide range of functions and are the main civil court. A large majority of civil cases start here, although fewer than 5 per cent result in actual trials, cases usually being settled by the parties. Cases in contract and most types of tort can be dealt with in the county courts, as well as adoption, bankruptcy, divorce, trust disputes, the winding up of companies and the land and estates of deceased people. Since 1973 the county court has operated a small claims procedure in which individuals can represent themselves. As a result of the Courts and Legal Services Act 1990, there has been a significant extension of the county courts' jurisdiction.[4] Thus, claims for damages in respect of personal injuries must now be commenced in the county courts if the value of the action is less than £50,000 (previously £5,000). Actions with a value of less than £25,000 will normally be tried in the county courts and those valued at £50,000 or more in the High Court. Various criteria (such as complexity of the case) are set out for determining where actions involving sums between these figures should be heard. Many more employment cases, including for example, claims for damages for breach of the contract of employment and actions in debt for wages owed, as well as claims for damages for personal injuries, will now be tried in the county courts rather than in the High Court.

High Court

This comprises three divisions – Queen's Bench, Chancery and Family. The Queen's Bench Division hears all cases in contract and in tort. The Chancery Division's work includes land, financial matters (such as taxation) and company law. The Family Division's remit takes in cases involving children and those involving matrimonial matters. Each of the three divisions has a 'divisional' court. The Queen's Bench Division divisional court hears criminal appeals from the Crown and magistrates' courts. It also exercises the supervisory jurisdiction of the High Court over inferior courts, tribunals and public officials, including local authorities. This is known as judicial review. It is done by means of prerogative orders:

- *certiorari* – quashing unlawful decisions.
- *mandamus* – instructing a public body to carry out its statutory duty.
- *prohibition* – instructing an inferior court to stop hearing a case which is not within its jurisdiction.

In practice, the foremost of these is the most relevant to employment law because it has been sought to quash dismissal decisions. A decision may be quashed if:

- the body making it had no jurisdiction or was exceeding its jurisdiction;
- the rules of natural justice were not followed, for example, someone was a judge in their own cause, or a person was given no opportunity to state their case (see below, pp. 179–80);
- there is an error on the face of the record, that is, a mistake of law in the written reasons for the decision;
- the body making the decision took into account matters that they should not have taken into account, or failed to consider matters that they should have considered;
- the decision was unreasonable, such that no reasonable authority would have come to it (for instance, the redundancies declared by Liverpool City Corporation as a result of setting an illegal rate (see below, p. 198).

To obtain a judicial review the person applying must have *locus standi* – that is, be affected by the decision about which they are complaining.

Important features of the system

The distinction between common and statute law
As far as the civil law is concerned it should be noted that the courts system reflects the division between statute and common law. Thus common law employment cases (such as damages for breach of contract) have to be pursued through the common law courts (county court or High Court) while cases based on breaches of statute (such as

claims for compensation for unfair dismissal) have to be dealt with by statute law bodies (such as industrial tribunals). However, this is not universally true, a number of breaches of statutory duty by trades unions (for example in respect of elections) being within the jurisdiction of the High Court. (The statutory Certification Officer also has jurisdiction but is limited to making declarations.) Moreover, the government is proposing to extend the jurisdiction of industrial tribunals to cover certain contractual matters.[5]

Appeals

A major feature of the system is the right of appeal. This is granted by the body which has just decided the case or by the appeal body itself. Appeals go to the appropriate division of the Court of Appeal, where they will be heard by three judges, and may go to the House of Lords which constitutes a court comprising five law lords. On matters involving EC law an appeal to the European Court of Justice may be possible.

Precedent

In deciding a case, attention will be paid to whether similar cases have already been decided by the courts. Precedent can be ignored if there is some difference between the cases being considered, that is, one case is distinguished from another. Otherwise precedent will usually apply unless the court has the authority to overturn an earlier decision on the grounds that it was wrong. Courts are normally bound by the precedents set by other courts which are of higher authority, for example, the Court of Appeal is bound by House of Lords decisions and the High Court by Court of Appeal decisions.

The Personnel of the Law

Solicitors

Solicitors have to pass the examinations of their professional body – the Law Society – and obtain a certificate if they wish to practice. Usually they are self-employed, often in partnerships. They tend to be generalists rather than specialists, although as law firms grow in size some specialization is occurring. A large majority are in private practice. Most of the others are salaried employees working in private industry or in public authorities such as local government. Solicitors are not allowed to act as advocates in the higher courts (for example, Crown Court, High Court and above), although recent reforms may alter this to some extent.[6]

Barristers

Barristers have a monopoly of representation in the higher courts, although this may now be at an end. Occasionally they can also be seen in the humble surroundings of industrial tribunals. They tend to be specialists both in the practice of advocacy and in terms of particular areas of law, although the latter is not always true. They need to pass their professional body – Bar Council – examinations in order to practice. They do not deal directly with the client. The client deals with the solicitor, who then hires (and pays) the barrister. Barristers are referred to as Counsel, and senior barristers as Queen's Counsel, entitling them to use the letters QC after their name and to be referred to as 'silks'. Barristers are self-employed, working in chambers, but are not allowed to form partnerships with each other.

Judges

Judges are drawn primarily from the ranks of practising barristers. Most of them are assigned to geographical circuits (hence circuit judges) taking in both county court and Crown Court work. Judges are appointed by the Queen on the advice of the Lord Chancellor. Senior judges, such as those who sit in the Court of Appeal, are appointed by the Queen on the advice of the Prime Minister, but the Lord Chancellor is consulted. Below the level of the circuit judge there are junior judicial posts in the Crown and county courts respectively. Immediately senior to the circuit judge (Judge Wisely) is the High Court judge (Mr Justice Wisely, or Wisely J).

Magistrates

Magistrates are one of the most visible examples of 'ordinary' people being involved in the administration of the law. They are appointed by the Lord Chancellor on the advice of local advisory committees. They are often people prominent in local life, for example, in political parties or other voluntary bodies such as charities or trades unions. They are appointed for their soundness of judgment and responsible attitude rather than any legal knowledge. In large cities there is often a full-time, salaried (stipendiary) magistrate.

The Specialist Institutions of Employment Law

Advisory, Conciliation and Arbitration Service (ACAS)

ACAS was set up by the Employment Protection Act 1975 and is financed by government. However, it is independent in the sense that its activities are not directed by government. It prefers to operate through the use of voluntary methods. Like the other statutory bodies of employment law its functions are regulated by statute. Its objectives are to improve industrial relations, especially by developing, and where necessary reforming, collective bargaining machinery, and extending collective bargaining. This means it has a brief to improve the procedures and institutions used by employers and unions to settle employees' terms and conditions, as well as any disputes. It is also charged with extending the range of issues subject to collective bargaining, and the spread of bargaining. The latter would involve workers being unionized and unions being recognized by employers in hitherto non-union workplaces. There was a legal procedure to help achieve this, the Grunwick case being the best-known example of its use (see below pp. 227–8). The relevant law was repealed in 1980 after having had only a minimal impact. ACAS can still help in recognition disputes, but will be able to get involved properly only if the employer is willing, there being no legal supports for recognition.

ACAS is governed by a council comprising employers, trades union officers and academic industrial relations specialists. The council members are all part-time. In addition, ACAS has a full-time chairman, and staff based at a head office in London and various regional offices.

Because ACAS has a role to play in the settlement of major disputes and at such times is high-profile in terms of media attention, there is a danger of seeing the resolution of major disputes as its main activity. In fact, it has a number of functions as laid down in the Employment Protection Act 1975. These are as follows:

- Conciliation in trade disputes.[7]
- Arbitration.
- Conciliation in cases of individual complaints to tribunals.
- Advice.

- Enquiry.
- Production of codes of practice.

It is important to recognize the difference between processes such as conciliation and arbitration. If the services of ACAS are used, it will be necessary to establish terms of reference. This will always be the case when a third-party is being used. The minimum involvement of a third-party in industrial relations problems is probably when advice is sought and nothing more. ACAS advice services are available – free – to individual employees, union officials and employers.

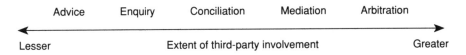

Figure 1.5 Forms of third-party assistance

Enquiry is a method by which government seeks to resolve important disputes. An enquiry puts pressure on the parties to settle; but more importantly it helps clarify points of dispute and identify avenues through which solutions might be reached. Reports of enquiries usually attract media attention.

Conciliation means bringing the sides together. A crucial point here is that the conciliator does not make decisions – the parties themselves – unions and employers – do this. Conciliation can be taken a little further by a process known as mediation. Here a third-party will suggest solutions – but the parties still make the decision. Finally, arbitration is quite different. Here the parties have decided that it is impossible for them to reach an agreement. The arbitrator is asked to make a decision. He or she, therefore, imposes a solution upon them. None of these are legally-enforceable decisions. Their ability to bind depends ultimately on the willingness of the parties to accept them; they are sometimes described as being 'morally binding'.

Conciliation is performed in trade disputes (that is, disputes between workers and their employer over matters of employment) and in cases where individuals complain to industrial tribunals (for example, over unfair dismissal). Most of the ACAS work is performed by its full-time staff. An exception is its arbitration role, where it uses a panel of part-time arbitrators, usually academic industrial relations experts.

ACAS has a responsibility to produce codes of practice as required under statute. It produced three in the late 1970s – disciplinary procedures, time off for union officials and disclosure of information to unions for bargaining purposes. The time off code has been revised recently to take account of changes brought about by the Employment Act 1989 (see below, pp. 231–3). Also, ACAS has issued detailed advice to supplement its code of practice on discipline (see below, pp. 177–80). More recently, codes of practice have been produced by the Department of Employment, reflecting the government's desire to bypass ACAS because of its consensus approach to industrial relations and the involvement of union leaders on its governing body.[8] These have dealt with picketing, closed shop agreements and arrangements and trades union ballots and industrial action. Codes of practice can be important. A breach will not give rise to any legal liability in itself, but in a case before a court or tribunal because of the infringement of an Act or regulation, the breach can be cited and if relevant must be taken into account by the body judging the case. More generally codes of practice are useful in encouraging good industrial relations.

Industrial Tribunals[9]

These were originally set up under the Industrial Training Act 1964 to hear employers' appeals against levies made against them under that Act. In 1965 the responsibility for redundancy payments disputes was added. The 1971 Industrial Relations Act introduced unfair dismissal, which operated from the end of February 1972. Since that time, unfair dismissal claims have made up the vast majority of the cases heard by tribunals. Subsequently equal pay, sex and race discrimination and other cases were also put within the tribunals' jurisdiction.

The jurisdiction of industrial tribunals is found in United Kingdom (UK) statutes, but it now appears that complaints may be pursued directly on the basis of European law in the absence of a UK statutory right (see p. 4 above). Some common law jurisdiction is likely to be added in the future (see below, p. 296). The current jurisdiction of industrial tribunals on the basis of UK statutes is as follows:

1 *Unfair dismissal*
   (a) Complaints of unfair dismissal.
   (b) Refusal to give written reasons for dismissal.
2 *Health and safety at work*
   (a) Appeals against improvement and prohibition notices.
   (b) Time off work with pay for union safety representatives.
   (c) Right to receive pay on suspension on medical grounds.

3 *Race relations*
   (a) Complaints of race discrimination in the employment field.
   (b) Appeals against non-discrimination notices.
   (c) Applications by the Commission for Racial Equality (CRE) relating to discriminatory advertisements, instructions to discriminate and pressure to discriminate.
   (d) Applications by the CRE prior to county court actions.
4 *Equal pay, sex discrimination and maternity*
   (a) Complaints of breaches of the Equal Pay Act 1970 (as amended).
   (b) Complaints of discrimination on grounds of sex or marital status in the employment field.
   (c) Appeals against non-discrimination notices.
   (d) Applications by the EOC relating to discriminatory advertisements, instructions to discriminate and pressure to discriminate.
   (e) Applications by the EOC prior to county court actions.
   (f) Time off work for antenatal care.
   (g) Decisions on equal access clauses under the Occupational Pension Schemes (Equal Access to Membership) Regulations 1976.

Complaints of unfair dismissal for reasons connected with pregnancy will fall within (b) above, or, if there is two years' or more qualifying employment, under the unfair dismissal provisions. The same is true of selection for redundancy on grounds of pregnancy. A failure to allow a woman to return to work following absence because of maternity is also within the unfair dismissal provisions.

5 *Redundancy, reorganization and transfers of undertakings*
   (a) Complaints that a recognized, independent trade union has not been consulted about proposed redundancies.
   (b) Right to receive payment under a protective award made by an industrial tribunal.
   (c) Right to receive a redundancy payment and questions relating to the amount of such payments.
   (d) Paid time off in the event of redundancy to look for other work or to make arrangements for training.
   (e) Complaints of failure to inform or consult with trades unions in cases of transfers of undertakings.
   (f) Complaints of failure to pay compensation arising out of (e) above.
   (g) Compensation for loss of office on reorganization under various statutes such as Local Government (Compensation) Regulations 1974 and British Transport (Compensation to Employees) Regulations 1970.
   (h) Right to be paid by the Secretary of State certain debts owed by an insolvent employer.

(i) Right to be paid by the Secretary of State occupational pension scheme contributions owing on behalf of employees of insolvent employers.

(j) Cases whare a redundancy payment is sought from the National Insurance Fund.

(k) Redundancy payments for civil servants.

Complaints that a redundancy involved unfair selection or was otherwise unreasonable fall within the unfair dismissal provisions. The same is true of complaints that dismissal occurred because of the transfer of an undertaking.

6 *Pay and other terms*

(a) Failure to give written particulars of the main terms of employment.

(b) Failure to provide an itemized pay statement.

(c) Failure to provide guarantee pay during lay-offs.

(d) Unauthorized deductions from wages (or repayments)

(e) Wages deductions (or repayments) made outside the 12-month time limit.

(f) Failure to notify the worker of total liability in cases of repayments for cash shortages or stock deficiencies.

(g) Payments or deductions exceeding 10 per cent of gross pay.

7 *Trades union membership or non-membership*

(a) Unjustifiable discipline by a trades union.

(b) Unreasonable exclusion or expulsion from a union in a closed shop.

(c) Right of a union to hold secret ballots on an employer's premises.

(d) Action short of dismissal taken for union membership or activities, or to compel union membership or payments in lieu of such membership.

(e) Paid time off for union duties.

(f) Time off for union activities.

(g) Interim relief where dismissal is for union membership or activities or non-membership.

(h) Unlawful refusal of employment on grounds related to union membership or non-membership.

Complaints of dismissal for union membership or activities, or non-membership, fall within the unfair dismissal jurisdiction. The same is true for selection for redundancy on these grounds and for cases involving dismissal for not making payments in lieu of union membership.

8 *Other*

(a) Time off for public duties.

(b) Failure to consult recognized, independent unions over an application for a contracting-out certificate relating to an occupational pension scheme (including determination of questions of independence and recognition).

(c) Appeals against training levies.

(d) Appeals formerly heard by referees or boards of referees under certain statutory provisions.

It should be noted that the 1991 Green Paper proposes (p. 24) that individuals should have the right to apply to an industrial tribunal for a remedy where they have been excluded from a trades union because of previous membership of another union or because some other union has sole recruitment rights in respect of their present employment.

Employment Appeal Tribunal (EAT)

Appeals against industrial tribunal decisions can be made to the EAT in most cases only on a point of law (that is, not generally on the grounds that the tribunal got its facts wrong). The appeal will need to show some incorrect legal interpretation, approach or procedure by the tribunal, or that no reasonable tribunal could have made the decision it did on the basis of the evidence before it.

Despite its modest sounding title, the EAT has the status of the High Court. It comprises a High Court judge, a senior union-nominated person, and a senior employer nominee. Sometimes there may be a tribunal of five rather than three people. This might occur where the EAT is deciding an issue which has hitherto been the subject of conflicting EAT judgments. Appeals have to be made within 42 days of the publication of the industrial tribunal decision.

Central Arbitration Committee (CAC)

The CAC was set up by the Employment Protection Act, 1975.[10] It is a standing arbitral body comprising a chairman (usually a lawyer), a Trades Union Congress (TUC) nominee and a Confederation of British Industry (CBI) nominee. There is no appeal from CAC decisions but they may be subject to judicial review. These days the CAC has a very limited role. Its main work is determining complaints by unions that employers have not disclosed information for bargaining purposes. (See below, pp. 233–5).

Certification Officer

The Certification Officer was established as a result of the Employment Protection Act (EPA) 1975, commenced operation on 1 February 1976,[11] and replaced the Registrar of Friendly Societies. His office is part of the Department of Employment and he is an independent statutory authority. The Certification Officer's role is to exercise the functions specified in various statutes, and comprises the following:

1 *Trades union political activities*
   (a) Ensuring compliance with the statutory requirements for adopting political objects and operating political funds.
   (b) Approving political fund rules, including any changes.
   (c) Approving the ballot rules of unions.
   (d) Dealing with complaints about breaches of political fund rules.
   (e) Dealing with complaints about political fund ballots.
2 *Trades union mergers*
   (a) Ensuring compliance with procedures for amalgamation, transfer of engagements and change of name.
   (b) Dealing with complaints from members about the conduct of merger ballots.
3 *Union listing and independence*
   (a) Maintaining lists of trades unions (and employers' associations).
   (b) Determining whether trades unions are independent.
4 *Union financial and administrative matters*
   (a) Ensuring that trades unions and employers' associations have accounting records, have their accounts audited and submit annual returns.
   (b) Ensuring that unions' superannuation schemes for members are actuarially examined.
The government has recently proposed an increase in the Certification Officer's powers in this area.
5 *Membership registers and principal executive committee etc. elections*
   (a) Ensuring that unions keep up-to-date membership registers and that they are open for inspection by members.
   (b) Dealing with complaints about union elections to principal executive and related positions.
   (c) Dealing with complaints about membership registers.
6 *Public funding for union ballots*
   (a) Reimbursing certain union expenditure on ballots (see below, pp. 267–8).

As a result of changes introduced by section 22 of the Employment Act 1988 the CO may now restrict disclosure of the identity of complainants. He or she may also make payments in connection with the expenses of claimants attending hearings (for example, travel, accommodation, loss of earnings). These are payable only to complainants (not to their representatives, nor to representatives of the respondent unions) in cases involving complaints about union elections, mergers, political rules and membership registers. The 1988 Act also offers protection to trades union members making complaints to the CO. Such complaints fall within the definition of matters for which discipline would be unjustifiable (see below, pp. 259–61).

Standing commissions

Commissioner for the Rights of Trade Union Members
The Commissioner was established by virtue of section 20 of the EA 1988.

Scope of the Commissioner's assistance Court proceedings that can qualify for assistance from the Commissioner are set out in the Employment Act 1988. They all relate to denials by trades unions of the statutory rights of members.

The Commissioner may grant assistance in connection with applications to the court which arise out of complaints by a union member that his union:

- has, without the support of a properly conducted secret ballot, authorized or endorsed industrial action in which he and other members are likely to be (or have been) induced to take part;
- has not observed statutory requirements in respect of elections to its principal executive committee;
- has applied its funds for party political purposes in breach of statutory requirements;
- has failed to comply with the rules approved by the Certification Officer in any ballot, or proposed ballot, on the use of funds for party political purposes;
- has failed to bring or continue any proceedings to recover union property applied to pay or compensate any individual for any penalty imposed for an offence or for contempt of court;
- trustees have caused or permitted, or propose to cause or permit, any unlawful application of the union's property;
- has denied his statutory right to inspect its accounting records;
- has not observed statutory requirements in connection with membership registers.

Forms of assistance Assistance provided by the Commissioner may include:

- paying for any legal advice and/or representation; or
- making arrangements for such advice and/or representation to be provided; or
- a combination of both of the above.

Qualifications for assistance In general, a person will be eligible to bring proceedings if:

- they were a member of the union concerned at the time when the unlawful act was committed; and

- the act complained of was unlawful at the time it took place.

A union member who applies for the Commissioner's assistance is protected against being disciplined by their union because they have done so.

Changes introduced by the Employment Act 1990 The words 'assisted by the Commissioner for the Rights of Trade Union Members' may appear in the title of proceedings after the name of the person being assisted. Presumably this is to hasten the listing of the case.[12] Furthermore, the Commissioner is now able to assist union members in cases of alleged breaches or threatened breaches of certain union rules, *viz*: those relating to:

- appointment or election to, or removal from office;
- disciplinary proceedings, including expulsion;
- the authorizing or endorsing of industrial action
- the balloting of members;
- the application of the union's funds or property;
- the imposition, collection or distribution of any levy for the purposes of industrial action;
- the constitution or proceedings of any committee, conference or other body.

For assistance, the breach must (or may) affect members other than the applicant, or similar breaches have affected (or may affect) other members.[13]

Decisions to assist The Commissioner has discretion, and can assist in cases which may not be successful if they involve a point of principle, are complex, or raise a matter of substantial public interest. The Commissioner must assist if the case follows a CO decision about a union election, membership register or political fund ballot and there is a reasonable prospect of obtaining an order.

Recovery of money Where an assisted person knowingly made a false statement to the Commissioner, or where they recklessly made a statement which was false, the Commissioner may recover the cost of the assistance. If an assisted person has costs or expenses ordered in their favour, or these are part of an agreed settlement, the Commissioner may recover the cost of assistance from these.

Race and sex discrimination

In addition, the Equal Opportunities Commission (equal pay and sex discrimination) and the Commission for Racial Equality (race relations) have responsibilities in the employment field as well as in other fields. Each has the aims of working towards the elimination of discrimination and of promoting equality of opportunity in its respective sphere. There is also a responsibility to review the working of the legislation and propose changes if necessary. The role and powers of the two organizations are also the same:

- Research and education.
- Producing annual reports.
- Conducting formal investigations and issuing non-discrimination notices.
- Seeking injunctions to stop discrimination which has been declared unlawful by an industrial tribunal.
- Applying to industrial tribunals for declarations, for example, in the case of discriminatory advertisements.
- Providing assistance to individuals (including representation at industrial tribunal hearings).
- Production of codes of practice. There is a sex discrimination code of practice and a race relations code.

Health and Safety Commission
The Commission began to operate in 1974 and has the following general duties:

- To assist and encourage persons concerned with matters relevant to HSWA's general purposes to further those purposes. (The Act's general purposes are to secure the health, safety and welfare of persons at work and to protect those not at work from the activities of persons at work.)
- To make arrangements for and encourage research, publication of research findings, provision of information and training in relation to the Act's purposes.
- To provide an advisory and information service for those concerned with the Act's purposes.
- To make proposals for regulations.

The Commission reports to and is under the direction of the Secretary of State for Employment. Members of the Commission are appointed by the Secretary of State from among those concerned with, or knowledgeable about, health and safety at work.

The Health and Safety Executive (HSE) is the Commission's operational arm and includes the various inspectorates – factories, mines and quarries, nuclear installations and so on. (The role and powers of inspectors are dealt with in chapter 4). The Health and Safety Commission is responsible for guiding other enforcement agencies for example, local authorities, which are outside the HSE.

The medical arm of the HSE is the Employment Medical Advisory Service.

Wages councils

These are statutory bodies comprising equal numbers of employers' and workers' representatives and up to five independent members, one of whom is the chairman. The function of a wages council is to set minimum wages for workers in a particular industry. The industries covered by the wages council scheme include clothing manufacture, catering and retail distribution. An employer paying less than the statutorily-fixed minimum wage will be guilty of a criminal offence. The scheme is enforced by the wages inspectorate. (See below, pp. 66–7).

Notes

1 Technically, there are three European communities: the Coal and Steel Community (set up by the Treaty of Paris, 1951), the Economic Community (Rome, 1957) and the Atomic Energy Community (Rome, 1957). Operationally there is a unified structure combining all three communities, and the term European Community (EC) is commonly used to refer to this.
2 There is also an Economic and Social Committee, which has to be consulted on proposals relating to economic or social matters. The committee is an advisory body made up of representatives of employers, unions and consumers. It has 189 members of whom 24 come from the UK.
3 Section 17 of the Criminal Justice Act 1991 *c.* 53, provides that the maximum amounts specified in the standard scale of fines shall be as follows:

Level	£
1	200
2	500
3	1,000
4	2,500
5	5,000

The new scale operates from October 1992.

4 Courts and Legal Services Act, 1990 *c.* 41. See The High Court and County Courts Jurisdiction Order, SI 1991/724, issued under Ss. 1 and 120 of the Act, and operative from 1 July 1991.

5 This could be done by an order bringing into operation s. 131 of the EP(C)A 1978 but new legislation seems likely.

6 Courts and Legal Services Act 1990, *c.* 41.

7 The term trade dispute in relation to ACAS conciliation and arbitration is defined in EPA s. 126A and is wider than the definition in s. 29 of TULRA which governs the question of trade union immunity. See below, p. 236.

8 Under s. 3 of EA 1980. EA 1990 allows the Secretary of State to amend or revoke ACAS and DE codes subject to Parliamentary approval.

9 See chapter 12 'Handling an industrial tribunal case' for more detail.

10 EPA, s. 10 and Schedule 1.

11 EPA, s. 7.

12 EA 1990, s. 11.

13 EA 1990, s. 10 (5).

2

Recruitment, Selection and Appointment

Employment of Workers who are Subject to Specific Legislation

Disabled workers

This is the only area of law where employers are actually required to employ a particular category of worker.[1] The Disabled Persons (Employment) Act 1944 established a voluntary register of disabled people. Employers with 20 or more workers have a duty to employ a quota of people with disabilities who are registered under the Act. The quota is three per cent. Government departments and the National Health Service (NHS) are excluded.

It is not an offence to be below the quota, but in this situation an employer has a further duty to engage suitably-registered disabled people if any are available when vacancies arise. An employer who is below the quota must not engage anyone other than a registered disabled person without first obtaining a permit from the Department of Employment (DE). Nor must an employer dismiss a registered disabled person without reasonable cause if below quota, or if he would fall below quota as a result of the dismissal.

A permit may be issued to enable employers to fill immediate vacancies if there are no suitable registered disabled people available. A more general permit may be issued allowing employers to recruit a specified number of people in a six-month period providing the DE is notified of the vacancies and any registered disabled people who apply are considered sympathetically.

The legislation allows certain occupations to be reserved for people with disabilities. This is the Designated Employments Scheme. Entry into the occupations of car park attendant and passenger electric lift attendant is reserved for registered disabled people, and these people do not count towards fulfilment of the quota.

Employers covered by the legislation must keep records and these must be available for inspection by officials of the DE. Under separate legislation, companies employing an average of more than 250 employees in the financial year must include in their directors' report a statement about the employment of people with disabilities.[2] This applies to disabled people generally and is not restricted to the registered disabled.

There is a code of practice on the employment of disabled people but it has no legal status.[3] The code encourages public sector employers not covered by the quota scheme to adopt its requirements and states that the three per cent should be applied to all the disabled people within the workforce rather than just to the registered disabled.

Foreign nationals

If an employer wishes to employ a foreign national, the first consideration will be whether or not a work permit is required. A work permit will not be required if the person is an EC national, or falls into one of a number of categories of commonwealth citizen, for example, those who can show that one of their grandparents was born in the UK. A limited number of others may work permit-free, for instance, representatives of overseas firms. To be such a representative and thus be exempt from the need for a work permit the person's overseas business must still be fully operational at the time of entry (*R. v. Immigration Appeal Tribunal ex parte Lokko*). It is not unlawful discrimination for an employer to require proof of the applicant's right to work in the UK (*Dhatt v. McDonald's Hamburgers Ltd*).

Generally, a non-EC national will require a work permit as well as meeting any other requirements e.g. passport, visa etc. An employer wanting to employ such a person will have to apply for a work permit on his behalf, specifying the name of the worker and the job to be done. Permits are normally granted for jobs where skilled or professional workers are required. (The category 'key worker' was widened with effect from 1 October 1991.) An employer will need to show that the vacancy cannot be filled from normal sources, including from EC nationals. An application should be made at least eight weeks before employment is due to commence, and proof of the worker's skills, qualifications and experience should be provided. A new 'fast-track' application procedure was introduced in 1991 for cases which clearly merit approval. Offers of jobs to foreign nationals should be conditional upon them obtaining a work permit and meeting any other entrance requirements. Permission is also needed from the DE if there is to be a change of job.

It is a condition of granting the permit that the worker must have terms and conditions no less favourable than other workers in the same job in that area. The worker will be covered by UK employment legislation in the same way as any other worker, including discrimination law. If the worker is in breach of the terms of the permit, any dismissal for this reason may fall under the heading of 'statutory bar' in dismissal law (see below, pp. 171 and 175). However, it will need to meet the test of reasonableness. Continuing to work in breach of the conditions of the permit may make the contract of employment illegal, and therefore unenforceable.

Women, children and young persons

Employment of children and young persons

In law, anyone under the age of 18 years is a minor, and anyone under the minimum age for leaving school is a child. Anyone over minimum school leaving age but under the age of majority is a young person.

As far as children are concerned, employment below the age of thirteen is generally unlawful.[4] Employment in relation to children is defined to include working without reward providing the trade or occupation is carried out for profit.[5] A child must not lift, carry or move anything so heavy as is likely to cause injury to them.[6] Local authorities have powers to supervise the employment of children (for example, to require registration of employment) and may restrict or prohibit employment.[7] They can also pass bye-laws restricting the employment of children.[8] The precise legal requirements in relation to the employment of children can, therefore, vary from area to area.

The Employment of Children Act 1973 provides for regulations to be made to standardize the position nationally, but no regulations have yet been made.[9] Where children are employed in performances a set of regulations does apply.[10] The general legislation restricts not only the type of work on which children can be employed but also their hours. This is dealt with below, p. 72. Work experience is discussed below, pp. 275–6

Much legislation relating to the employment of young persons was repealed by the Employment Act 1989.[11] The Act removed all specific statutory restrictions on the hours and holidays of young persons and removed some of the restrictions on the work that young people can do. However, it did not remove those restrictions on the employment of young persons which are necessary for health, safety and welfare purposes, for example, in respect of working with dangerous machinery or hazardous substances. Anyone aged under 18 years is prohibited from working in places selling alcohol (except bars which are solely the subject of table licences) and in betting shops.[12]

In general, minors do not have the capacity to enter into a binding contract. They can, however, enter into such a contract if the contract is for 'necessaries' (that is, the supply of goods and services) and is for the minor's benefit. Thus, an employment contract will not be binding upon a minor unless the contract is, on the whole, beneficial to them, but will be binding upon the employer.

Employment of women

The Employment Act 1989 lifted various restrictions on the employment of women, who may now, for example, work underground in mines.[13]

Nevertheless, some protective legislation remains. There is still a prohibition upon employing women in certain lead-manufacturing processes, there are still restrictions under the Ionising Radiations Regulations and it remains unlawful to employ a woman in a factory within four weeks of her giving birth.[14] The full list is contained in Schedule 1 to the Employment Act 1989.

More generally, discrimination is lawful if it is necessary in order to comply with the requirements of existing statutory provisions concerning the protection of women or with relevant statutory provisions within the meaning of the Health and Safety at Work etc Act. 1974.[15] In both cases the discrimination will be lawful only if necessary to protect women in relation to pregnancy, maternity or other circumstances giving rise to risks specifically affecting women.

Ex-offenders

Under the Rehabilitation of Offenders Act 1974, convictions do not have to be revealed if:

- they relate to offences included in the spent convictions scheme;
- the rehabilitation period has elapsed;
- no excluded offence has been committed during rehabilitation; and
- the sentence has been served.

There are minor exceptions to this last point. A further 'scheme' offence during a rehabilitation period creates a new rehabilitation period. The excluded offences, to which the scheme for spent convictions does not apply, are more serious ones attracting sentences of over 30 months. The maximum rehabilitation period for a scheme offence is ten years.

The effect of completion of a rehabilitation period in relation to offences covered by the spent convictions scheme is that the conviction becomes spent. This means that the offences are to be treated as if they were not committed and the person as if not charged or convicted of the offence. There are exceptions here for various legal proceedings. A job applicant can treat questions about their previous criminal record as *excluding* the spent convictions. If asked, 'Do you have a criminal record?' they can answer 'No', and refusal to disclose a spent conviction cannot give rise to any legal liability. For example, it cannot constitute a breach of the term of trust in an employment contract. Moreover, spent convictions can be excluded from references, without the referee incurring any legal liability. However, a referee may include details of spent convictions providing that the information is true and the disclosure is done without malice. Dismissal on the grounds of a spent conviction or a failure to disclose one will be unfair. Refusing employment because of a spent conviction will also be unlawful. It is not just the spent conviction itself that is protected, but the circumstances surrounding it. Thus, a dismissal because of the nature of the offence which is the subject of the spent conviction would also be unfair. An employee may pursue an unfair dismissal claim or an action for breach of contract. It is not clear what remedy is available for a refusal of employment; an action for breach of statutory duty may be possible.

The right to be silent about spent convictions and the Act's protection against exclusion and dismissal are subject to numerous exceptions where suitability for employment is to be ascertained. The excepted professions, offices, employments and occupations include medical practitioners, barristers, solicitors, nurses, accountants, midwives, pharmacists, dentists, opticians, police constables, veterinary surgeons, firearm dealers, those involving access to minors and health service employment which involves access to patients. There are others and the Secretary of State has power to amend the list.[16]

Anyone applying for work in these occupations can be asked about spent convictions, must disclose them and can be refused employment on the basis of them or dismissed for them or failing to disclose them.

Such dismissals will be permitted under the Rehabilitation of Offenders Act but must still stand the tests of unfair dismissal law. In the case of excepted employments, requests for references are not protected from questions about spent convictions. In such cases, the applicant (or referee) must be told that the exception order applies.

Anyone employed or seeking employment as an officer of a building society may be asked about spent convictions, but only within a range of offences connected with fraud, dishonesty or building society, company and related legislation. The person must be told that the order applies. Spent convictions may be the subject of questioning and grounds for exclusion or dismissal in the interests of national security, but again the individual must be told that the order applies.

As regards unspent convictions, a job applicant is under no general legal duty to voluntarily disclose them. However, the position may be different if a person is asked specifically about any unspent convictions and gives dishonest answers which are discovered later, although a dismissal in these circumstances will not necessarily be fair. Relevant questions are: How long ago was the conviction? What length of good service has there been with the employer? Is the offence relevant in any way to the job now being done? In general, is the employee now unsuitable for their job? Proper procedure will also need to be used.

The Requirements of Discrimination Law

Meaning of unlawful discrimination

Discrimination is unlawful at any stage of the recruitment and selection process. Before analysing the legal aspects of that process, therefore, it is necessary to describe the requirements of discrimination law. It is unlawful in relation to employment to discriminate against a person because of their sex, because they are married, or on grounds of colour, race, nationality or ethnic or national origins. Discrimination takes the following forms.[17]

- Direct – treating a person 'less favourably' than another person is or would be treated, on one of the prohibited grounds (such as colour). This includes segregation on racial grounds.
- Indirect – applying a 'requirement or condition' which is or would be applied equally (for instance, to women and men) but which is such that the proportion of one group (say, women) who can comply with it is 'considerably smaller' than the proportion outside that group who can comply.

● Victimization – treating a person less favourably because they have, or are suspected of having used the legislation, or because they intend to use the legislation, or have properly alleged breaches of the legislation.

The legislation referred to is the Sex Discrimination Act 1975, the Equal Pay Act 1970 and the Race Relations Act 1976. It should be noted that discrimination practised against either sex is unlawful. Thus, in *Jeremiah* v. *Ministry of Defence*, there was unlawful sex discrimination because only the men had to do the unpleasant jobs. Sexual harassment can be unlawful sex discrimination and may amount to a detriment (*Strathclyde Regional Council* v. *Porcelli*).

The Equal Pay Act applies to terms of employment (see chapter 3). By contrast the two other discrimination Acts apply to:

● recruitment and selection arrangements – for example, a discriminatory interview as in *Brennan* v. *J. H. Dewhurst Ltd*;
● the terms on which jobs are offered;
● refusals to offer employment;
● opportunities for promotion, transfer or training, or access to any other benefits, facilities or services;
● dismissal or any other detriment.

The Race Relations Act additionally contains provisions relating to terms of employment, conferring a right equivalent to that contained in the Equal Pay Act for women. Establishing direct discrimination falls upon the applicant, although once a prima facie case is made out the employer will then have to to show that the different treatment was accorded for reasons other than sex, race and so on. (However, in *King* v. *The Great Britain-China Centre*, the Court of Appeal denied any shift in evidential burden. Tribunals are entitled to seek explanations from employers where the primary facts point to the possibility of discrimination, and they can legitimately draw inferences from such explanations or the absence of explanations.) The issue of unlawful discrimination is not affected by the question of whether or not discrimination was intentional. Thus acts based on generalized assumptions relating to sex – such as sacking a woman rather than a man, because the latter is assumed to be the 'breadwinner' – constitute unlawful sex discrimination (*Skyrail Oceanic Ltd* v. *Coleman*).

In cases of indirect discrimination the applicant has to adduce evidence to establish the 'requirement or condition', the 'considerably smaller' proportion who can comply with it, and the fact that they have suffered detriment because they cannot comply with it. The employer's defence would be that the requirement or condition was justifiable irrespective of the prohibited grounds. Justifiable means that it has to be related to the needs, rather than merely the convenience, of the business (*Steel* v. *The Post Office*). Tribunals will ask if there is a non-discriminatory way of achieving the same objective. In *Price* v. *The Civil Service Commission* the respondents were concerned about age structure and limited entrants to a particular grade to the age of under 28 years. The complainant was qualified for that grade but was well over the age limit. She argued that because of women's child rearing duties a considerably smaller proportion of women could comply when compared with the proportion of men. The EAT accepted this view and recommended that the respondents should balance their age structure by other means. The European Court of Justice has held, in *Bilka-Kaufhaus GMbH* v. *Weber von Hartz*, that the exclusion of part-time employees from an occupational pension scheme may amount to unlawful indirect discrimination under EC law, but see *R.* v. *Secretary of State for Employment*, below, p. 71. (See also *Rinner-Kühn* (below, p. 71) and *Nimz* (see below, p. 278).

'Justifiable' requires the employer to show a real need for the measures, and that they are appropriate and necessary to meet that need. The discriminatory effects of the requirement or condition must then be weighed against the real needs of the employer – the principle of proportionality (*Hampson* v. *Department of Education and Science*).[18] Appropriate means that the measure is suited to the achievement of the particular need. 'Necessary' means that no other measures are available. In a hypothetical case, where a bookshop proprietor insists that staff are at least six feet tall so that they can reach the top shelves, there is clearly a rule with which a considerably smaller proportion of women can comply. The rule is detrimental to women who apply for jobs in the bookshop and cannot meet the height requirement. Is it justifiable? Certainly it is important for staff to be able to reach the books, and the rule is appropriate in the sense that it does ensure that staff can do this. But is it necessary? Clearly it is not, because other measures are available, for instance, stepladders could be used. Therefore, it is not justifiable and would constitute unlawful, indirect sex discrimination. Industrial tribunals will not award compensation in indirect discrimination cases because the discrimination is unintentional. They may, however, order that the discriminatory rule be abandoned.

Other unlawful acts

There is, in addition to discrimination, a series of other unlawful acts:

- Discriminatory practices which are so successful that no discrimination is ever committed, so no individual could ever take a case.
- Discriminatory advertisements.
- Instructions to discriminate.
- Pressure to discriminate.
- Aiding or assisting in committing unlawful acts.

An employer is liable for the acts of an employee in the course of their employment, along with the employee themselves. An employer will not be liable, however, if they show that they took whatever steps were necessary to prevent an employee from discriminating. Positive discrimination is not permitted, for example, restricting a post to black applicants in order to alter the occupational structure in favour of blacks.

Where discrimination is lawful

Single race or sex training schemes are permitted, if that race or sex has been under-represented in a particular type of work during the last 12 months. Moreover, both Acts allow discrimination where it is a 'genuine occupational qualification' (GOQ).[19] This means that it is lawful in such cases to restrict recruitment to persons of a particular sex or race. The circumstances are limited, and there are differences between the two Acts.

Race Relations Act, GOQs
To be of a particular race is a GOQ where:

- a person of a particular race is needed for authenticity in a dramatic performance or other entertainment;
- the need is for authenticity on the part of an artist's or photographer's model;
- authenticity is needed in an establishment providing food or drink within a particular setting;
- the job holder provides a particular racial group with personal welfare services and these can best be provided by a person from that racial group.

Sex Discrimination Act, GOQs
To be a man (or a woman) is a GOQ where:

- reasons of physiology require it (excluding physical strength or stamina);
- decency or privacy require it (for example, physical contact; undressing);
- the job is in a single-sex special care institution (for example, prison; hospital)
- living-in is necessary, and no separate accommodation exists;
- the job is in a single-sex special care institution (for example, prison; hospital)
- personal welfare services can best be provided by a person of that sex;
- duties outside the UK will be subject to laws or customs which make it difficult for a person of the other sex to do the job;
- the job is one of two held by a married couple.

Not only are they limited but also the courts are likely to interpret them quite strictly and the monitoring commissions, (the Equal Opportunities Commission, EOC, for sex equality; and the Commission for Racial Equality, CRE) may well be involved. In *CRE* v. *London Borough of Lambeth*, the CRE successfully pursued a complaint against an employer who was using race as a GOQ outside the terms of the Act. Where an employer relies on a GOQ the responsibility for proving GOQ rests with them. If an employer is in doubt about whether a job can be restricted to a particular sex or racial group, they should seek the advice of the EOC or CRE beforehand. Such advice is available free of charge.

Under the original terms of the Sex Discrimination Act (SDA) 1975, it was lawful to discriminate in order to comply with legislation enacted prior to the SDA. The Employment Act (EA) 1989 overrides these statutory requirements and gives the Secretary of State power to repeal them. In alleged indirect discrimination cases it will be for the party who claims there is no discrimination to show that the pre-SDA legal requirement is justifiable.[21] Discrimination will still be lawful, however, if it is to comply with specified protective legislation (see p. 31 above). Discrimination in respect of certain educational appointments also remains lawful.[22]

Complaints and remedies

A questions procedure exists under both Acts to help people decide whether to institute proceedings, and help them formulate and present their case. There are prescribed forms which applicants may serve on respondents, and on which respondents may reply. These are provided by regulations issued under the Acts.[23] The questions ask why the respondents did what they did. The answers are admissible in any proceedings, and an equivocal or evasive answer, or no answer at all, may be interpreted, at the tribunal's discretion, as evidence of the committing of an unlawful act. The procedure may be invoked before or within 21 days of an application to an industrial tribunal.

The remedies for unlawful discrimination are obtained by applying to an industrial tribunal within three months of the act which is the subject of complaint. ACAS conciliation is built into the complaints process, but information communicated to ACAS is 'privileged'. Complainants have no right to legal aid but the EOC or CRE may assist and such assistance may extend to representation at any hearing. The tribunal may make a declaration of rights, an order for compensation (including for injury to feelings) of up to £10,000 and a recommendation that the respondent take a particular course of action. Failure to abide by such a recommendation can result in increased compensation, but not above the limit. More generally, an attempt to obtain compensation in excess of the limit through direct reliance on EC law has been made in *Marshall* v. *Southampton and South West Hampshire Area Health Authority No 2.* (The House of Lords has now referred the matter to the ECJ.) Some recent decisions under the Race Relations Act have emphasized that compensation can be awarded for injury to feelings and may include aggravated damages which compensate for the manner of or motive for the discrimination (*Alexander* v. *The Home Office*; *Noone* v. *North West Thames Regional Health Authority*). Where there is oppressive, arbitrary or unconstitutional action by public servants, exemplary damages can be awarded in order to punish the offender and deter others from similar unlawful conduct (*City of Bradford Metropolitan Council* v. *Arora*).

In discrimination cases employers will be seeking to show that they did something for reasons other than discrimination. Tribunals will have to look carefully at these reasons because no admission of a discriminatory act is likely to occur except in the case of indirect discrimination. Tribunals, and complainants and indeed employers may be helped if certain information is disclosed. For example, consideration of the application forms of other candidates for a job, including that of the successful candidate, will help a tribunal decide whether the employer's reason is genuine. An employer may refuse to disclose such information to the complainant but ultimately a tribunal chairman may order disclosure.

Discriminatory provisions in collective agreements and works rules are void, but discrimination in relation to death and retirement is permitted except for retirement provisions which affect promotion, demotion, dismissal, training and transfer. This exemption was originally much wider but was narrowed considerably by the Sex Discrimination Act 1986, following the decision of the European Court of Justice in *Marshall* v. *Southampton and South West Hampshire Area Health Authority* in which discriminatory retirement ages were held to be a breach of EC law. Other exemptions (e.g. small firms) were removed by the same Act following *Commission of the European Communities* v. *UK*, a case in which the European Court found UK sex discrimination law to be in breach of European legislation.

Both the Race Relations Act 1976 and the Sex Discrimination Act 1975 have accompanying codes of practice.[24] While a breach of these codes does not give rise to any legal liabilities, such a breach is admissible and must be considered if relevant in any proceedings under an Act. Both codes recommend to employers that they adopt and implement equal opportunities (EO) policies and that these policies should be monitored.[25] No legal liability flows from not having an EO policy, or from having a policy but not monitoring it, and a failure to apply a policy will not automatically constitute discrimination (*Qureshi* v. *London Borough of Newham*). However, absence of a policy or monitoring, or failure to apply a policy, can constitute background evidence from which a tribunal may draw unfavourable inferences. Where policies are adopted, and monitoring used, employers will have to be prepared to disclose the results of that monitoring. The practice of ethnic monitoring has been given further support by the Court of Appeal, as has the use of its results for evidential purposes when claims are brought.

In *West Midlands Passenger Transport Executive* v. *Singh* it was held that an employer can be ordered to disclose statistical evidence of the ethnic origins of staff recruited since an EO policy was implemented. The general drift of case law on disclosure of information in race and sex discrimination cases has been to favour disclosure. As a rule, it should be granted if it is necessary for disposing fairly of the proceedings (*Science Research Council* v. *Nasse*). However, disclosure will not be ordered if it is oppressive, for example, the information could be provided only at great expense or trouble (*Singh*). More recently, the EAT has made it clear that the duty of the employer to disclose documents applies only to existing documents. An employer cannot be ordered to collect statistics not already collected (*Carrington* v. *Helix Lighting Ltd*). Nor can claims for further particulars be used to obtain this sort of data in the absence of monitoring. They are for elaboration of cases rather than for eliciting supplementary evidence. Furthermore, tribunals do not have the power to order interrogatories – written questions to be answered under oath by the other party. Instead, complainants can rely on the tribunal to draw inferences from:

- the failure of the employer to monitor;
- the failure to reply to, or adequately reply to, the statutory questions procedure (*Carrington*).

Recruitment and Selection

Discrimination is the main area of law likely to be relevant here. There must be no discrimination at any stage of the recruitment and selection process. There are three types of discrimination which are unlawful:

- race (bearing in mind the definition on p. 33);
- sex (including discrimination against married persons, see p. 33);
- union, that is, on grounds of union membrship or non-membership

The last-mentioned is a relatively recent addition to the law, having been introduced by the Employment Act 1990.[26] There is no legislation outlawing discrimination on grounds not mentioned above, such as age.

Advertising jobs

Race and sex discrimination
Attention has already been drawn to the dangers of indirect discrimination – placing requirements upon candidates which have the effect of being discriminatory. By contrast, direct discrimination – treating someone less favourably than a person of the opposite sex, or of a different racial group – would occur where a job is not genuinely available irrespective of race or sex. Thus, in what must be one of the few cases where direct discrimination has been admitted in writing, a firm of solicitors wrote to a female applicant for a job saying that what they wanted was a man. The tribunal at the resultant hearing came to its decision without difficulty. Except in the limited circumstances where sex or race is a GOQ, such restrictions will be unlawful.

As regards sex discrimination – and similar but not identical provisions apply in relation to race – it is unlawful to publish or cause to be published an advertisement which indicates or could be taken to indicate an intention to commit unlawful discrimination. Use of job descriptions which have sexual connotations (for example, salesgirl, waiter, postman, stewardess) are to be taken as showing an intention to discriminate unless the advertisement indicates to the contrary.[27] Thus, if both male and female terms are not used in the advertisement, it would be advisable to insert a phrase indicating that applicants of both sexes will be welcomed. There is no statutory requirement for job titles to be changed. However, occupational descriptions giving both sexes (for example, manager/ess, salesman/woman) or appearing in neutral form (for example, cowperson, with experience of milking and herd-rearing) make an employer's non-discriminatory policy clear. Where there are doubts about terminology (that is, fears that it might imply one particular sex) a phrase of the sort mentioned above might be inserted. In any case, where there is an EO policy, it might be helpful to draw attention to it. It is not advisable to advertise, as one employer who subsequently visited an industrial tribunal did, 'overhead crane driver/ess – to satisfy damn silly employment legislation'. As regards race relations, confining advertisements to areas or publications which would disproportionately exclude a particular racial group is likely to constitute unlawful discrimination.

An employer should not tell a publisher that an advertisement is lawful unless they know it to be so. Making such a statement knowingly or recklessly which is materially false or misleading constitutes a criminal offence punishable by fine. Advertisement for the purposes of both race and sex discrimination law includes every form of advertisement, whether public or not, and whether:

- in a newspaper or other publication;
- by television or radio;
- by display of notices, signs, labels, showcards or goods;
- by distribution of samples, circulars, catalogues, price-lists or other material;
- by exhibit on of pictures, models or films;
- in any other way.[28]

This definition would seem to include careers advertising and films, direct mail and in-company advertising as well as advertising in the public media. The legal requirements apply in relation to each advertisement. It should be noted that the placing of a discriminatory advertisement and the instructing of someone else to place such an advertisement are unlawful acts in themselves. The failure to subsequently offer a person a job on the grounds of sex or race would constitute a further unlawful act.

Employers may target some of their publicity towards a particular sex or race where a particular sex or race is under-represented among the existing staff.

Union discrimination

It is unlawful to refuse someone a job on the grounds that they are, or are not, a trades union member. An advertisement containing such a requirement will not in itself be unlawful, but it will be taken as conclusive evidence that an unlawful act was committed if a non-unionist or union member is subsequently refused employment, does not have the required status as specified in the advertisement and makes a claim to an industrial tribunal. Any requirement that a person must agree to join or leave a union if appointed is also unlawful. Union discrimination is unlawful whether practised by an employer directly, or indirectly through an employment agency.

Claims are made to an industrial tribunal within three months against employers, employment agencies or both. Provision exists for joining parties to the proceedings (for example, a trades union insisting on union members only being recruited, or an employer if the original action is against an employment agency). Remedies are a declaration and such compensation as is just and equitable including for injury to feelings. The tribunal can make a recommendation of action to ease the complainant's position, and increase the compensation if it is not complied with. Maximum compensation is £10,000. It should be noted that advertisement is defined widely to include any notice even if it is not made public.

Contracts of employment

Stating certain requirements in job advertisements will generally strengthen the employer's case if there is a subsequent dispute with the employee. Telling applicants in advance that the organization operates a no smoking policy, or that mobility is required, provides evidence that the individual knew these things *before* agreeing to become an employee, the inference being that these terms were accepted as part of the contract of employment.

Application forms and further particulars

Application forms and further particulars also provide an opportunity to inform the employee in advance of his employment that certain requirements must be met. The employer will have records showing that the prospective employee has been sent these documents, and in the case of an application form the employee's signature indicates that he or she wishes to apply for the job, perhaps on the terms as stated. For example an application form containing the words 'I agree to work shifts' and signed by the employee is strong evidence that this was an agreed term of the contract and could be important if the matter later turned out to be in dispute. There is some value, therefore, in specifying the main, and particularly any potentially controversial terms.

It is possible for the application form itself to give the impression that it could be used in a discriminatory way. Thus, where questions about sex or race are asked, it should be made clear that the reason is for EO policy monitoring purposes only or in order to ascertain whether the applicant will need a work permit. Moreover, care needs to be taken not to use the application form as a test of English literacy unless that can be demonstrated to be necessary for the job.

Information supplied by applicants

It is a matter for the prospective employer to check the authenticity of data supplied by job applicants: *caveat emptor* – let the buyer beware. This may be done by asking the applicant for certificates proving that stated qualifications are actually held, by taking up references, by pursuing issues with the applicant at an interview, by testing and so on. If the employer does not make a reasonable enquiry any dishonesty on the part of the applicant which is discovered later, although not excused, may be more difficult to deal with. In any case there is a possibility of recruitment being negligent (see pp. 45–6 below). Other than in exceptional cases, there is no duty upon the job applicant to volunteer information about themselves except in response to direct questions (*Walton* v. *TAC Construction Materials Ltd*).

Under the Theft Act 1968, it is a criminal offence to dishonestly obtain a job and a person doing so may be prosecuted. When the dishonesty is discovered, dismissal may be justified but this is not automatically the case (see chapter 7). It can be useful for an application form to contain a statement whereby the applicant confirms the correctness of the information provided and acknowledges that deliberately providing false information could result in dismissal.

Where information is sought about criminal convictions, the

provisions of the Rehabilitation of Offenders Act 1974 may apply, as indicated earlier. Where a medical report is required, the provisions of the Access to Medical Reports Act 1988 might apply (see below, p. 280).

Interviews and tests

The interview stage usually marks the appearance of the candidate on the employer's premises. Therefore, the employer's general duty of care as owner or controller of the premises is brought into effect. The main danger at this stage, however, is that employers act contrary to discrimination law. A problem is that the boundary between lawful and unlawful is not altogether clear. What is clear is that in an interview the candidates should not be asked different questions because they are of a different race or sex. This does not mean that all candidates must be asked the same questions. Interviewers may legitimately frame their questions in the light of what the candidate has said on an application form or in a letter of application.

One of the difficulties is that some of the matters which employers need to be reassured about could give rise to questions which lead to accusations of discrimination. For example, employers may wish to enquire about a woman's family circumstances as a means of judging the candidate's likely work commitment. This is a potentially discriminatory line of questioning which some would say is based on a stereotyping of women's roles. Similarly, enployers will want to be sure that candidates from ethnic minorities have sufficient command of the English language. Again, such a line of questioning is potentially discriminatory. So too is questioning about union member-ship or non-membership. All that can be said is that evidence of such questioning may lead to unfavourable inferences being drawn by a tribunal. This has prompted some employers to drop such questions from interviews, and indeed to omit questions of this sort from application forms. It should be remembered that an industrial tribunal may well have the application forms of all of the candidates before it. It is quite likely that disclosure of these would be ordered by a tribunal if resisted. Finally, it should be noted that if interviewers are being called as witnesses there is nothing to stop their contemporaneous notes being submitted as evidence – doodles and all. A record of the proceedings of an interview could also provide evidence.

The main problem with testing is that the tests themselves may be discriminatory. This is less likely to be the case with sex discrimination but has been alleged in relation to race. Here it is said that testing in part reflects cultural values, so that candidates from cultures other than the dominant one are disadvantaged. Another way in which tests might be discriminatory is by setting educational standards which amount to indirect discrimination and which cannot be justified in terms of the job. A high standard of written English as a requirement to pass a test would be difficult to justify in relation to a job where little or no writing was needed and a considerably smaller proportion of people from ethnic minorities would be able to comply.

Selection

The carrying out of a discriminatory interview or test is not of itself unlawful. Apart from discriminatory advertisements and other unlawful acts (see p. 36), the law is broken only where a person is denied access to a job on grounds of discrimination. If the selection is based heavily upon a discriminatory interview or test it is likely that selection will be unlawful. If selection is based on a number of factors, one of which is a discriminatory test, then the critical factor will be how much weight was put upon the test result. Where recruitment is done by word of mouth it may be discriminatory if it reduces the opportunity of members of a particular sex or race to apply for jobs. It may perpetuate the existing make-up of the workforce especially if it is the only method used. If the workforce is largely black, or largely white, in the context of a multi-racial labour market, using this method alone may be unlawful.

The freedom to discriminate positively has already been mentioned in relation to training. However, that freedom does not extend to the selection process. Restricting offers of jobs to those of a particular sex or race constitutes unlawful discrimination. An industrial tribunal recommendation that an applicant (who had been unlawfully discriminated against in the recruitment and selection process) should have preferential treatment in future went too far (*Noone* v. *North West Thames Regional Health Authority*).

Another potential constraint on the selection process is procedure. In the public sector an abuse of procedure could possibly be open to challenge by means of judicial review. This could occur, for example, where recruitment is in breach of the principles of natural justice, as it would be if (some of) those doing the selection knew one of the candidates and favoured that candidate in the selection process.

Finally, recruitment could be negligent if a person appointed to a post proves to be unsafe in it. There is a common law duty to take reasonable care in making the appointment, especially with certain kinds of jobs. In *Hicks* v. *Pier House Management Ltd*, the company employed a night porter at a block of flats, but did not adequately check his background. He had a long list of convictions and many spells in prison for theft and/or burglarly. He went on to commit several burglaries at the flats which were in his charge. One of the tenants, who had been burgled, successfully sued the company for damages for negligence.

Appointment and the Contract of Employment[29]

The contract of employment and its terms

It is on appointment that the employer enters into what is the central relationship in employment law. Once the employer makes an offer and the candidate accepts, there is a contract of employment. The offer may be conditional in which case it expires if the condition is not met, as in *Wishart* v. *National Association of Citizens' Advice Bureaux Ltd*, where satisfactory references were not provided. (Satisfactory means to the satisfaction of the employer in question rather than to the satisfaction of a notional 'reasonable employer'.) More generally, an offer terminates after a fixed period, if specified, or otherwise after a reasonable length of time has elapsed. It should be noted that the concept of a contract of employment has common law origins. There is no Act of Parliament determining that the employer-employee relationship shall be one of contract. In essence the contract is an agreement in which the employee agrees to work for wages and the employer agrees to pay for the work done. Exchange is at the root of the contract – there must be consideration for the services rendered. Describing the contract as an agreement (rather than a document) is a reminder that the contract is unlikely to be committed to paper. Even if there are no pieces of paper arising out of the enployment transaction the contract is still legally enforceable. The absence of paper may, however, make it more difficult to establish evidence of the contract terms.

The contract begins when it is made – the date of the agreement (that is, once the employee accepts the employer's offer) – rather than when the employee actually starts to perform the work. Thus if either party changes their mind between agreement and the commencement of work the other party has a potential claim for breach of contract.

It is appropriate before going on to look at the sources of the terms of the contract to consider the relationship between the contract and any collective agreement which may have been made between the employer and one or more trades unions. Unless the parties specifically state otherwise, the collective agreement will not be legally enforceable.[30] This emphasizes the key legal status of the contract of employment between the employer and the individual employee. An important feature of the contract, however, is the incorporation of terms from the collective agreement. Thus terms from the non-enforceable collective agreement may become incorporated into the individual contract of employment, and by being so become enforceable between the employer and individual employee. The incorporation is not automatic – it may occur expressly by terms in an individual contract being linked to a union agreement, or impliedly by the custom of wages and other terms being adjusted when changes occur in the collective agreement. Incorporation of terms which limit the right to take industrial action is subject to rules laid down in the Trade Union and Labour Relations Act (TULRA)[31] (see below, pp. 229–30).

Although statute limits to some extent what can be included, much of the substance of the contract stems from what the parties themselves agree. The terms of the contract, therefore, have a number of sources, and it is the totality of what is derived from these which constitutes the contract. The main sources are as follows:

Expressly agreed terms
These will be directly agreed between the employee and employer either in writing (for example, the letter of appointment and a reply of acceptance) or orally (for example, at the end of the interview). The employee needs to know the standards of performance and conduct required and the consequences of not meeting them.

Terms incorporated from collective agreements
These are terms that are collectively negotiated by an employer (or employers) and one or more trades unions. These terms are agreed by the union(s) on behalf of the employee and have become expressly or impliedly incorporated into the individual contract of employment.

Works rules
It is necessary to have non-discriminatory rules and apply them in a non-discriminatory way. Rules, other than instructions, are likely to be contractual, especially in the case of disciplinary rules.

They will either be expressly contractual, or become contractual by the employer giving reasonable notice of them and the employee working under them.

Custom and practice

Where there are no express terms or other evidence on a particular point, custom or practice may be used to imply a term. This will be the case only where the custom is widely known, reasonable and certain (that is precisely-defined).

Terms implied by common law

Like the statute-imposed terms the implied terms are of particular importance because they lay down some ground rules for all employment contracts. The following obligations are prominent:

Employer	*Employee*
To pay wages for work done.	To obey the employer's lawful commands.
To take reasonable care for the employee's safety.	To take reasonable care and skill in going about the work.
To act in good faith.	To give faithful and honest service and not to act manifestly against the employer's interest.

The main employee duties can be seen to be co-operation, care and fidelity. It is submitted that co-operation includes a duty to adapt to reasonable change (*Cresswell* v. *Board of Inland Revenue*; *MacPherson* v. *London Borough of Lambeth*). The employer has no general duty to provide work, but in the absence of a term to the contrary the common law holds that payment will nevertheless be due. The employer's duty to treat the employee fairly and reasonably, on the one hand, and the employee's duty to give faithful and honest service, on the other, import into the contract a term of mutual trust and confidence (*Woods* v. *W. M. Car Services* (Peterborough) Ltd). An employer may be under a duty to inform an employee about contract terms which have not been agreed with the employee individually and about which the employee could not reasonably be expected to know. (*Scally and ors* v. *Southern Health and Social Services Board and ors*). An employer is under no duty to provide a reference.

Terms imposed by statute

These are terms which Parliament has decreed will be put in contracts of employment generally, for example, contracts have an equality clause as a result of the Equal Pay Act and minimum notice requirements under the Employment Protection (Consolidation) Act (EP(C)A).

The courts may, in any dispute about the terms of a contract, imply a term. The aim is to decide what the parties intended, in the absence of express agreement. The approach taken is that such a term should be so obvious that the parties did not feel a need to state it expressly. In practice, it is often difficult in the absence of express provisions to decide what was intended by the parties. Sometimes evidence can be found in the terms of collective agreements, or in custom and practice. In other cases, the courts may simply imply what is reasonable. Thus, in *Coslett Contractors Ltd* v. *Quinn*, they implied a term that expenses reasonably incurred in the course of employment would be reimbursed.

Courts will generally enforce contract terms without reference to their fairness to the respective parties, providing that the contract itself is not illegal, the terms are not contrary to public policy and are not made void by statute, and the contract was entered into willingly. In *Electronic Data Systems Ltd* v. *Hubble* the Court of Appeal set aside (pending trial) a judgment of the High Court that the employee should pay a refund of training costs because he left within a specified time. This term had been contractually agreed but was potentially in restraint of trade. In the event, the case was settled without going to trial. Courts may restrict the operation of terms if they consider them too wide, especially if they are in restraint of trade or made under duress. In *United Bank Ltd* v. *Akhtar*, where an employment contract had a widely-drawn term allowing geographical mobility, the court implied a further term requiring the employer to handle any relocation in a reasonable way (for instance, with adequate notice). Where a court finds a particular term of a contract is void, the remainder of the contract terms will still be enforceable if the offending term can be severed.

Letters of appointment and other documents

It is clear from what has been said about the contract of employment that there is considerable potential for dispute about terms. Having unambiguous evidence of what was agreed is therefore important. A letter of appointment may be a key document, especially if it sets out some of the main terms, including anything perceived as an area of potential dispute. Successful candidates might be encouraged to reply in writing stating that they accept the offer on the terms laid down in a letter of a particular date.

Special care needs to be taken in relation to three areas which often give rise to problems: location, hours of work and duties. In all three cases, as generally, an employer has much to gain by drawing the contract terms widely. This is because an employer may legitimately alter an employee's terms *within* the contract, but may be at risk of legal challenge if the alteration is not permitted by the contract. For example, if it is a term of an employee's contract that they will work at any of the health district's establishments, the employer (all other things being equal) will be free to effect the change. However, if it is a term of the contract that the employee works at a particular hospital, the employer may risk a legal challenge if he or she goes ahead. Similar problems often occur in relation to hours of work and duties. In relation to the latter, job descriptions may offer useful evidence of contract terms.

Another important document is one containing disciplinary rules. This should set out the dos and don'ts of employee behaviour indicating what sorts of punishments are likely, and in particular what may lead to dismissal. It is useful for employers to have evidence that the employee has received a copy of such rules. The law will then assume that the rules are known and the employer has a defence to claims that the employee did not know the rules. The clearer and more widely-known the rules, the stronger is this defence. The documentation should also contain the disciplinary procedures. The rules themselves (which may include those posted on boards or at clocking stations or circulated as memos) will generally be taken to be part of the contract of employment. Procedural aspects may not be, although, depending on the facts, a disciplinary procedure can be part of the contract of employment (as in *Dietmann* v. *London Borough of Brent*).

Types of contract

If the relationship is to be one governed by a contract of employment it will be necessary to determine the type of employment contract to be used. There are four principal types:

Permanent contract

This is the most usual type of employment contract. It is open-ended in that no date of expiry is fixed. The parties assume that the contract will continue indefinitely, although provision is made for termination by notice.

Fixed-term contract (FTC)

A fixed-term contract has a definite starting date and a definite expiry date. Provision for notice to end the contract during its term does not prevent it from being an FTC. An FTC terminates when the expiry date is reached, and constitutes a dismissal.[32]

'Performance' contract

A contract discharged by performance is a contract of employment for the performance of a specific task. It terminates when the task is completed. The ending of the contract is not a dismissal.

Temporary contract

A temporary worker is employed for a limited period but not under a fixed-term contract or a performance contract. In general a temporary worker will have the same rights as a permanent employee if he or she acquires sufficient continuous employment. Dismissal of a temporary replacement for someone medically suspended or on maternity leave will normally be a fair dismissal.

Task contracts are clearly relevant where the job will last as long as the work itself, and the work lasts for an unspecified period of time – until completion. Because the ending of a task contract is not a dismissal, no question of redundancy or unfair dismissal arises. By contrast a fixed-term contract, upon expiry, constitutes a dismissal, but it may be shown to be fair if challenged (for example, because of redundancy). Some employers use rolling fixed-term contracts, giving substantial advance notice of renewal (for instance, at the end of the second year of a three-year contract). Since task and fixed-term contracts end automatically – by completion of the work in the former case, and by completion of the term in the latter – notice is not required to bring them to an end. Notice would be required, however, to end them at an earlier stage.

Most contracts of employment are open ended – they are assumed to continue indefinitely. Termination may be mutual, by the employee resigning, by the employer dismissing or by force of law – frustration of contract. Frustration of a contract occurs where one of the parties, for unexpected and unintended reasons, is unable to perform the contract in the manner agreed. Prison sentences and long-term sickness are the main examples in the employment field. Tribunals are reluctant to apply the concept of frustration because it has the effect of removing he employee's statutory rights to claim unfair dismissal. This arises out of the fact that frustration, and not dismissal, is the cause of termination. There have been occasional examples of frustration in employment law, as in *F. C. Shepherd and Co Ltd* v. *Jerrom* where the Court of Appeal held that a borstal sentence of nine months frustrated a four-year contract of apprenticeship. There is no particular length of time by which frustration occurs – this will depend upon the circumstances of the case (See below, pp. 86–7).

Task and fixed-term contracts are types of temporary contract but temporary contracts can also be open-ended. The expectations of the parties are different from those where the contract is permanent. The legal position is not dissimilar however, perhaps with one exception – temporary employees might have less protection in a redundancy. Otherwise, normal legal rights accrue with continuous employment and several temporary contracts nose to tail (or even sometimes with gaps in between) are treated as continuous. There is no legal requirement to make a temporary contract permanent at any stage unless this has been specifically agreed. However, in the long term it is possible that a stream of temporary contracts might suggest that in practice there has been a mutually-agreed variation of the contract terms.

Written particulars of main terms

While the law does not require a contract to be in writing (except in certain cases such as apprenticeships), it does require that within 13 weeks of the commencement of employment the main terms are put in writing to the employee. These details have to be included in a written statement, or in other documents to which the written statement refers. Crown servants, and employees who normally work outside Great Britain are excluded, as is anyone working under 16 hours a week (or under eight if they have five years' or more continuous employment). The statement must identify the employer and employee, the date when the employment began and whether any employment with a previous employer counts as continuous employment, and if so, when the continuous employment began. It must include the following:

- The rate of pay or method of calculating it.
- The interval of payment.
- Any terms and conditions relating to:
  - hours of work;
  - holiday pay, sufficient for holiday pay entitlement to be calculated;
  - sick pay;
  - pensions.
- Length of notice on both sides.
- The title of the job the employee is employed to perform.

If there are no terms under any of these headings the statement should say so. An additional note should specify disciplinary rules and procedures, and grievance procedures, and whether a pensions contracting-out certificate is in force.

The above details do not have to be actually provided in the statement. The statement can simply refer the employee to other documents containing the details (for example, works rules or collective agreements). The employee must have 'reasonable opportunities of reading' such documents 'in the course of his employment', or the documents must be 'reasonably accessible in some other way'. An employer must keep reference documents up to date within one month of any changes, or issue new statements. A new statement must be issued upon change of ownership, although this is not required if there has simply been a change of name, or where continuous employment is preserved (as under the Transfer of Undertakings Regulations). An application can be made to a tribunal to determine the question of continuity, to determine what should have been provided in a statement or to determine the accuracy or sufficiency of the written particulars. If written particulars have been issued the employer also has the right of application to an industrial tribunal to seek determination. If the employment has been terminated, the application period is three months from termination.

Provision has been made for tribunals to handle certain breach of contract cases but this jurisdiction has not yet been activated by order. Thus once the terms of the contract are established by the industrial tribunal the remedy for failure to abide by the terms is a contract matter which cannot be pursued through the tribunals. The government has announced that it will introduce new legislation in this area.

As a result of the Employment Act 1989, firms employing fewer than 20 employees need not give details of disciplinary rules and procedures.[33] They would be ill-advised not to, however, because this offers an employee who is being disciplined the possibility of arguing that they did not know the rules.

The Proof of Employment Relationship Directive, (91/553/EEC; OJ L 288/32) adopted by the EC in 1991, requires domestic legislation to be in operation by 30 June 1993. No draft of proposed legislation is yet available, but it appears that employers will have to provide the main details of employment within two months of the employee commencing work. Of considerable importance is the likelihood of the legislation applying to employees (and perhaps some other workers) working for more than eight but less than 16 hours per week without the current five-year continuous employment qualification. The information to be provided is largely the same as that already required under EP (C) A, section 1. It will need to be provided, on request, to those already in employment, within two months of the request.

Workers who may not have contracts of employment

There is no universal legal definition of 'worker' but in general the term includes not only those who have entered or work under a contract of employment but also those who personally carry out work or services. Four particular types of worker may not have contracts of employment: the self-employed, staff supplied by employment agencies, office-holders and trainees. The last-named are dealt with below, pp. 274–8. In addition the position of Crown servants is not always clear.

The self-employed

The criteria for determining whether a contract is for services or is a contract of employment are described below. The significance for the individual worker is that only employees can benefit from the general body of employment law since the law gives rights to *employees*. The exceptions are discrimination law and the Wages Act, which confer rights on *workers*, which includes employees. Sometimes courts have decided that contracts of employment did not exist in cases where workers clearly felt that they did (see, for example, *O'Kelly* v. *Trusthouse Forte*).

An employee is defined as 'an individual who has entered into or works under (or where the employment has ceased, worked under) a contract of employment'. A contract of employment means 'a contract of service or apprenticeship'.[34] Unfortunately this does not get us very far, since the critical question 'How is it to be decided if the worker is employed under a contract of service?' is left unanswered. In fact the common law of contract and recent case law provide some tests to be applied, although no single test is generally conclusive. The issue is whether the worker is an employee, working for an employer under a contract of employment (or service), or a person in business on their own account providing services for a customer under a contract for services. (A worker's contract does not have to be one of these. Depending on the facts, a middle road is possible, that is, 'a contract of its own kind', see *Ironmonger* v. *Movefield Ltd*). Tribunals should consider the following:

- Who has the right to control the manner of work? (The 'control' test).
- Is the worker integrated into the structure of the organization? (The 'organizational' test.)
- Whose business is it – who takes the risks, who takes the profits? (The 'entrepreneurial' test.)
- Who provides the tools, instruments and equipment? (However, some employees by custom provide their own tools.)
- Is the employer entitled to exclusive service?
- Are there wages, sick pay and holiday pay? If yes, who pays them? A fixed payment for a specified period suggests a contract of employment. Payment by task argues for a contract for services, but not conclusively.
- Who has the power to select and appoint, dismiss, fix the place and time of work and fix the time of holidays?
- Is there a mutual obligation – the employee to work, the employer to provide it? (*Nethermere (St Neots) Ltd* v. *Gardiner and Taverna*).
- What contractual provisions are there?
- Is there a duty of personal service?
- What arrangements are there for tax and National Insurance, for example, is tax deducted via PAYE?
- Is the relationship genuinely one of self-employment or is there an attempt to avoid protective legislation?

If all the relevant circumstances are considered, the matter is one of fact for the tribunal to decide, and can be appealed only if there is an error of law (*O'Kelly* v. *Trusthouse Forte plc*). This would include a tribunal coming to a conclusion that no reasonable tribunal could have come to on the evidence before it. The House of Lords has ruled, however, that where a written contract determines the relationship the issue is a matter of law (*Davies* v. *Presbyterian Church of Wales*). The tribunal will examine and decide the real nature of the relationship on the facts even if the parties have themselves agreed, for example, that the worker is self-employed (*Oyston Estate Agency Ltd* v. *Trundle*).

Homeworkers are not self-employed by virtue of working from home. Indeed, homeworking is now becoming more widespread because of information technology, so that homeworkers include managerial and technical staff as well as the more traditional makers of cuddly toys and garment repairers. To determine whether homeworkers are employees or working under contracts for services it is necessary to apply the normal range of tests.

It should be noted that what a tribunal decides is a contract for services for employment legislation purposes may not be so for Inland Revenue purposes. Definitions of employee and self-employed may differ between the two.

Workers provided by employment agencies

Clearly one can expect a contract for services between the agency and the organization in which the work is taking place. The key question, however, is whether the individual worker is an employee of that organization. Possibly the worker could be an employee of the agency. A further possibility is that the individual worker has a contract for services with the agency, and so is self-employed. Much will depend on the details of each particular case and the criteria set out on p. 55 above should be applied.

Office holders

This is a special category of people whose employment is not governed by a contract of employment. Judges, magistrates and other people holding public office or positions in voluntary bodies fall into this category. The definition of 'worker' in TULRA does not extend to office holders. Some office holders may also have a contract of employment.

Crown servants

The traditional approach has been that a Crown servant was not employed under a contract of employment, but rather held office at the Crown's pleasure. Until recently the issue was not decided, although it did seem that Crown service and employment under a contract of employment were not incompatible. The intention of the Crown was thought to be a critical factor (*R.* v. *Civil Service Appeal Board ex parte Bruce*). The High Court has now ruled that a civil servant works under a contract of employment (*R.* v. *Lord Chancellor's Department ex parte Nangle*). In any case, the EP (C) A 1978 expressly extends various employment rights to Crown servants so that they are treated as employees. Moreover, the Employment Act 1988 requires Crown servants to be treated as being under contracts of employment for the purposes of establishing liability in tort for industrial action, the right to hold a ballot before industrial action, the right not to be unjustifiably disciplined by a trades union and removal of immunity for industrial action to enforce union membership (see chapters 9 and 10) .

Notes

1 Disabled Persons (Employment) Act 1944, as amended by the Disabled Persons (Employment) Act 1958.
2 Companies Act 1985, s. 235 and Schedule 7, Part III.
3 *Code of Practice on the Employment of Disabled People*, London, DE, 1988. (Original version: 1984).
4 Children and Young Persons Act 1933 *c.* 12, s. 18; Children and Young Persons (Scotland) Act 1937 *c.* 37.
5 1933 Act, s. 30.
6 1933 Act, s. 18.
7 Employment of Children Act 1973, s. 2.
8 Children and Young Persons Acts 1933–69.
9 Employnent of Children Act 1973 *c.* 24.
10 The Children (Performances) Regulations, SI 1968/1728.
11 Employment Act 1989, s. 10 and Schedule 3.
12 Licensing Act 1964, s. 170; Betting, Gaming and Lotteries Act 1963 s. 21.
13 Employment Act 1989, Schedule 2.
14 Factories Act 1961 Ss. 74, 128 and 131; Ionising Radiations Regulations, 1985 (Parts IV and V of Schedule 1); Para 118 of the Approved Code of Practice under the Control of Lead at Work Regulations, 1980; Public Health Act 1936, *c.* 49, s. 205.
15 HSWA 1974, s. 53. Relevant statutory provisions comprise Part I of HSWA, health and safety regulations (including agriculture) and any other existing statutory provisions.
16 Rehabilitation of Offenders Act 1974, *c.* 53; the list of exceptions is to be found in the Rehabilitation of Offenders Act 1974 (Exceptions) Order, SI 1975/1023 as amended by the (Exceptions) (Amendment) Order, SI 1986/1249 and the (Exceptions) (Amendment) (No. 2) Order, SI 1986/2268.
17 SDA 1975, Ss. 1, 3 and 4; RRA 1976, Ss. 1–2.
18 The Court of Appeal's decision was overturned by the House of Lords but on a point other than the interpretation of 'justifiable'.

19 SDA 1975, s. 7; SDA 1986, S.1(2); RRA 1976, s. 5.
20 Added by SDA 1986, s. 1(2).
21 EA 1989 amends SDA 1975, s. 51.
22 EA 1989, s. 5.
23 *The Sex Discrimination (Questions and Replies) Order*, SI 1975/2048, issued under Ss. 74 and 81(4) of the SDA 1975.
The Race Relations (Questions and Replies) Order, SI 1977/842, issued under Ss. 65 and 74(3) of the RRA 1976.
24 Sex Discrimination Act 1975 *c.* 65 as amended by the Sex Discrimination Act 1986 *c.* 59 and other legislation; Race Relations Act 1976; *Race Relations Code of Practice*, CRE, London, 1983; *Sex Discrimination Code of Practice*, EOC, Manchester, 1985.
25 SD Code paras 34 and 37; RR Code Part 1, paras 1 and 33.
26 Employment Act 1990.
27 SDA 1975, s. 38; the race relations requirements are in RRA 1976, s. 29.
28 SDA 1975, s. 82(1); RRA 1976, s. 78(1).
29 The security and confidentiality aspects of the information gathered during the recruitment process are dealt with in chapter 11. (Changes to contract terms are dealt with below, pp. 76–85.)
30 The Green Paper, *Industrial Relations in the 1990s*, p. 36, proposed that the position should be reversed, so that there is a presumption of legal enforceability. However, the government announced in January 1992 that it would not proceed with this proposal.
31 TULRA 1974, s. 18 (see chapter 9).
32 EP (C) A, s. 55.
33 EA 1989, s. 13. On the other hand, the government is considering making it a requirement that changes in the main terms of employment must be notified direct to the employee (*People, Jobs and Opportunity*, p. 16).
34 EP (C) A, s. 153.

3

Pay and Other Main Terms

The Legal Framework

The key problem areas are clearly those relating to the employee's entitlement (to pay, holidays and so on) and to management's ability to make changes to terms. These issues are much more likely to hinge upon questions of contract than upon the provisions of statute law. Indeed, one of the notable features of the legal context within which pay and other terms are set is the relatively small amount of statute law governing specific terms. Discrimination law covers the whole area, so that anyone treated less favourably on grounds of sex, race or union membership or activity or non-membership will be able to invoke legal remedies. Thus in *National Coal Board* v. *Ridgway and Fairbrother* it was unlawful to pay more to members of one union than to members of another.

The applicability of discrimination law to the recruitment process was considered in chapter 2 and it was noted that it covered discrimination in the terms offered. Once employment has commenced, it embraces the terms as applied. Continuing discrimination in relation to terms of employment is an act extending over the period of employment (*Barclay's Bank plc* v. *Kapur*). It will be treated as if it were done at the end of the period of employment rather than at the time the decision was made.[1] Race and sex discrimination law covers workers employed under a contract of employment as well as those who may not be employed under such a contract. The latter will be people under contracts personally to execute work or labour – contracts for services. In contrast, once employment has commenced, union discrimination law applies only to those working under contracts of employment (including contracts of apprenticeship).

Pay

Overview

For the purposes of this chapter the terms pay, wages and salary are used interchangeably. The Wages Act 1986 defines wages as 'any sums payable to the worker by his employer in connection with his employment'.[2] What is to be included in this definition is described later (see below, pp. 61–2). The European Court of Justice has also contributed to the definition of pay by developing what might be termed the European concept of pay (see below pp. 70–1).

The most significant point is that there is no legislation requiring a minimum level of pay generally, although the Wages Act 1986 makes provision for minimum wages in certain industries and services (see below, pp. 66–7) and the TUC and Labour Party are committed to the introduction of a generally applicable national minimum wage. In the absence of legislation employees cannot complain in law that their pay is too low. They can complain, however, if their pay is less than the amount due under their contract of employment, that is, if it is less than was agreed. If there is a dispute about what was agreed, the courts will rule on entitlement. Employees may also complain even where there is no dispute about entitlement if their employer has not paid them. Section 131 of the Employment Protection (Consolidation) Act 1978 allows industrial tribunals to deal with such contractual matters where they arise on termination of employment or can be brought alongside some other issue which is already within the tribunal's jurisdiction, but has not yet been made operational. In fact, the government has recently announced that new legislation will be enacted.

The position in relation to deductions is quite different. This is provided for by legislation, although part of the statutory test is based upon contractual arrangements. The Wages Act 1986 restricts the deductions that can be made from wages (or the payments that can be obtained from workers) and allows complaints to industrial tribunals about unauthorized deductions or payments.[3] Finally, there is legislation requiring itemized pay statements.

Deductions

There is a general restriction on deductions which applies to both manual and non-manual workers. The Wages Act refers to workers rather than employees, so has a broad application similar to that of the equal pay, sex and race discrimination laws. Therefore, a self-employed person working under a contract for personal services might be protected. A deduction from wages may not be made unless it is authorized:

- by statute;
- by a relevant provision of the worker's contract; or
- by the worker in advance, in writing.

These rules apply equally to payments obtained by an employer from a worker. Statutory authorization will include such deductions as National Insurance premiums and PAYE (pay as you earn). A relevant provision of the worker's contract means that there must be a term of the contract permitting deduction, as there is in the case of occupational pension contributions. Moreover, the employer must provide a copy of that term, or notify it to the worker in writing in advance of any deduction. Posting a notice on the board where the worker has an opportunity to read it may amount to notification (*McCreadie* v. *Thomson and MacIntyre (Patternmakers) Ltd*). Neither contractual changes nor the worker's agreement can be used to authorize deductions retrospectively.

As regards deductions, the Wages Act has general applicability. There are no hours restrictions or qualifying periods of employment. However, unlike previous legislation it does not actually specify whether any particular type of deduction is reasonable. It simply aims to prevent deductions being made which have not previously been agreed. In this respect the law applying to pay is like much of the law relating to terms of employment more generally – it is imbued with the spirit of the doctrine of freedom of contract. This means that the parties can (up to a point) agree what they like: in the main the law will intervene only to enforce what was agreed (but see below, p. 79–80).

The term wages includes weekly and monthly pay, including salaries. It includes any holiday pay, commission, bonuses and other pay, whether contractual or non-contractual, as well as statutory sick and maternity pay and various statutory payments such as guarantee pay and pay for time off. It does not include advances of wages, payments of expenses, pensions, ex gratia payments, redundancy payments or payments to the worker otherwise than in his capacity as a worker. Payments or benefits in kind are excluded from wages, except for vouchers with a fixed monetary value (e.g. luncheon vouchers) which are capable of being exchanged for money, goods or services.

The rules about deductions apply only to wages. Certain deductions from wages are not subject to the above rules. These include deductions made by an employer to recover over-payment of wages. However, according to the EAT in *Home Office* v. *Ayres*, the recovery of over-payments can be dealt with under the Wages Act if it is not lawful at common law. The recovery of over-payments will not automatically be lawful (see below).

If it transpired that the dispute was about entitlement to wages rather than the lawfulness of recovery of over-payment then the case would turn on the terms of the contract, and whether or not there had been a breach. Deductions to allow payments to third parties are also excluded providing the contract permits it or the worker agrees to it in writing. This would cover the check-off system of deducting union subscriptions, see below, p. 263. The employer will not be bound by the rules for deductions in the event of a strike or other industrial action.

The provisions do not apply to the Armed Forces, to those ordinarily working outside Great Britain, or to merchant seamen on non-UK registered ships, or those merchant seamen working wholly outside or living outside Great Britain. The provisions do apply to Crown employment and the NHS.

In addition to the general restrictions on deductions there are special restrictions applicable to retail employment. This includes, not just shop assistants, but many others handling money – bus conductors, drivers who collect fares, cashiers, ticket clerks and so on. The provisions apply to deductions for cash shortages or stock deficiencies including those arising from the dishonesty or negligence of the worker. The restriction is not on the amount that can be recovered by the employer, but simply on the rate at which he can make recovery. The deduction is limited to ten per cent of gross wages on any pay-day although there is no limit at the termination of employment. Deductions, or the first of a series of deductions, must be made within twelve months of the employer's discovery of the shortage or deficiency, or from any earlier date when the employer ought reasonably to have made the discovery. If the deduction is one of a series arising from the same shortage the repayment may continue beyond the twelve-month limit. Wages cannot be agreed as being net of cash shortages to avoid the ten per cent rule.

The rules governing deductions also apply to repayments. That is, there must be statutory or contractual authorization or the worker's agreement in writing. In retail employment the demand must be in writing and made on a pay-day, and the total liability must be stated before any repayment is received. The ten per cent and twelve-month rules apply. A worker's failure to repay removes the ten per cent rule and there is no limit to the percentage deduction on termination of employment. The employer may take the usual steps for recovery providing that within twelve months of the discovery of the shortage or deficiency he has made a demand for repayment in the above manner. If the worker is still in that employer's employment any court order will be limited by the ten per cent rule.

The time limit for complaint to a tribunal is three months. The tribunal, if it finds for the applicant, will make a declaration to that effect. Any unauthorized deduction will have to be repaid in full. Any over-deduction (for example, more than the ten per cent in the retail employment case) will result in repayment of the excess. Further attempts to recover the same amount from a worker after a tribunal order will be unlawful. The right of application to a tribunal replaces the worker's right to go to the county court over the matters contained in the Wages Act. Where the amount properly payable to the employee is disputed, a tribunal will need to determine this matter before deciding the issue of whether or not a deduction is lawful. Wages in lieu are damages for breach of contract and are not claimable under the Wages Act (*Delaney* v. *Staples*).

Manner of payment

There has been much interest in this area in recent years as government and employers have recognized the financial and security gains to be made from payment other than in cash. The various Truck Acts gave manual workers a right to be paid in cash (coin and notes) and so these were seen as an obstacle. The Wages Act 1986 repealed them.

The repeal of the Truck Acts means that manual workers no longer have a statutory right to be paid in cash. The issue will be subject entirely to matters of employment contract and union-employer negotiation. It may well be that those employees paid in cash before 1 January 1987 have an implied term in their contracts that cash will be the method of payment. Cashless pay, therefore, may result in claims for damages or breach of contract, or perhaps less likely, in resignations followed by tribunal applications for compensation for unfair constructive dismissal. For employees starting on or after 1 January 1987 employers are likely to insist on cashless pay as part of the contract, unless unions can persuade them otherwise.

The abolition of the manual worker's statutory right to be paid in cash also raises the question of payment in kind. How does modern law deal with this? The answer is that it does not deal with it directly. Rather, the Wages Act defines what is meant by wages (see above). Anything else, such as payment by cans of beer, bags of potatoes or car components will not constitute wages. Therefore, it follows that due wages will not have been paid, leaving an entitlement to claim under contract for damages for non-payment.

Frequency of payment

None of the above changes introduced by the Wages Act 1986 affect the frequency of pay (weekly or monthly) which remains a matter of contract and collective bargaining. Nor, indeed, is there any law in this area other than the terms of the contract of employment. Thus it is open to the parties to agree whatever frequency they wish. Courts might intervene however if an employee were foolish enough to agree that they would accept payment once a year, on the grounds that there had been duress or that such a frequency breached an implied term of reasonable frequency. In any case, at what stage does this amount to non-payment?

Over-payment

Occasionally employers may pay an employee more than he or she is due. This may arise purely through arithmetic error, or through incorrect interpretation of legal or other requirements (in relation to tax, pensions or National Insurance for instance). The law generally distinguishes between these two types of case, seeing the former as a genuine mistake which all of us are allowed to make from time to time. In such circumstances the employee will be required to make good the over-payment. In the second type of case the employer may be held to be culpable and the money may not have to be repaid.

The position is not clear-cut. Considerations which also apply are the length of time which elapsed between over-payment and discovery, the employee knew that they had money not due to them and whether the employee had relied upon the money (that is, spent it). Where the time period is long, the employee did not know and there has been reliance, the employer's position will be at its weakest, especially if the over-payment represented misinterpretation rather than mistake (see *County Council of Avon* v. *Howlett*).

In reclaiming repayment of overpaid monies, due regard will need to be given to the pay of the employee. There is no legislation on this point, but clearly as a matter of contract the employee has a right to expect that he or she will not be put in financial difficulties as a result of what was, after all, a mistake made by the employer rather than the employee.

Pay statements

The Wages Act 1986 does not affect the employee's rights under the 1978 EP (C) A to have an itemized pay statement.[4] This is a right to have deductions notified, compared with the Wages Act right not to have unauthorized deductions made. The EP (C) A requires the employer to provide an itemized pay statement on or before the time of payment of wages or salary. It must show:

- the gross amount of wages or salary;
- the amount of any variable or fixed deductions and the purposes for which they are made;
- the net amount of wages or salary payable; and
- where different parts of the net amount are paid in different ways, the amount and method of each part payment.

Separate details of fixed deductions need not be given providing the employee has been issued with a standing statement of fixed deductions. This must be issued at least every twelve months, and updated as necessary.

An employee may apply to an industrial tribunal in order to have determined what should be included in the itemized pay statement or standing statement of fixed deductions. If the employee is no longer employed by the employer the application must be made within three months of termination. The tribunal must make a declaration if they find unnotified deductions, and may order the employer to pay a sum amounting to the total of any such deductions made in the thirteen weeks preceding the tribunal application.

As already indicated, there is no qualifying period of employment needed for the rights under the Wages Act 1986. This is also true for the right to have an itemized pay statement. The latter however is restricted to those with contracts for or working sixteen hours or more per week (unless they have five years' continuous employment, in which case the figure is eight hours or more), while the Wages Act provisions have no such restrictions. Both apply to Crown employment.

Minimum wages

As noted earlier, there is no general minimum laid down by law. There are however minimum levels laid down for certain industries through the medium of wages councils. Originally trade boards, under the Trade Boards Act of 1909, they were to afford protection to employees in industries which were low-paid, and where trades union organization was weak. They now operate under the Wages Act 1986.[5] A wages council consists of equal numbers of employers' and workers' representatives appointed by their respective organizations, and up to five independent members, one of whom is the chairman. Small business interests are specifically required to be represented on the employers' side. Wages orders are enforceable as implied terms of the contract of employment, and implementation is monitored by a wages inspectorate. In fixing minimum rates wages councils must consider the possible effect on levels of employment. The orders cannot be retrospective. A period of 28 days exists for objections to the proposed rate.

Where there has been under-payment, a worker may sue for arrears for up to six years, but the wages inspector can institute civil proceedings on behalf of a worker when instigating criminal proceedings. In such circumstances the worker may obtain up to two years' arrears, and the employer may be fined. It is an offence if false records are kept or false statements made. Just over two million workers are covered by the wages council system in industries such as clothing manufacture, catering, hairdressing, toy manufacture, retail distribution and laundries. A notice of the current wages order must be displayed and homeworkers notified. The employer must keep records. Orders may set a single minimum rate of remuneration for all hours, or fix a minimum basic and a minimum overtime rate, and set a limit on deductions in respect of living accommodation The orders do not apply to anyone under the age of 21 years. Under-payment may allow an employee to resign and claim unfair constructive dismissal. Any redundancy payment must be based on a figure no less than the statutory minimum, otherwise an application may be made to a tribunal to establish the proper amount of the payment. A system similar to wages councils – wages boards – operates in agriculture.

Guarantee pay

The Employment Protection (Consolidation) Act of 1978 provides for a daily guarantee payment where the employer is unable to provide any work at all during a day when the employee's services would normally be required.[6] Crown employment is included. One month's qualifying employment is needed and any employee on a fixed-term contract of three months or less, or on a specific task contract expected to last for three months or less is excluded, unless there is already three months' continuous employment under a contract for, or working 16 hours or more per week (eight hours or more if there is already five years' continuous employment).

If the failure to provide work stems from industrial action in the employer's firm or any associated employer's firm, no payment will be due. Nor will it be due if suitable alternative employment (even if not permitted by the contract) is unreasonably refused, or if the employee does not conform to the employer's requirements relating to availability for work. The amount of the daily payment is the number of normal hours multiplied by the hourly rate, subject to a statutory maximum of £14.10. No payment is due where there are 'no normal working hours on the day in question'.[7] The maximum number of days' guarantee pay is five in any three-month period. An employee may complain to an industrial tribunal that their employer has not paid part or all of the guarantee payment. This complaint must be made within three months of the day to which the application relates. Any remuneration for the day may be offset against the liability to pay statutory guarantee pay. Where there is a collective agreement on guarantee pay, and at the request of the parties, the Minister may issue an order exempting from the statutory provisions the employees covered by that agreement.[8] Guarantee pay has no bearing on the issue of whether the employer has a right under the contract to dispense with some or all of the employee's pay during a lay-off or short-time working when there is insufficient work. This will depend on the terms of the contract.

Equal pay

British legislation and case law
The Equal Pay Act 1970 operates by inserting an equality clause into the contract of employment. This means that there should be equality where a man and a woman are employed:

- on 'like work' – work of the same or a broadly similar nature;
- on 'work rated as equivalent' – work of equal value under a non-discriminatory job evaluation scheme; or
- on work which is of equal value.

'Like work' does not mean that the work has to be the same (*Capper Pass Ltd* v. *Lawton*). It can be 'broadly similar', but the differences must not be of any 'practical importance.'[9] The time at which the work is done does not affect whether it is 'like work' (*Dugdale* v. *Kraft Foods Ltd*). What has to be examined is the work actually done, rather than what could be done under the contract (*Electrolux Ltd* v. *Hutchinson*). Job evaluation schemes allow a comparison of different jobs for the purposes of equal pay claims. The scheme must be non-discriminatory, impartial and must constitute a proper analysis (*Eaton Ltd* v. *Nuttall*; *Bromley and ors* v. *H & J Quick Ltd*).

In 1982 the European Court had decided that the British Equal Pay Act was not sufficient to meet the requirements of the EC Directive on Equal Pay[10] (*Commission of the European Communities* v. *UK*). A woman must be able to claim equal pay for work of equal value, hence the 1983 regulations, operative from the beginning of January 1984 and issued under the European Communities Act 1972.[11] These mean that equal pay can be claimed irrespective of the jobs being completely different, provided that the demands made 'under such headings as effort, skill and decision' are of equal value.

The British legislation states that equal value claims are permitted only if neither 'like work' nor 'work rated as equivalent' claims are possible. In *Pickstone and ors* v. *Freemans plc*, however, the House of Lords held that this was a restriction of the wider European right to pursue an equal value claim. Thus, the present domestic law is deficient and complainants can rely on the wider European interpretation. This means, for example, that the existence of a man doing work that is the same as the complainant's and being paid the same does not preclude an equal value claim using some other man as the comparator.

The Act does not apply solely to pay. It extends to other terms. However, the House of Lords has rejected the argument that the whole remuneration package has to be considered, rather than just pay. The basic rate must be the same regardless of other contractual benefits (*Hayward* v. *Cammell Laird Shipbuilders Ltd*). The Act applies to both men and women. The comparator has to be in the 'same employment' as the claimant.[12] This means employed by the same (or an associated) employer at the same establishment, or at a different establishment if there are common terms (see *Leverton* v. *Clwyd County Council*). A woman may compare herself with a male predecessor (*MacCarthys* v. *Smith*). It is not provided under the Act, however, for comparison to be made with a 'notional' man (i.e. to argue that a man doing the same job *would* have been paid more). It will be for the applicant to establish like work, equally-rated work and the same employment. Conversely, these issues will provide a basis for the employer's defence.

If the applicant succeeds in establishing the comparison, the employer may then argue that the variation in male/female terms is nothing to do with sex. The equality clause does not operate if the variation is 'genuinely due to a material factor'[13]. In 1978, the Court of Appeal stressed personal factors (such as skills, training and experience) when it looked at material difference in *Clay Cross (Quarry Services)* v. *Fletcher*. In the same year, however, the EAT accepted that different hours of work (part-time as opposed to full-time) were a material difference because of the differential contribution made towards offsetting the firm's overhead costs (*Handley* v. *H Mono Ltd*). By 1981 the EAT, after a reference to the European Court, decided that a difference in hours (full-time rather than part-time) was not in itself a material difference, but could be if it gave economic advantages to the employer (*Jenkins* v. *Kingsgate (Clothing Productions) Ltd No 2*). Thus material difference could include economic factors, an interpretation later confirmed in *Rainey* v. *Greater Glasgow Health Board*. Different pay structures can also be a material factor as in *Leverton* and in *Reed Packaging* v. *Boozer and Everhurst*. When an industrial tribunal is comparing a woman's pay with that of a man whose work is of equal value, the tribunal may take into account that their notional hourly rates of pay are similar but that she both works shorter hours and is entitled to longer holidays in order to infer that the difference between their annual salaries is genuinely due to a material factor other than sex (*Leverton*). The onus of proof is on the employer to show a material factor. Such factors must be justifiable, that is, caused by a real need on the part of the undertaking, appropriate to meet that need and necessary (*Bilka-Kaufhaus GmbH* v. *Weber von Hartz*).

The decision in *British Railways Board* v. *Paul* makes it appear that there is no time limit for complaints made by individuals to industrial tribunals, nor, by inference, for applications by employers. However, the interpretation of the statute in this case is perhaps doubtful. It may be wiser to regard the time limit as being six months from the date of termination. Applications can also be made where employment is continuing. The Secretary of State may take cases to tribunals, either while the complainant is still employed or within six months of leaving. Where the claim is successful the remedies are damages and up to two years' arrears of pay. A special procedure operates for equal value claims. First, the tribunal must dismiss the claim if it is satisfied that there are no reasonable grounds for determining that the jobs are of equal value. Second, if the case progresses, an expert (from a panel drawn up by ACAS) will be called in to do an assessment of the value of the respective jobs and to present a report to the tribunal.

The Act is comprehensive in its application. Few occupations are excluded and there are no hours or length of employment qualifications for making a claim. It applies to those who are 'employed', which is a wider category than 'employees' (see *Quinnen* v. *Howells*).[14] Until recently equality of retirement and death provisions was excepted apart from access to pension schemes. However, in *Garland* v. *British Rail Engineering Ltd*, a case which the House of Lords referred to the European Court, differential travel concessions after retirement were found to be a breach of article 119 of the Treaty of Rome, which overrides UK legislation. Similarly in *Worringham and anor* v. *Lloyd's Bank Ltd* an enhanced gross salary for men to compensate for pension contributions which they had to pay, but which women did not pay, constituted a breach of European law, notwithstanding the exception in the UK legislation. That exemption has subsequently been narrowed considerably by the Sex Discrimination Act 1986 so that pay provisions relating to retirement and concerning demotion, dismissal, promotion, transfer or training must not be discriminatory.[15]

The European approach to equal pay

Article 119 of the Treaty of Rome, which established the European Economic Community, holds that there should be 'equal pay for equal work'. An Equal Pay Directive requires member countries to give effect to this principle through their own legislation.

Although the British equal pay legislation includes contractual terms other than pay, it does not go as far as the concept which has been developed by the European Court of Justice. Recent ECJ cases show that contractual and statutory sick and redundancy pay, and occupational pensions, are pay within the meaning of article 119. Therefore, they are subject to the principle of equal pay and article 119 can be directly relied upon in preference to the narrower domestic legislation.

This appears to have two possible effects. First, any differences in terms – pay, in the wider, European sense – on grounds of sex will be unlawful because they are in breach of European equal pay legislation. Thus, differences in pensionable age and in benefits payable under an occupational pension scheme are a direct breach of the principle of equal pay as laid down in European law (*Barber* v. *Guardian Royal Exchange Assurance Group*). Second, exclusion of groups of people from particular terms (for instance, part-timers from redundancy pay) where those groups are predominantly of one sex may constitute indirect sex discrimination if it cannot be objectively justified by factors unrelated to sex. (Such discrimination was held to be objectively justified in *R.* v. *Secretary of State for Employment*. See below, p. 156.) Thus, since statutory sickness payments made by an employer are pay under article 119, denial of such pay to part-timers, affecting women more than men, constitutes indirect sex discrimination (*Rinner-Kühn* v. *FWW Spezial-Gebäudereinigung GmbH & Co. KG*). Similarly, since severance payments under a collective agreement were pay, the exclusion of part-timers, most of whom were women, constituted indirect sex discrimination and there was an entitlement to proportionate benefits (*Kowalska* v. *Freie und Hansestadt Hamburg*).

Moreover, there is, in another recent decision, the basis of an approach to the equal pay comparison which is entirely different from that used in the UK (*Handels-OG Kontorfunktionaerernes Forbund i Danmark* v. *Dansk Arbejdsgiverforening* (*acting for Danfoss*)). Domestic legislation requires a woman to use one or more individual comparators as the basis for her case. By comparison, the ECJ in *Danfoss* stated that it was sufficient for the complainant to show a statistical imbalance between men's and women's pay to throw the burden of proof onto the employer to justify the imbalance. The context was one in which discretionary elements of pay were being distributed between individuals on a basis which was not clear.

Hours of Work

There is no legislation operating to generally determine hours of work. Traditionally, the hours of work of women and young persons have been restricted, but this legislation has now been repealed. The restrictions on the employment of children (persons under minimum school-leaving age) remain. They must not be employed before the close of school hours on any day when required to attend school, nor before 7am nor after 7pm on any day. The maximum number of hours of employment on any day when required to attend school, or on a Sunday, is two hours. These provisions are found in the Children and Young Persons Acts 1933-69, which also give local authorities the power to make bye-laws extending the regulation.[16]

In addition to the provisions concerned with children, there is a small amount of legislation relating to the hours of work of people in a number of specific occupations: vehicle drivers, underground miners, sheet-glass workers and shop assistants.[17] Agricultural wages board orders may also regulate hours.[18] Otherwise, hours of work will be in accordance with the contract of employment. Usually, this will provide for some normal or standard number of hours per week, beyond which hours constitute overtime. The rate at which overtime is paid, is, like ordinary pay, not governed by legislation. Rather it is a matter of contract.

The requirement to work a reasonable amount of overtime may be a term of the contract. Whether an employee can lawfully refuse to work overtime in these circumstances will depend on such factors as the number of hours overtime sought by the employer, the frequency of overtime working, the extent of advance notice given by the employer, any health and safety considerations and the need of the business for the overtime. An employer cannot lawfully require an employee to work for so many hours that there would be a foreseeable risk of injury to his health (*Johnstone* v. *Bloomsbury and Islington Health Authority*).

Even where an employee is required to work a reasonable amount of overtime as part of the contract of employment the overtime worked will not necessarily be of a contractual nature. This will be true even if the overtime is frequent, regular and substantial. The test of whether overtime is contractual is whether the employer must provide it and the employee must work it. Thus, even if the work the overtime is intended to produce is not there, the employer must pay and the employee must be available. Contractual overtime is characterized by overtime pay being included in pay during absence (for example, for sickness or holidays).

The treatment of overtime and hours of work generally for the purposes of computation of unfair dismissal compensation and redundancy payments is dealt with in chapters 7 and 8 respectively. The law has developed a concept of 'normal working hours' for these purposes.[19] 'Working hours' is the more general legal concept meaning hours of work as determined by the contract of employment.[20]

Holidays and Time Off

Holidays

There is no general legislation concerning holidays. A small amount of legislation exists in relation to specific occupations – shop assistants and agricultural workers – but otherwise there is only the statutory provision for bank holidays.[21] This does not, however, confer a statutory right to take holidays on those days. The most that can be said is that there may be an implied term in many contracts of employment that bank holidays will actually be provided as paid holidays. Clearly this will not be the case in those industries (such as hotels and catering) where bank holidays are traditionally busy work periods although there might be an implied term that there will be time off in lieu; nor will it be the case where there is an express term to the contrary.

As with pay, there is generally no legal remedy for the employee's complaint that he does not have sufficient holidays. Disputes over holidays, therefore, are more likely to be about entitlement (i.e. what was agreed) or timing, or perhaps failure to return to work on time. Contractual terms may be relevant to such problems.

Time off for public duties[22]

An employee is entitled to time off for duties arising out of holding one of the following public positions:

- justice of the peace;
- member of a local authority;
- member of a statutory tribunal;
- member of an NHS trust or authority (including a family health services authority);[23]
- member of the National Rivers Authority;
- member of the governing body of an educational establishment maintained by a local authority, a grant-maintained school or a higher education corporation; or
- member of a board of visitors for prisons, remand centres and so on.

The amount of time off is what is 'reasonable in all the circumstances'. There is no obligation upon an employer to pay for the time off. Any employee refused time off may apply to a tribunal within three months. The tribunal may make an award which is 'just and equitable' taking into account any loss sustained and the infringement of rights.

Time off for maternity reasons

There is statutory maternity leave (see chapter 6 for Statutory Maternity Pay) and statutory time off for antenatal care.[24] These rights are limited to employees, and exclude the police, armed forces, share-fisherwomen and those ordinarily working outside Great Britain. There is no statutory paternity leave, although there are employments where this has been agreed with trades unions and may have become incorporated as a term in individual contracts, and there may be cases where it is a direct and expressly agreed term of the contract.

There is no minimum qualifying employment or hours requirement for the right to paid antenatal time off. The woman must have an appointment. For any second or subsequent appointment she must, if requested, provide a medical certificate as proof of pregnancy, and evidence of the appointment, such as an appointment card. Any complaint to a tribunal must be made within three months of the appointment for which paid time off has been refused. An employer may defend such a claim by arguing that the refusal was reasonable.

Statutory maternity leave is expressed as the right to return to work. It applies until the end of the period of 29 weeks beginning with the week in which the child is born, although it may be extended in certain circumstances. The qualifying period of employment is two years at 16 or more hours, or five years at eight or more, up to the eleventh week before the expected week of confinement, as medically certified. (The requirement for a period of qualifying employment is likely to be removed to allow the UK to conform with the EC's proposed Directive on the Protection of Pregnant Women at Work.) The woman must continue to be employed, but does not necessarily have to be at work, up to the eleventh week before confinement. She must give all the following information to her employer in writing at least 21 days before maternity absence, or as soon as it is reasonably practicable:

- that she will be (or is) absent from work in order to have a baby;
- that she intends to return to work afterwards;
- the expected week of confinement (or actual week if it has already occurred).

If requested by the employer she must produce the medical certificate showing the expected week of confinement. The employer has the right to send a written request not earlier than 49 days from the notified date of the beginning of confinement asking for confirmation of intention to return. He must explain that a failure to give written confirmation within 14 days (or as soon after as is reasonably practicable) will lose the employee the right to return. She must in any case notify the employer in writing of her proposed date of return at least 21 days beforehand.

The return to work must be within 29 weeks of the week in which the child was born unless illness prevents it, in which case the period may be extended by up to four weeks. The same is true where the employer gives specified reasons for delaying the return, and notifies the employee of a later date. Where there is industrial action the return will be as soon as practicable after the dispute or within 28 days if no date has been notified. The return can also be delayed by mutual agreement, according to the EAT in *Dowvona* v. *John Lewis plc*. The period of absence does not break continuity, and counts for the computation of length of employment for statutory purposes. Whether it counts for seniority, pension and other length of employment payments such as pay increments, depends on the terms of the contract (but see below, p. 151, in relation to pensions and the third EC Equal Treatment Directive).

The right to return will not apply if there has been a redundancy and there is no suitable alternative work, or if an offer of such work is unreasonably refused. Similarly, if the employer can argue that it is not reasonably practicable to take the woman back in her original job, but that suitable alternative work has been offered, which she has unreasonably rejected, the right to return will be lost. An employer with five or fewer employees can argue that it was not reasonably practicable to take her back nor to offer her suitable alternative work. 'Suitable' means that the terms, conditions and location are not substantially less favourable than those of her employment prior to maternity absence.

Time off for other purposes

There is statutory time off for union officials and members to pursue various union activities. These provisions are outlined in chapter 9. Separate rights to time off exist for union safety representatives (see chapter 4). A person under notice for reason of redundancy has a statutory right to time off to look for another job or to arrange training (see chapter 8). Reservists called up to serve in the Armed Forces have their employment rights protected by the Reserve Forces (Safeguard of Employment) Act 1985. There is no statutory provision for time off for other purposes, for instance, short-term leave to cope with family emergencies, or extended leave for carers, although there is probably an implied contractual term allowing time off to attend court as a juror or a witness.

Making Changes to Terms and Conditions of Employment

There are a number of ways in which employers can make changes to terms and conditions of employment. Some are lawful, others are not. The various types of change are described below and summarized in figure 3.1.

Agreed variation of contract terms

Express agreement
The contract of employment is at the centre of the employment relationship and changes in terms can easily give rise to problems. In law the contract is an agreement entered into voluntarily by the parties. In theory, the parties have equal status and power. The mutuality principle extends to changes in the terms – where both parties agree, the terms may be varied. This is known as mutual or consensual variation. Such variation occurs frequently and by definition is rarely problematic. For example, an exployee agrees to a change in work location; the employer agrees to a financial package to compensate.

Variation by conduct
There are also situations in which changes are made unilaterally by one party but are accepted by the other party by implication. That is, they are not challenged, and over a period of time – unspecified, as is usual in law – it will be taken that 'silence is consent'. For example, an employee's hours are reduced from 32 to 26 per week. After initial protest the employee continues working until made redundant three years later. The change was agreed. The employee's conduct is interpreted as indicating acceptance of the change.

Incorporation of terms from collective agreements
Employers may also be able to make changes to contract terms by securing agreement with a trades union. Again, the change may be willingly agreed by a union or be accepted because the union is unable

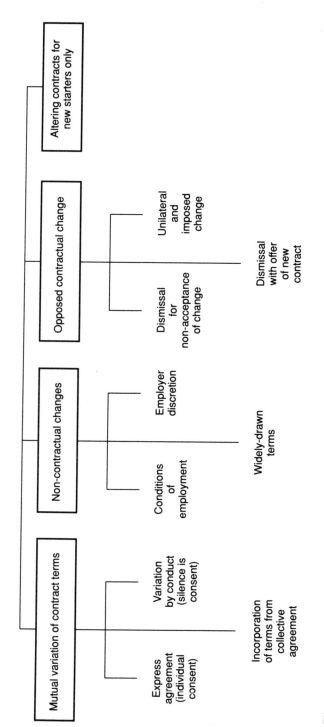

Figure 3.1 Making changes to terms and conditions of employment

in practice to prevent it. The change will alter the contracts of employment of individual employees only if the terms of the collective agreement become incorporated into those contracts. This may be provided for expressly – where it is stated that contract terms will be as negotiated from time to time between the company and the trades union – or be implied. (For implied terms see p. 49.) In the latter case, individual contract terms are altered in practice by collectively bargained changes. Contract terms may be altered by collective bargaining where, for example, employers have succeeded in negotiating work flexibility agreements with unions.

Non-contractual changes

Conditions of employment
Not all changes to terms and conditions of employment involve contractual changes. A distinction can be drawn between terms and conditions. The former may include the amount of holidays, the latter when the holidays may be taken. Terms are based on contractual agreement whereas conditions are laid down by an employer unilaterally – they are a *condition* of employment. Changes in conditions may be seen as relatively minor, perhaps even as administrative changes. Clearly, however, changes made to such as the timing of holidays, method of payment or method of work may give rise to legal and/or industrial challenges. Nevertheless, it is submitted, an employer may argue that a change does not amount to a change in terms but is merely a change in conditions which lies within the legitimate authority of the employer.

Employer discretion
Some aspects of employment may be neither terms nor conditions. They may be elements provided by an employer on a goodwill basis, with nothing specific sought in exchange. It follows that the withdrawal of such items may well be at the discretion of the employer. This applies particularly to matters such as Christmas bonuses and the private use of company cars. In effect these are gifts made by management since the employee is not required to contribute anything to the organization in exchange. However, much will depend on the circumstances of the case; for example, the private use of a company car could be expressly agreed as a contractual term. Where something is required in exchange (for instance, good attendance as a

qualification for entitlement to a bonus) the relationship assumes more of a contractual character.

Widely-drawn terms

Contract terms may be sufficiently wide to allow a change to be effected within the contract without any breach occurring. For example, if the employee's contract provides that they will work at any of the organization's sites, a change of location will be permitted by the contract. It is then a matter for the employer to ensure that the move is reaeonably handled; that sufficient warning and perhaps financial assistance are provided (*United Bank Ltd* v. *Akhtar*).[25] Another example is where a contract includes a description of specific duties but also provides that the employee will perform whatever else his manager may require. Courts will look at the reasonableness of such requirements, particularly in relation to the normal job duties and status of the employee. Therefore, a university lecturer with such a term in his contract need not feel unduly troubled about refusing a request to clean out the lavatory. A further example of a widely-drawn term is where an employer expressly reserves the right to vary terms.

The courts will use common law principles looking closely at widely-drawn terms and at anything involving penalties (e.g. payments in relation to discrepancies; repayment of training costs). By doing this they have developed the practice of limiting the effect of what the parties have agreed. This happened in *Akhtar* where an implied term that there should be proper warning was found. In *Johnstone* there was no absolute right to require 88 hours of work (including hours on call) despite a contractual term to this effect. A lack of reasonableness can also give rise to a finding that the employer has breached that term of the contract which requires mutual trust and confidence. Finally, if a term is too widely drawn the courts may regard it as uncertain in its application. Although a valid term, the courts may nonetheless refuse to enforce it.

Opposed contractual change

The legal position

Problems often occur when an employer wishes to change what is clearly a contractual term and this is against the wishes of the employee (and perhaps their union). Where agreement to the change is not forthcoming an employer may contemplate unilateral change. Generally speaking, any unilateral change which is not accepted opens the way for a claim that one or more of the contract terms have been breached. If the breach is substantial and the term is one which goes to the very root of the contract – pay, for example – the breach may be said to be a fundamental one. That is, the employment contract has been repudiated – the employer has, in effect, said that he or she no longer intends to be bound by the terms of the contract. Putting someone on a half-time, half-pay contract after a full-time, full-pay one was a pay cut and a demotion amounting to a fundamental breach of contract. The fact that a part-time contract was accepted afterwards did not mean that the change was affirmed. The employee accepted the employer's repudiation and brought the former contract to an end (*Hogg* v. *Dover College*).

The employee, faced with any breach of contract (whether a repudiatory (fundamental) breach or not) may elect to affirm the contract and continue. In doing so he or she can either accept the change, or reject it by standing on the original terms and suing for damages. Thus, in *Ferodo* v. *Rigby*, where a wage cut was imposed on employees despite their opposition and the opposition of their union, the resulting breach of contract allowed them to sue for damages for the amount of the reduction. This was also the position in *Burdett-Coutts and ors* v. *Hertfordshire County Council*. Similarly, in the absence of an agreed variation of terms, an employee was entitled to claim lost pay caused by a shorter working week being introduced unilaterally by his employer (*Miller* v. *Hamworthy Engineering Ltd*).

If the breach is repudiatory, the employee can accept the repudiation and treat it as grounds for terminating the contract. In such circumstances the employee must at some stage choose between acceptance and affirmation. Provided he makes clear his objection to what is being done, he may continue to work and draw pay for a limited period of time without being taken to have affirmed the contract (*Marriott* v. *Oxford Co-operative Society*). However, in a later ruling – also by the Court of Appeal – it was stated that if the employee 'continues for any length of time without leaving he will lose his right to treat himself as discharged'. (*Western Excavating (ECC)* v. *Sharp*). The EAT subsequently adopted the softer line of *Marriott* but noted that a prolonged delay in electing for acceptance of repudiation may be evidence of an implied affirmation (*W. E. Cox Toner (International) Ltd* v. *Crook*). After accepting repudiation, the employee may sue for damages or pursue a claim for compensation for unfair (constructive) dismissal, or both.

The employee has the right to treat the contract as terminated only if the breach is fundamental. Where the breach is not fundamental, the employee's action is to stand on the original terms and sue for damages.

Effecting the change: the employer's options
Can an employer ever defend a contractual breach as lawful? There are three options here, all of which, ultimately, might need defending at law. First, an employer may give notice to the employee (that is, notice of termination of contract) and offer a new contract containing new terms (*Gilham and ors* v. *Kent County Council*). Continuity is automatically preserved for statutory purposes and can be preserved for other purposes by agreement. A second option is to enforce the change by informing the employee that if they do not accept it they will be dismissed with due notice. The third option is to impose the change and wait for the employee to either consent to it by his conduct or commence legal proceedings.

Possible responses by employees
Whichever option the employer chooses it will result in a dismissal, although this will be true in the third case only if the breach is fundamental and is accepted as a repudiation. For the dismissal to be found fair, if it is challenged, an employer will have to demonstrate to a tribunal that there was a valid reason. A dismissal for unwillingness to accept contractual change constitutes 'some other substantial reason' under unfair dismissal law (see chapter 7). An employer will need to show that the business had a real need for change of the type that has been effected. For example, acute financial difficulties caused by a lack of competitiveness might warrant changes in the duties of employees in order to increase productivity and reduce unit costs. Less dramatically, an employer wishing to introduce a no smoking policy and dismissing someone who would not accept it might argue that the need to comply with section 2 of the Health and Safety at Work etc. Act 1974 (HSWA) was a substantial reason.

Once a fair reason is established, the fairness of the dismissal will then depend upon how it was handled. For example, were the need for and details of the change explained to the employee? Was there advance warning (if it was possible)? Was there assistance, if necessary (for example, where there is a change of location) or training (for instance, where duties are changed)? In addition, has the proper procedure been followed – has an opportunity been given to the employee to state his or her case?

The employee may respond in other ways (see figure 3.2). Where the contractual change is a wage reduction, an employee may be able to apply to an industrial tribunal under the Wages Act 1986, that is, in respect of an unauthorized deduction. More generally, there is the possibility of suing for breach of contract. This will not be an option if the employer has dismissed with due notice, but will apply where a change has been unilaterally imposed. Dismissing with due notice for non-acceptance of change or by offering a new contract thus restricts the employee to a tribunal claim (if there is eligibility) and removes the prospect of a claim in respect of breach of contract. Claims in respect of breach of contract are dealt with in the common law courts – the county court and High Court – and there is the common law remedy of damages. In as much as an employee is able to claim damages for breach of contract these will normally be restricted to the notice period since the contract could have been ended lawfully if due notice had been given, although this principle was not accepted as applying in *Ferodo*.

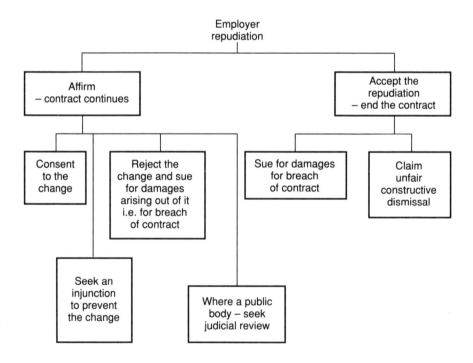

Figure 3.2 The employee's options when an employer repudiates the contract

There are also equitable remedies, *viz.* injunctions and orders for specific performance. It is considered inappropriate to force continuation of an employment relationship when one of the parties is opposed to it, so specific performance is rarely granted. Trust and confidence would need to have been preserved between the parties and there would need to be some benefits arising from continuation. However, in a recent case the test applied was less stringent: the relationship had to be 'workable' (*Robb* v. *London Borough of Hammersmith and Fulham*). In any case, it would need to be established that damages would be an inadequate remedy. Sometimes a temporary injunction may be granted where breach of contract is alleged (see *Hill* v. *C. A. Parsons* and *Irani* – wrongful dismissals chapter 7, and *Hughes and ors* v. *London Borough of Southwark* – change of work duties and location). On the other hand, the High Court would not grant an injunction in *MacPherson* v. *London Borough of Lambeth* to stop the employer withholding pay because the employees would not operate a new computer. The employees were not able and willing to perform their contractual duties.

To decide whether an injunction should be granted the courts apply what is known as the balance of convenience test (*American Cynamid* v. *Ethicon Ltd*). The court asks:

● Is there a serious issue to be tried?
● Would damages provide an adequate remedy for the plaintiff if the injunction was refused but he or she subsequently succeeded at a full hearing of the case?
● Would the employer be adequately compensated by damages if the injunction was granted but he or she subsequently succeeded at a full hearing of the case?

The Court is not required to look at the relative strength of the parties' cases.

It will not be possible for employees to seek remedies of any sort for breach of contract, however, if the contract itself is illegal, for example, because the employee is a child, or because there was a deliberately illegal purpose such as defrauding the Inland Revenue. This would also prevent unfair dismissal and other claims such as sex discrimination although perhaps not if the employee was unaware of the illegality.

Many employees faced with a repudiatory breach of contract by an employer will prefer the simpler, quicker and cheaper route of claiming unfair constructive dismissal to processing a claim for damages. This may, perhaps, be less true where a claim for damages is compatible with continued employment, and where the legal services of a trades union are available (both of these applied in *Ferodo*). In practice, many employees will probably reluctantly accept the employer's imposed change because of the need to keep their job.

Where the employer is a public body, there is also the possibility of a decision being open to challenge by judicial review. There will have to be a public law issue at stake, otherwise the case would be a straightforward private law matter (for example, a claim for remedy for breach of contract) (*R.* v. *East Berkshire Health Authority ex parte Walsh*). However, the decisions of local authorities to reduce wages by dismissing and offering new employment on inferior terms were subject to judicial review, although orders to quash them were not granted (*R.* v. *Hertfordshire County Council ex parte NUPE and ors*; *R.* v. *East Sussex County Council ex parte NUPE and ors*). A decision to withhold the pay of teachers because they were unable to work when caretakers were involved in industrial action was quashed in *R.* v. *Liverpool City Corporation ex parte Ferguson*. A decision of the same council to declare redundancies (following the setting of an illegal rate) was also quashed (*R.* v. *Liverpool City Corporation ex parte Ferguson and Smith*) (see chapter 8).

Altering the contract terms for new starters

If an employer is worried about the response that existing employees and/or their trades union might make to a change in terms, there is the possibility of restricting the change to new entrants. The individual nature of the contract of employment makes this relatively easy to achieve. New entrants would be offered terms different in some way from those of existing staff. For example, new staff might have a wider term in relation to where the work is to be carried on – they may be required to work in more than one place or to transfer from time to time between places. Existing staff may have contracts specifying one place of work. Care would need to be taken in relation to any collective agreements. A confusing situation would arise if the employee's written particulars specified that terms were to be as determined from time to time by agreements with a union, whereas in fact one or more of the terms differed fron that laid down in the collective agreement. It would need to be clear that the express incorporation of collectively-bargained terms did not extend to the particular term(s) in question.

Continuity of Employment

Significance and computation

Various rules are set down for establishing whether or not a person's employment is continuous. Many employment law rights depend on a person having a minimum period of continuous employment, so that entitlement to use the legislation will be governed by whether there is the necessary length of continuous employment. In addition continuity will be a factor determining the number of full years of employment for compensation purposes. An employer who establishes that there has been a break in continuity may succeed in barring the employee's claim altogether, or in reducing the compensation that has to be paid.

Employment means employment under a contract of employment or apprenticeship, and the continuity provisions (except where they specifically relate to a change of employer – see below) apply to employment by one employer. Once the fact of a contract of employment is established, and a starting date proven, employment is presumed to be continuous. An employer would need to bring evidence to the contrary if he or she wanted to rebut the presumption. Continuous employment will begin on whatever date the contract specifies for the start of work, even if it is not a working day – the date specified might be the first day of the next month, and this might be a Sunday (see *The General of the Salvation Army* v. *Dewsbury*). For the purpose of claiming a statutory redundancy payment (RP), but not for claims for remedies for unfair dismissal etc., employment before the age of 18 years does not count towards continuous employment. Changes in the terms of contracts do not interrupt continuity of employment.

Two major issues which arise in the computation of continuous employment are:

- What counts towards continuity?
- What breaks continuity?

Any week in which the employee works under a contract for 16 or more hours counts, even if the actual hours worked are fewer than 16. Alternatively, a week counts if the actual hours are 16 or more. Where contractual hours fall from 16 or more to eight or more (but under 16) continuity is preserved for up to a further 26 weeks. A person who has been employed for five years working eight or more hours per week establishes continuity. Anyone working fewer than eight hours will never, however, obtain any continuous employment. These hours requirements may be of considerable importance, therefore, and need to be borne in mind. For example a 30-hour a week job, subject to a 50/50 job share, would result in neither of the employees having continuity until a five-year period had elapsed. This might or might not be what an employer intends.

Continuity preserved by contract or statute

An employer and an employee may agree, either expressly or impliedly, that the contract of employment will continue even in the absence of the employee. An express agreement may be found in cases of secondment, career break or maternity leave. Continuity in respect of the last of these (as far as the statutory period is concerned) is in any case preserved by statute, providing the woman returns to work, and the weeks also count. More problems are likely to be caused by cases involving long-term sickness or absence occasioned by employees serving prison sentences. Here, the general rule will be that the contract is taken as continuing unless terminated by the employer or employee. However, there is also the possibility that the contract may be frustrated. This is a useful argument for an employer to put, because if successful it means that there is no dismissal. Hence, no questions of unfair dismissal or redundancy arise. Frustration means that the contract comes to an end by force of law because one of the parties cannot perform it at all, or can only perform it on terms radically different from those originally appertaining. The reason is likely to be neither foreseeable nor the direct fault of the parties. Long-term illness and imprisonment are the main examples. There are some cases where it is obvious to all that the contract must be regarded as being at an end. There are others, however, which are less clear, for instance, a prolonged illness where the outcome is uncertain. The EAT in *Egg Stores (Stamford Hill) Ltd* v. *Leibovici* put forward a number of factors which should be considered in such cases:

- length of previous employment;
- expected future length of employment;
- nature of the work;
- nature, length and effect of the injury or illness;
- the employer's need for the work to be done and the need for a replacement to do it;

- the risk to the employer of a replacement employee acquiring employment protection rights;
- whether the employer has continued to pay the employee; and
- whether a reasonable employer could be expected to wait any longer for the employee to return.

An 18-month absence because of illness did not frustrate the contract in *Marshall* v. *Harland and Wolff Ltd* because there was no evidence that the contract could not again be performed, or that it could be performed only in a way radically different from that originally intended. This was a large firm. On the other hand, a borstal sentence expected to last nine months did frustrate a four-year apprenticeship in a relatively small company (*F. C. Shepherd and Co. Ltd* v. *Jerrom*).

Statute specifically preserves continuity in a number of situations where there is no contract, and the weeks also count. First, absence due to injury or illness may result in continuity being preserved for up to 26 weeks. This would be in addition to any contractual sick leave. The same is true of absence due to pregnancy, although here the 26-week period can be extended through the provision of statutory maternity leave. Absence from work, without a contract, due to a temporary cessation of work (other than because of industrial action in which the employee takes part) does not break continuity, and also counts. What is temporary is a matter of fact for tribunal to decide (*Ford* v. *Warwickshire County Council*). The reason for any temporary cessation is not relevant to the question of continuity. It is also possible to have continuous employment in the absence of a contract where there is a custom or arrangement to that effect.

Strikes do not break continuity but neither do they count when computing the period of employment. They do count if the employee cannot work because of a strike by someone else. An employee dismissed during a strike and later re-engaged has his continuity preserved, but the days on strike do not count towards the period of employment. The days on strike postpone the start of the period of continuous employment. As regards lock-outs, there is no break in continuity and the days also count.

Changes of employer

The above description has related to continuous employment with one employer, but statute also makes provision for continuity to be preserved, in certain cases, when there is a change of employer.

Where the respective employers expressly agree to continuity there is unlikely to be a problem. The difficulty is likely to arise where an employer finds unexpectedly that one of their employees can count employment with a previous employer and themself as continuous.

Statute preserves continuity where a business is transferred as a going concern, that is, including assets and goodwill. Another instance of continuity is where an employee transfers to an associated employer – where one firm controls the other, or both are controlled by a third person. Local authorities are to be treated as if they were associated for continuity for RP purposes.[26] Finally, continuity is preserved by statute if there is a transfer which falls under the Transfer of Undertakings Regulations (see chapter 8). In the above situations an employer will need to check whether he has inherited any continuous employment. Continuous employment with a previous employer should be specified in the written particulars of terms of employment given to new starters.

Notes

1 Race Relations Act 1987, s. 68(7) (a) and (b). These apply rather than (c) so an application some years later would not be time-barred as it would have been if there had been a 'deliberate omission'. By contrast, an alleged discriminatory grading was a one-off decision rather than a continuing act and the claim was time-barred (*Sougrin* v. *Haringey Health Authority*).

2 Wages Act 1986, *c*.48, s. 7(1).

3 Wages Act Ss. 1-11.

4 EP (C) A, s. 8.

5 Wages Act Ss. 12-16.

6 EP (C) A, s. 12.

7 EP (C) A, s. 14(1).

8 EP (C) A, s. 18.

9 Equal Pay Act 1970 *c*.41.

10 75/117/EEC under article 119 of the Treaty of Rome.

11 Equal Pay (Amendment) Regulations, SI 1983/1794. These were issued under the European Communities Act 1972, *c*.68.

12 EqPA, s. 1(2).

13 EqPA, s. 1(3).

14 EqPA, s. 1(6).

15 Sex Discrimination Act 1986 *c*.59, s. 2.

16 Children and Young Persons Act 1933 *c*.12, s. 18. There is a separate Act for Scotland.

17 See: Transport Act 1968 *c*.73 (Part VI) ; Coal Mines Regulation Act 1908 as amended; Hours of Employment (Conventions) Act 1936, s. 3 (hours of work in automatic sheet-glass works) and the Shops Acts 1950–65. The Coal Industry Bill published in November 1991 provides for the repeal of the Coal Mines Regulation Act 1908.
18 Agricultural Wages Act 1948 *c*.47, s. 3, (wages, holidays and other terms).
19 EP (C) A, Schedule 14.
20 EP (C) A, s. 32.
21 Shops Acts 1950–65; Agricultural Wages Act 1948.
22 EP (C) A, s. 29.
23 Previously family practitioner committees (National Health Service and Community Care Act 1990 *c*.19, s. 2).
24 Employment Act 1980 *c*.42, s. 13.
25 The EAT has subsequently stressed that the rule in *Akhtar* does not require any general test of reasonableness: it requires no more than that an employer should not act in a way which prevents the employee fulfilling his side of the contract (*White* v. *Reflecting Roadstuds Ltd*). However, an employer must behave responsibly by having sufficient reason for instituting change and must not destroy the employee's trust and confidence in him (*Reflecting Roadstuds*).
26 Redundancy Payments (Local Government) (Modification) Order, SI 1983/1160, as amended.

4

Health and Safety: the Legal Framework

Introduction

Breach of statute law in this area gives rise to criminal offences, with prosecutions taken by the Health and Safety Executive or the appropriate local authority, and to claims for damages by injured parties for breach of statutory duty. Civil claims for such breaches are not, however, permitted on the basis of the general sections of the Health and Safety at Work etc. Act 1974 (HSWA). Nevertheless injured parties might be able to sue for damages for negligence (see below). Much of the legislation laying down specific duties is in the form of regulations made under one of the major Acts, predominantly HSWA, although some specific duties are laid down in the major Acts themselves. Regulations have the full force of law and are frequently backed by approved codes of practice. These have the object of providing practical guidance on the requirements contained in Sections 2 to 7 of HSWA, or in regulations, or in any of the existing statutory provisions. Approved codes of practice have a specific status: while failure to observe any provision of an approved code is not in itself a criminal offence, where in criminal proceedings a person is alleged to have contravened a statutory requirement the court must admit in evidence any provision of an approved code of practice which appears to be relevant (see below, p. 105).

In addition to the statutes, the common law imposes duties upon employers (and employees). A major source of these duties is the law of torts (civil wrongs) under which an employer has a duty of care arising out of his or her position as employer and as owner or controller of premises. The latter means that the duty extends to people who are not employees. The duty of care towards employees is also found as part of the employment contract. It should be noted that criminal proceedings may be taken under the common law. Where negligence is gross, or behaviour reckless, a prosecution for manslaughter may occur. The prosecution would need to establish that the accused was aware of an obvious and serious risk as well as being guilty of the act or omission itself. Where senior employees who are in control of the organization were aware of such a risk and allowed such acts or omissions to occur, a charge of corporate manslaughter may accompany the charges against individuals. This happened in the prosecution following the capsizing of the ferry Herald of Free Enterprise, although the prosecution was unsuccessful.

A number of features of legislation in the health and safety field are worth stressing. First, the law is often invoked, particularly in respect of the more serious cases. Second, one incident often gives rise to two separate cases – a civil case, usually pursued in the High Court, and a criminal case, usually prosecuted in the magistrates' (but sometimes Crown) court. Third, different parts of the legislation set different standards. Thus, some requirements are mandatory (that is, there is an absolute duty) and others need to be met as far as is practicable or as far as is reasonably practicable. Finally, health and safety is an area where EC law plays an increasingly important role. EC health and safety legislation is subject to the qualified majority voting process in the Council of Ministers (see above, pp. 3–7 and below, pp. 135–9).

Statutory Duties

Health and Safety at Work etc. Act 1974

General duty of employers to their employees
The philosophy behind this legislation is that the duties of employers should be set out in broad terms covering all sorts of employment situations – shops, offices, factories etc. The Act covers all persons at work except domestic servants in private households. Sets of regulations issued under the Act then deal with different types of work situations or different health and safety issues.

It should be noted that all those receiving training or work experience from an employer in the workplace, and who are not employees, are deemed to be employees for the purposes of health and safety legislation.[1]

The essence of HSWA is a general duty imposed upon employers which requires them 'to ensure, so far as is reasonably practicable, the health, safety and welfare at work' of all their employees.[2] This general duty includes health and safety in relation to the:

- provision and maintenance of plant and systems of work;
- arrangements for use, handling, storage and transport of articles and substances;
- maintenance of the place of work and access to and egress from it;
- working environment;

and includes the duty to provide:

- adequate welfare facilities;
- necessary information, instruction, training and supervision,

and to consult with union safety representatives if there are any. A notice containing the main provisions of the Act must be posted.[3]

Employers must prepare a written statement of their policy with respect to the health and safety at work of their employees, and show it to an inspector if requested to do so. The statement must indicate the organization and arrangements in force to give effect to the policy and must be revised as often as is appropriate. The statement, and any revision of it, must be brought to the notice of all the employees.[4] There is a provision for exceptions, but the only exemption granted to date is for employers who employ fewer than five employees.[5] The number of employees relates to the undertaking rather than the site or establishment, and trainees on the Youth Training Scheme count as employees for the purposes of these and other health and safety requirements (see below, pp. 276–7).

The Department of Employment has produced an outline safety policy statement for small businesses.[6] The statement is in three sections. The first makes a general declaration of the employer's obligations under HSWA. It also indicates who is responsible for health and safety – for example, in overall terms and in particular places. The second section deals with the arrangements made by the employer in order to meet the legal requirements as regards first-aid, fire safety, training and so on. The remaining section covers the arrangements made to deal with particular hazards such as those arising from the use of electrical equipment and dangerous substances. Policies, and the way they operate, should be reviewed annually.

By virtue of section 235 of, and schedule 7 to the Companies Act 1985, the Secretary of State has power to prescribe by regulations information to be contained in directors' reports about a company's arrangements for ensuring the health, safety and welfare of its employees, but this power has not yet been invoked.

Where, under HSWA,[7] a safe system of work for the employer's own employees involves giving information and instruction to persons other than his or her own employees (the employees of a contractor, for instance) it must be given (*R* v. *Swan Hunter Shipbuilders Ltd and Telemeter Installations Ltd*). Thus, employers have a duty to provide relevant safety information to the employees of other employers working on their premises.

Meaning of practicable and reasonably practicable

'Practicable' means something less than physically possible. It means feasible – possible in the light of current knowledge and invention. Where the requirement is that something should be as safe as is practicable this means that the duty must be performed unless it is unreasonable to do so (*Marshall* v. *Gotham and Co. Ltd*). The word 'reasonably' requires that a comparison be made between the risk of injury (including the severity of any injury which might occur) and the time, trouble and expense of preventive action. If there is gross disproportion between them (that is, the risk is insignificant compared with the preventive measures needed), the defence that an employer has done what was reasonably practicable will succeed (*Edwards* v. *National Coal Board*). Because reasonably practicable involves weighing the risks against the costs of prevention, employers will need to adduce evidence about the risks and costs involved, so influencing what is reasonably practicable. For example, in assessing the likelihood of risk a relevant consideration would be the length of time the employee is exposed to the risk. When considering preventive measures, doubts about the efficacy of those measures in reducing risk may be of relevance as may be the size and resources of the employer. The onus of proof lies upon the accused to show that it was not practicable or reasonably practicable to do more than was done.[8]

Duties owed to non-employees

The HSWA operates where people are at work rather than by specifying particular types of workplace. With the exception of where there is Crown immunity, it therefore covers all premises including vehicles, movable structures and off-shore installations. Under the Act employers have a responsibility to show the same standard of care towards non-employees (such as visitors and contractors) as they are required to show to their employees and, as noted, this duty includes provision of information and instruction (*Swan Hunter*).[9] The duty is not restricted to the employer's premises. A self-employed person has similar duties. Both the self-employed and employers may be required to provide information to non-employees about the way in which their undertakings might affect such people's health and safety.

Persons who have 'to any extent, control of premises'[10] (but not domestic premises) or control access to or egress from such premises, have duties to persons other than employees and must take such measures as are reasonable for a person in that position to take, as far as is reasonably practicable. This does not extend to taking measures to guard against unexpected events (*Austin Rover Group Ltd* v. *HM Inspectorate of Factories*). Whether precautions in relation to someone else's use of the employer's premises are reasonable will depend upon:

- the employer's knowledge of the anticipated use of the premises;
- the extent of control and knowledge of actual use.

In *Austin Rover*, contractors' employees were in breach of safety rules and the controller of the premises (Austin Rover) could not reasonably have been expected to foresee and to guard against this.

The Act also covers control of the emission into the atmosphere of noxious or offensive substances from prescribed premises. These are premises and substances laid down in the Health and Safety (Emissions into the Atmosphere) Regulations 1983 as amended.[11] The duty imposed is to use the 'best practicable means' for preventing the emission and to render harmless or inoffensive any substances emitted. (Part I of the Environmental Protection Act 1990 and regulations thereunder introduce new controls over air pollution.)

Duties of designers, manufacturers and others

Duties are also placed upon designers, manufacturers, importers and suppliers to require the safe design and construction of articles, testing and examination and the provision of information indicating the designed use and precautions needed to avoid risks. Designers and manufacturers must carry out necessary research. Those erecting or installing articles are also responsible for safety. Parallel requirements exist in relation to manufacturers, importers and suppliers of substances. The standard of care is what is reasonably practicable to achieve safety and the absence of risks to health. This section of the Act has been strengthened by the Consumer Protection Act 1987.[12] Manufacturers and others must now consider reasonably foreseeable risks. Moreover, these risks are to be considered in relation to handling, maintenance and storage, as well as use. The requirement to provide health and safety information is also widened so that it covers revision (for example, in the light of new knowledge), applies not just to use, and covers situations such as foreseeable errors by users. Manufacturers and others must also take account of non-domestic premises other than workplaces to which they supply substances. As a result of the Control of Substances Hazardous to Health (COSHH) regulations (see chapter 5) there is now a much clearer onus upon employers to obtain health and safety information, and data provided by suppliers are a major source.

Duties of employees
It is noted below that employees have a common law duty to go about their work with reasonable care. This is supplemented by the 1974 Act which lays upon employees a statutory duty of reasonable care towards themselves and those who may be affected by their acts or omissions. There is also a statutory duty to co-operate with the employer or any other person in meeting the statutory requirements. Reasonable care includes the use of equipment provided for employees' safety. The employer must make sure that employees know of the equipment and must take steps, as far as is reasonably practicable, to get them to use it. Standards for personal protective equipment are now set down by an EC Directive (see below, p. 137) so that it is important for the equipment to meet these standards if a successful defence is to be raised by an employer. The duties of employees include not intentionally or recklessly interfering with or misusing anything provided for health, safety and welfare purposes in pursuance of the statutory provisions. (This is a duty placed upon all persons and not just employees.)

Individual employees can be, and occasionally are prosecuted by the inspectors under these provisions. Moreover, as noted below (see p. 105) senior managers, as well as the organization, may be liable under HSWA section 37 where they consented to or connived at the commission of an offence or neglected their duties.

No charge must be made for anything done or provided in respect of any *specific* requirement of health and safety legislation. Thus, if a regulation states that eye protectors must be worn in a particular situation, there can be no charge. If an employer provided them simply in an attempt to fulfil their *general* duties under section 2 of HSWA, they could charge. The duties of employees apply to all employees including those who hold managerial positions.

Safety representatives

Regulations under the Act allow a recognized trades union to appoint safety representatives, with specified functions:

- to investigate potential hazards, dangerous occurrences and the cause of accidents;
- to investigate and process members' complaints about health and safety at work;
- to deal with management over general questions of health and safety;
- to carry out workplace inspections;
- to represent members in discussions with inspectors;
- to receive information from the inspectors;
- to attend meetings of health and safety committees.[13]

A code of practice and guidance notes give further detail. As far as is reasonably practicable a safety representative (SR) should have been employed by their employer for the previous two years, or have had at least two years' experience of similar employment.[14] Employers must provide facilities for SRs for inspections including for independent investigation and discussion. However, employers are entitled to be present during inspections.[15] SRs can have access to any documents kept by their employer for statutory health and safety purposes, except those relating to the health and safety of individuals, and in general are entitled to information which it is necessary for them to have to perform their duties. SRs are not entitled to information where:

- disclosure would be against the national interest;
- disclosure would result in contravening a statutory prohibition;
- it relates to an individual (unless the individual gives their consent);
- apart from health and safety effects, the information would cause substantial injury to the employer's undertaking, or where the information was supplied to the employer by some other person, to the undertaking of that other person;
- information was obtained for the purpose of any legal proceedings.

Disclosure is restricted to documents or parts of documents which relate to health, safety or welfare.

Safety representatives are the appropriate people to receive information from the inspectors about particular occurrences in the workplace, and any action that inspectors take or propose to take. The safety representatives are given a right to time off in order to perform their functions, and also for training.

A separate code of practice covers time off for training.[16] There should be basic training provided by the union as soon as possible after appointment. This training should be approved by the TUC or the independent trades union to which the SR belongs. There should also be further training for any special responsibilities or changes in legislation or work circumstances.

The basic training should provide an understanding of the role of the SR, the role of safety committees (see below) and of union health and safety policies; these should be related to the legal requirements, the nature and extent of workplace hazards and precautions and the employer's health and safety policy. The training should also develop skills, for example, conducting inspections; using legal and official sources. Management should be provided with a copy of the syllabus on request. Normally, a few weeks' notice should be given of the names of SRs nominated to attend a course. The numbers should be reasonable taking into account the availability of courses and the operational requirements of the employer. Union training for SRs should be complemented by employer training which should focus upon the technical hazards of the workplace, relevant precautions for safe methods of work and employer organization and arrangements for health and safety.

A safety representative may complain to an industrial tribunal if refused reasonable time off or refused pay for such time off. Where at least two SRs request it in writing, an employer is required to establish a safety committee. The overall function of such a committee is to keep health and safety measures under review.[17]

Factories Act 1961[18]

Until repealed and replaced by regulations under HSWA the Factories Act 1961 (FA) remains important. In general, the person or company in immediate control of the premises is responsible for ensuring compliance with the Act and the many sets of regulations issued under it.

Meaning of factory
A factory is a place where people are employed in manual labour in any process for or incidental to the making, repairing, altering, cleaning, adapting for sale or demolition of any article. With a number of exceptions (for example government, local authorities) this must be done for gain or for trading purposes. An employer will have rights of access and control. Manual labour means that the work is done

primarily or substantially with the hands. A number of specific processes are also defined as factory processes so that they are covered by the Act; these include shipbuilding or repairing or breaking up.

Health provisions

General conditions are laid down for cleanliness, overcrowding, ventilation and temperature but there are also specific and absolute requirements, either in the Act itself or in regulations under the Act which govern different types of process or industry. Thus walls and ceilings must be washed or cleaned every 14 months; if painted, they must be repainted every seven years, if not, whitewashed every 14 months. Each person should have not less than 11 cubic metres of space, although machinery can take up some of this. No space more than 4.2 metres above floor level may be counted. Temperature should be reasonable, and where most of the work is done seated, should be at least 60°F (16°C) after the first hour. Other provisions of the Act relate to lighting, ventilation and drainage.

Safety provisions

The Factories Act 1961 provides for the guarding or secure fencing of dangerous machinery. Certain machinery such as prime movers and transmission machinery is required to be guarded under all circumstances. However, for other machinery guarding is required to prevent employees coming into contact only with those parts which are dangerous. Though an absolute duty, the requirement for secure fencing of other dangerous parts of machinery has been the subject of considerable and extended judicial consideration. It is now established that the provision of secure fencing is required for those parts of other machinery which are a reasonably foreseeable cause of injury to anybody acting in a way in which a human being may be reasonably expected to act in circumstances which may be reasonably expected to occur.

Guards must be secured in position whenever the machinery is in motion or use. Though under certain very limited circumstances dangerous parts of machinery may be approached while in motion or use and unguarded, the strict requirements of the Operations at Unfenced Machinery Regulations 1938 must be observed. Practical guidance on machinery is contained in British Standard 5304:1974 *Safety of Machinery* and in other detailed guidance published by the Health and Safety Executive, industrial advisory committees and industry.

While the provisions of the Factories Act 1961 are concerned with preventing employees approaching dangerous machinery, there is no specific provision to provide for danger caused by the ejection of work pieces or parts of machines. While in some cases specific regulations cover this type of risk, for example the Woodworking Machines Regulations 1974, and the Abrasive Wheels Regulations 1970, this potential danger would be covered by the more general provisions of section 2 (1) of the Health and Safety at Work etc. Act 1974.

Various rules are laid down for lifting equipment (such as hoists, lifts and cranes) and lifting tackle (such as chains and ropes). The construction must be good, the material sound, the strength adequate and the maintenance proper. There are specific rules about testing, inspection and the marking of safe working loads. Workplace floors, stairs and gangways must be soundly constructed, properly maintained and as far as is reasonably practicable kept free of obstructions and slippery surfaces. There may need to be a handrail on staircases. Openings in floors must be fenced whenever practicable.

Provisions relating to works of engineering construction and building operations are to be found in sets of regulations issued under the Factories Act 1961. These provisions are briefly described in chapter 5.

The Factories Act 1961 contains provisions to protect people from being overcome by fumes in confined spaces and to protect against fire and explosion in such circumstances. There are sections dealing with steam boilers and air receivers. Specific requirements in relation to all pressure plant, including pipework and fittings, have recently come into force; these requirements relate to steam systems and any other systems operating at pressures in excess of 0.5 bar above atmospheric pressure.[19] (These are described below, see pp. 132–3.)

Requirements relating to general fire precautions such as means of escape in case of fire, fire fighting and fire warning are enforced by local fire authorities under the provisions of the Fire Precautions Act 1971 as amended by section 78 of the Health and Safety at Work etc. Act 1974. Enforcement in relation to process fire risks remains with the appropriate health and safety legislation enforcing authority; for most substantial workplaces this is the Health and Safety Executive.

Welfare provisions
The welfare provisions of the Factories Act require an adequate supply of drinking water, adequate and suitable washing facilities and accommodation for non-work clothing. Seats must be provided for

workers who have the opportunity to sit without detriment to their work. Where work can properly be done sitting, detailed rules apply. Requirements relating to first-aid are now set out in the Health and Safety (First-Aid) Regulations 1981 together with an approved code of practice and guidance. (See below, pp. 129–31.) Unlike early provisions relating to first-aid these regulations adopt a flexible approach to enable any particular undertaking to provide for effective first-aid arrangements. Provision of protective clothing is required by various sets of regulations under the Act. Eye protection is subject to the Protection of Eyes Regulations 1974, as amended.

Other provisions

The Act contains a number of other provisions. A list of any homeworkers must be provided to the local authority. A person intending to use premises as a factory must notify the inspector at least four weeks in advance. Where premises are occupied by separate factories, the owner is responsible for the common parts. Otherwise, the occupier is liable. Where a particular individual fails to fulfil a statutory duty imposed upon them and the employer has taken all reasonable steps, the employer will not be liable. An employee causing an accident by interfering with a guard would be in breach of their statutory duty not to wilfully interfere with or misuse anything provided in pursuance of the Act's objectives. There is also a duty upon employees to use anything provided under the Act for their health and safety. A breach of the Act by an employee may mean that both they and the employer are criminally liable. Women must not be employed in a factory within four weeks of childbirth.

Section 29(1) of the Act provides that, as far as is reasonably practicable, there must be a safe means of access to any place where a person has to work. Moreover, that place must be kept safe while the person is working there. There was thus a breach of the Act where a contractor's employee was working on an unsafe roof. Moreover, since section 155 casts the duty to comply with the Act upon the occupier, the occupier was guilty notwithstanding the facts that there was no evidence that he was in control of the work and that he believed the work could have been done by a different (and safe) method (*Dexter* v. *Tenby Electrical Accessories Ltd*).

Legislation covering other types of workplace

Offices, Shops and Railway Premises Act 1963

Most of the Act's provisions are similar to those of the Factories Act 1961 including the requirement to notify the business to the inspectorate. The Act applies where people are employed. It applies generally to all offices and shops, and to most railway buildings near the permanent way. It covers offices and shops which are part of buildings used for other purposes as well as associated areas like stairs, passages and toilets. There are specific requirements for the cleaning of premises and furnishings. Floors and steps must be swept or washed at least once a week. In a room where people work, there should be reasonable, generally not below 16°C after the first hour person and 11 cubic metres if the ceiling is lower than 3 metres. An exception is made where the room is open to the public. Temperature should be reasonable, and generally not below 16°C after the first hour and a thermometer must be prominently displayed. There must be adequate supplies of fresh or artificially purified air. The Act lays down requirements for toilets and washing facilities and for drinking water, storage of clothing and seats. Provisions similar to those in the Factories Act apply to stairs, passages and so on. There are provisions for the fencing of dangerous machinery and restrictions on the lifting of excess weights. The first-aid and fire provisions of the Act have been repealed. The former are covered by the Health and Safety (First-Aid) Regulations 1981 and the latter by the Fire Precautions Act 1971. Fire certificates issued under the Offices, Shops and Railway Premises Act 1963 (OSRPA) prior to the 1971 Act are deemed to have been issued under the 1971 Act. Generally, the occupier is responsible for complying with the Act, although some responsibilities are given specifically to employers (such as the duty to notify the inspectorate of the commencement of business). If the premises are used by more than one employer the owner becomes responsible for health and safety in the common parts. The defence against alleged breach of duty under the Act is that all due diligence was used[20].

Mines and quarries

The principal Act regulating the health and safety and welfare of those employed in the extractive industries in the Mines and Quarries Act

1954: the provisions of the Act have been substantially extended by regulations made under section 141. Also of note is the Mines and Quarries (Tips) Act 1969 and the associated Mines and Quarries (Tip) Regulations 1971: the 1969 Act resulted from the recommendations of the enquiry into the Aberfan disaster in 1966.

The 1954 Act is unusual in so far as it imposes specific duties on owners of mines and quarries to make provision for and ensure that the workplace is managed and worked in accordance with the requirements of the Act and relevant orders and regulations. The Health and Safety at Work etc. Act 1974 also applies. Part II of the 1954 Act, in the case of mines, and part IV, in the case of quarries, provide for the formal appointment of managers and specify their duties, powers and responsibilities. The duties under the 1954 Act and related legislation are extensive and complex and a detailed analysis is not attempted here.

Progress has been made on the gradual process of modification and amendment of health and safety legislation in relation to mines and quarries so as to bring it under the umbrella of the Health and Safety at Work etc. Act 1974 and related regulations and approved codes of practice: this will continue. It should be noted that whilst the provisions of the Electricity at Work Regulations 1989, the Noise at Work Regulations 1989 and the Control of Substances Hazardous to Health Regulations 1988 apply to both mines and quarries, Regulations 6 to 12 of the Control of Substances Hazardous to Health Regulations are specifically not applied to work carried out below ground at a mine.

Agriculture

Agriculture, including horticulture, forestry and associated industries, is subject to the Health and Safety at Work etc. Act 1974 and regulations thereunder including COSHH, Noise at Work and Electricity at Work (see chapter 5). In addition, there is the Agriculture (Safety, Health and Welfare Provisions) Act 1956 and a number of sets of regulations which apply specifically to agriculture. Part of the Food and Environmental Protection Act 1985 is also relevant.

The Agriculture (Avoidance of Accidents to Children) Regulations 1958 make it illegal to allow children under the age of 13 to drive or ride on tractors and self-propelled machines or to ride on machines in connection with an agricultural operation. It is illegal for them to ride on implements at any time. There is an approved code of practice.

The Agriculture (Stationary Machinery) Regulations 1959 prohibit an employer from causing or permitting an employee to work at stationary machinery unless certain components are guarded and the guards maintained. In addition, there are other requirements (such as those in relation to the guarding of inlets and outlets, stopping devices and lighting). Employees also have responsibilities. The Agriculture (Field Machinery) Regulations 1962 impose duties similar to those above but relate to machines other than those designed or adapted for stationary use only.

The Agriculture (Power Take-Off) Regulations 1957 require, among other things, that the power take-off on a machine should be shielded or covered. The Agriculture (Tractor Cabs) Regulations 1974 require approved safety cabs or frames to be fitted to tractors except where not reasonably practicable. The regulations contain other requirements. An approved code of practice, *Rider-Operated Lift Trucks – Operator Training*, came into force in 1989 to ensure that operators of various types of truck (for example an industrial counterbalanced lift truck) undergo proper training. The Agricultural (Circular Saws) Regulations 1959 concern the guarding, maintenance and operation of circular saws. Among other things, no young person may operate or assist at a circular saw unless supervised by an experienced person over the age of 18 years.

Part III of the Food and Environmental Protection Act 1985 deals with pesticides. The detailed requirements are to be found in The Control of Pesticides Regulations 1986. There is an approved code of practice on the use of pesticides in agriculture and horticulture, and standards for storage are set out in an HSE guidance note on chemical safety. The advertisement, sale, importation, supply, storage and use of a pesticide is prohibited unless it has been approved. Pesticides include insecticides, herbicides and fungicides as well as wood preservatives. The regulations do not apply to pesticides administered directly to farm livestock; these are controlled by the Medicines Act 1968. All reasonable precautions must be taken to protect the health of human beings, creatures, plants and the environment, and there are requirements that people should be competent and properly instructed. Certificates of competence are needed in some cases – anyone selling or supplying pesticides approved for agricultural use, for example. There is detailed control for aerial applications.

Enforcement of health and safety

Notices and prosecutions

Enforcement is principally by the HSE, although local authorities are responsible for enforcement in certain premises and for enforcing the implementation of general fire precautions. The allocation of enforcement responsibilities is determined by the Health and Safety (Enforcing Authority) Regulations 1989, issued under section 18 of HSWA.

These increased the local authorities' coverage by re-allocating premises including those used for leisure and consumer services, churches and other places of religious worship, and premises used for the care, treatment and accommodation of animals.[21] Certain lower risk construction work carried out in premises where local authorities already had enforcement responsibilities was also re-allocated. The 1989 regulations allocate to local authorities responsibilities for enforcing the Health and Safety at Work etc. Act 1974 and relevant statutory provisions, subject to certain specific exceptions, in all premises where the main activity is listed under schedule 1. Broadly speaking, local authorities have responsibility under the 1989 regulations for: premises where the main activity is the sale or storage of goods for retail or wholesale distribution; office activities; hotels and catering; places of entertainment. It should be noted, however, that the 1989 regulations allocate to the Health and Safety Executive sole responsibility for the enforcement of section 6 of the Health and Safety at Work etc. Act 1974 in relation to articles and substances for use at work including at those premises where the local authority would enforce the remaining provisions of the 1974 Act.

In terms of local authority enforcement, the principal role is performed by district councils and usually by the department which has an environmental health function. In addition, county councils (in England and Wales) and regional councils (in Scotland) have responsibilities such as those in relation to petroleum licensing, certain explosives, including fireworks, and the packaging and labelling of dangerous substances in consumer premises. Enforcement in these areas is carried out by trading standards officers or fire authorities as appropriate. Some of these 'county' functions, however, are performed at district level, for instance where the district is a metropolitan one or a London borough. If there is doubt about whether enforcement is in the hands of the HSE or a local authority (or which local authority), employers can check with the HSE. In each HSE area there is an enforcement liaison officer.

If there is a breach of duty an inspector may serve an improvement notice, or a prohibition notice, or may prosecute. An improvement notice will apply where the inspector alleges a breach of statutory duty. It will specify a time period within which the improvement(s) must be made. An employer may appeal to an industrial tribunal within 21 days against either the allegation of a breach or the shortness of the time period if, for example, this would cause undue difficulty for the production process. The appeal has the effect of suspending the notice. Where an inspector believes that there is a risk of serious personal injury he may serve a prohibition notice, which can have immediate effect. There is again a right of appeal but this does not suspend the notice unless an industrial tribunal so directs. The normal industrial tribunal costs rule – see chapter 12 – does not apply.[22] In these cases costs may be awarded against the losing party at the tribunal's discretion. Because the Crown cannot prosecute the Crown the Health and Safety Commission (HSC) issues Crown notices where improvement or prohibition notices would be used, (in the Civil Service for example) although these have no legal force. The NHS no longer enjoys Crown immunity[23] for the purpose of health and safety legislation.

Any breach of the general duties in the 1974 Act or of specific duties under other health and safety legislation is a criminal offence, as is obstructing an inspector or giving him false information. An employer will be liable for the acts of his or her employees during or arising out of the course of their employment. Where an offence is committed with the consent or connivance of, or due to the neglect off any director, manager, secretary or other similar officer the individual as well as the organization is to be held guilty.[24] Thus, in *Armour* v. *Sheen* the inspector prosecuted a senior employee because he had been given the responsibility for drawing up the health and safety policy, but had not done it. Where there is a breach of an approved code of practice issued under section 16 of HSWA this will be taken (in criminal proceedings) as conclusive proof of a contravention of a requirement or prohibition unless the court can be satisfied that there was compliance by some other method. Prosecution for breaches of HSWA is limited to inspectors save for permission otherwise by the Director of Public Prosecutions; nor can the Act be used for the purposes of civil claims, that is, for breach of statutory duty. Regulations under HSWA and legislation enacted prior to HSWA can be used for civil purposes unless they state otherwise.

A successful prosecution for a breach of HSWA requires proof beyond all reasonable doubt, as in criminal cases more generally. Thus, the relevant public authority may decide not to prosecute if they conclude that the evidence is not strong enough. This was the case in relation to th Piper Alpha oil platform disaster in the North Sea in 1988, which resulted in the death of 167 men.

Powers of inspectors[25]

The powers of the inspectors are substantial. They have the right to:

- enter premises;
- make examinations and inspections;
- take samples;
- take possession of articles and substances;
- take measurements and photographs;
- make recordings;
- keep things undisturbed;
- have something tested, removed or dismantled;
- obtain information and have answers to questions;
- inspect and copy any entry in documents required to be kept under statute.

Facilities and assistance must be provided for inspectors in connection with any of the above. Inspectors have any other powers necessary to fulfil their responsibilities. Where there is 'imminent danger of serious personal injury' an inspector may seize an article or substance and render it harmless.[26] An inspector does not need to give prior notice of a visit but an employer or occupier of premises is entitled to see proof of an inspector's identity prior to entry.

Powers of the courts

Maximum penalties for different types of offences are laid down in HSWA. On summary conviction the maximum is £2,000. The Criminal Justice Act 1991 provides for increases in the maximum levels of fine on the standard scale (see above, p. 26) and there are other proposals for a maximum fine of £20,000 in certain cases. A daily penalty of up to £100 can be imposed where there is a continued breach of an improvement or prohibition notice or court order. In the Crown Courts, on indictment, the fines are unlimited and in the case of certain offences there can also be up to two years' imprisonment. This applies, for example, where there is contravention of a prohibition notice or where a person acts without the licence necessary under a relevant statutory provision. In addition, the courts can order specific forms of action in order to ensure safety.

Employer defences

An employer's defence will be that there is no breach of statutory duty. For example, it might be maintained that there is little or no risk, therefore what has been done in the way of prevention is all that is reasonably practicable. An employer is unlikely to be successful in arguing that financial difficulties facing the firm mean that safety improvements cannot be afforded. It is submitted, however, that the costs of such improvements can be related to the overall size and resources of the firm as part of the weighing of the actions against the risks in order to determine what is reasonably practicable.

Common Law Duties

Types of action

An injured person may have three types of possible legal case under the common law, all of which involve a claim for damages:

1 Breach of statutory duty (this constitutes a tort).
2 Breach of contract (through negligence).
3 Negligence in tort.

In the absence of provision to the contrary, civil action can be taken for breach of a duty contained in a statute by someone injured as a result of the breach. In fact, there is such provision to the contrary in the Health and Safety at Work Act etc. 1974, so that breaches can be subject to legal action by the enforcement agencies but cannot be used as a basis for civil claims.[27] The same is not true of earlier legislation still in force, such as the Factories Act 1961. Thus employees may take a case on the basis of breach of statutory duty if a claim on the basis of negligence is ruled out, and vice versa. It should be noted that employer defences in the statue are in respect of criminal proceedings. They only indirectly relate to civil cases.

The basis of a worker's claim for damages arising out of an employer's negligence is as follows:

1 The employer owes the worker a duty of care.
2 The employer has not fulfilled that duty.
3 As a result, the worker has suffered injury or damage to health.

The origin of the duty of care is found in the law of torts (civil wrongs – see chapter 1). The liability of the employer which arises in this respect is in tort. However, a duty of care also flows from the contract of employment, so an action for damages for breach of contract would also be possible in cases where the relationship is governed by such a contract. Nevertheless such actions are rare because the basis for the action is narrower. Actions for damages in tort are not limited to parties to a contract and encompass provision for greater damages. Even where there is a contract of employment the duty of care in the law of torts does not arise from the fact of contractual relations; it arises from the fact of the employee working for the employer. The employer's liability goes beyond situations where the employee is acting in the course of their employment. The test is whether the circumstances were within the control of the employer.

The duty of care

Employers have a duty of reasonable care for the safety of their employees, and the responsibility extends to the premises of third parties to which they send their employees. They also have a duty of care towards independent contractors, although the degree of care is less in such cases.

What is meant by reasonable care? In general it means avoiding acts and omissions which a person can reasonably foresee would be likely to injure their neighbour (*Donoghue* v. *Stevenson*) A neighbour is anyone who is so affected by my acts or omissions that I ought reasonably to have these effects in mind. Liability arises, therefore, where there is not reasonable care to prevent reasonably foreseeable risk. Foresight has to be assessed on the basis of what is known (or should reasonably be known) at the time.

It follows that the degree of care required is determined by balancing risk against the actions necessary to prevent or reduce it. Risk is judged in terms of how likely it is that an injury will occur and how serious it would be. The cost of preventive action will figure highly in the equation. The degree of care may vary according to the worker, how experienced they are, for example. If the injury is caused by a manufacturing fault, the employer will not, ultimately, be liable if they could not reasonably tell that something was wrong. However, if the employer knew that there was something wrong and kept the machine in use they will be in breach of their duty of care. The Employers' Liabililty (Defective Equipment) Act 1969 provides that where an employee suffers injury in the course of their employment in consequence of a defect in equipment provided by their employer and the defect is wholly or partly attributable to the fault of a third party, the injury will be deemed to be attributable to the negligence of the employer. This leaves the employer to recover damages from the third party, for example the manufacturer of a machine.

The duty of care may be divided into a number of specific parts:

- safe premises;
- a safe system of work;
- safe plant, equipment and tools;
- safe fellow workers.

The duty to take reasonable care in relation to plant, equipment and tools has implications for testing and maintenance and may, ultimately, require the item to be replaced. Fellow workers will be safe if they have adequate training, instruction and supervision. Part of a safe system of work is the provision of safety equipment. In *Crouch* v. *British Rail Engineering Ltd*, the duty of care was not fulfilled by making safety goggles available for collection from a point about five minutes away. The lack of immediate availability encouraged risks to be taken. In *Pape* v. *Cumbria County Council*, the employers provided gloves for cleaners handling chemical cleaning materials but the duty of care went beyond this; it extended to warning the cleaners about handling such materials with unprotected hands and instructing them as to the need to wear gloves at all times.

Negligence

Negligence occurs where there is a breach of the duty of care. In terms of the above definition of the duty of care this means that the actions taken by an employer to prevent or reduce risk were inadequate for the level of risk which was reasonably foreseeable. It should be noted that an employer cannot use a contract term or a notice to exclude or restrict liability for death or personal injury resulting from negligence.[28] The onus of proof of negligence lies with the plaintiff, who must also show causation, that is, that the negligence caused the injury, and that the employer had a reasonable and safer alternative to what they did. However, in the absence of an explanation of the cause of the injury there is what almost amounts to a presumption of negligence. This is because courts may infer from the immediate facts of the case that negligence occurred. It is particularly likely where *res ipsa loquitur* –

the thing speaks for itself. Therefore, the plaintiff can establish a prima facie case on the immediate facts even if there is no direct proof that a negligent act or omission caused the injury. This discharges the plaintiff's burden of proof, leaving the defendant to rebut the inference of negligence by showing that the cause of the injury was not negligence.

If the action is against the defendant in the capacity of employer it will need to be established that the plaintiff was acting in the course of their employment when they received their injury. Where the injury was sustained in working hours on the employer's premises this is likely to prove difficult to challenge, especially if the employee was performing tasks in the employer's interest. Acting in the course of employment means carrying out acts which have been authorized by the employer, as well as some that have not been authorized, in order to fulfil contractual obligations. The latter, however, must be connected with authorized acts in that they can be regarded as ways of performing such acts. Anything normally and reasonably incidental to a day's work, such as going to the toilet, to the canteen or to collect tools or materials, will also be included.

In contrast to the above, there was breach of statutory duty under the Offices, Shops and Railway Premises Act 1963 even though an employee had no authority to be where he was. The legislation applies regardless of whether an employee is in the course of his employment. Since there was no warning of danger there was no contributory negligence on the part of the employee (*Westwood* v. *Post Office*). More recently, in *Smith* v. *Stages and Darlington Insulation Co. Ltd*, the House of Lords set out guidelines for helping to decide when travel associated with work is in the course of employment. An employee paid wages (rather than a travelling allowance) to travel in their employer's time to a workplace other than their regular workplace will, prima facie, be acting in the course of their employment. The guidelines are as follows:

- Travelling from home to a regular workplace will be in the course of employment if the employee is compelled by the contract of employment to use the employer's transport, unless there is an express condition to the contrary.
- Travelling in the employer's time between workplaces will be in the course of employment.
- Receipt of wages (as distinct from a travelling allowance) is indicative of travel being in the course of employment.

- Travel in the employer's time from home to a workplace other than the regular workplace will be in the course of employment.
- Incidental deviation or interruption to a journey taken in the course of employment will not take the employee out of the course of employment, but anything more would do.
- Return journeys are to be treated on the same footing as outward journeys.

Where the action lies against the defendant in the capacity of occupier of premises the test is again whether there has been a breach of the duty of care. As a result of the Occupiers' Liability Act 1957, a statutory duty of care is owed to persons authorized to be on the premises.[29] The occupier's actual degree of control over the premises will be an important factor in determining liability. The Occupiers' Liability Act 1984 defines the duty owed to trespassers.

Actions for damages

The Law Reform (Personal Injuries) Act 1948 gave employees the right to sue their employer by abolishing the principle that employees in common employment accepted the risks of their work. In the process, vicarious liability was allowed. The general rule now is that employers (principals) will be liable for the acts and omissions of their employees (agents); that is, they will be vicariously liable. The limiting factor is that the employee's act or omission must be in the course of employment or linked with it in the ways described earlier. Moreover, the courts have held that the person entitled to tell the employee how to do work would generally be liable for that employee's negligence, even if the employee is an employee of another company. (See *Sime* v. *Sutcliffe Catering (Scotland) Ltd*).

Vicarious liability does not mean that individual employees, whether managers or not, cannot be sued, since under the contract of employment (and in tort) the employee has a duty of reasonable care. In practice, however, the likelihood of a civil action is quite small since the sums involved in damages claims are larger than an individual could normally pay. The position would be entirely different if the individual had insurance cover. Most employers accept vicarious liability as a fact of life and the necessary insurance as an unavoidable cost of production.

The time limit for commencement of claims is three years from the time of knowledge of cause of action.[30] Where the person is fatally injured, the three years can be applied from the time of death or from the date of the personal representative's knowledge, whichever is later. Other exceptions are possible on grounds of equity.

Employers must be insured against such actions as a result of the Employers' Liability (Compulsory Insurance) Act 1969. The insurance must cover injury and disease arising out of and during the course of employment. Cases will be heard in the county courts or High Court (see above, p. 12 for details of the new allocation criteria). Convictions (for instance, under HSWA) are admissible as evidence so can be pointed to as relevant to civil liability. A breach of an approved code by an employer also substantially assists the plaintiff in discharging the burden of proof. A plaintiff may want to see the accident report in an attempt to establish their case. Such reports will be protected from disclosure by legal professional privilege only where use in possible litigation was the 'dominant purpose' of the report (*Waugh* v. *British Railways Board*). The dominant purpose of accident reports is usually to establish why the accident happened, so there may not be protection against disclosure. The plaintiff may also obtain information from an inspector.[31] Where the employer seeks a medical report, the provisions of the Access to Medical Reports Act 1988 may apply and where the employee seeks medical information from a health professional, the Access to Health Records Act 1990 may be relevant (see chapter 11).

Finally, the Civil Liability (Contribution) Act 1978 allows the plaintiff to take action against any of the tortfeasors (those who have allegedly committed torts), leaving the defendant to claim from others who contributed to the tortious act.

Damages are divided into special and general. The former covers provable loss to the date of the trial – loss of earnings, damage to clothing and so on. The loss of earnings is net loss. The general damages cover the remaining forms of loss such as pain and suffering before and after the trial and future loss of earnings. The broad aim is restitution – putting the injured person back where they were before the accident happened, in as much as money can do this. Where appropriate, a money value will put on disfigurement, loss of enjoyment of life, nursing expenses and the inability to pursue personal or social interests.

Under the Fatal Accidents Act 1976, certain dependent relatives can claim for the financial loss they suffer but not in England and Wales for the shock, grief and so on that they experience. Since 1985 a plaintiff may seek provisional damages and may return to apply for further damages in due course. However, the courts cannot declare that if a person dies before making that further claim their surviving dependants will have an entitlement to claim under the 1976 Act (*Middleton* v. *Elliott Turbomachinery Ltd and anor*). Under section 17 of the Judgments Act 1838 interest is payable on damages, but only from the date of the judgment in which the amount of damages is determined. Where there has been a split trial, interest is not backdated to the judgment on liability (*Lea* v. *British Aerospace plc*). A number of statutory social security benefits are deductible from awards of damages. This principle does not extend, however, to benefits under an occupational pension scheme (*Smoker* v. *London Fire and Civil Defence Authority*). The principle laid down by the House of Lords in *Parry* v. *Cleaver* is that the fruits of money set aside in the past, through insurance, cannot be appropriated by the tortfeasor. Nevertheless, employers and insurance companies are at liberty to draft pension schemes in such a way as to negate the effect of this principle.

Defences

Contributory negligence
An employer may argue that the injured person was careless or reckless and was solely or partly to blame for their own injuries by, for example, ignoring clear safety rules. Contributory negligence might include contribution to the seriousness of the injury by the failure to wear available safety equipment. Where the injured person is partly to blame, the Law Reform (Contributory Negligence) Act 1945 requires that the damages be reduced rather than the claim defeated.

Injuries not reasonably foreseeable
An employer may argue that the type and/or the extent of injuries sustained by the plaintiff were not reasonably foreseeable as a result of the employer's breach of duty of care. The plaintiff has the burden of proof in demonstrating that such injuries could be foreseen as arising out of that particular negligence.

Voluntary assumption of risk
In extreme cases an employer may succeed in escaping liability on the grounds that the employee had consented to taking risks as part of the job – risks other than those inherent in performing the job as safely as is reasonable practicable. This defence – *volenti non fit injuria* (one who consents cannot complain) – is argued on the basis of the plaintiff's knowledge and acceptance of the likelihood of the occurrence of a

tortious act. It can apply to negligence but cannot apply to breach of statutory duty because the effect would be to allow the employee to contract out of Parliamentary protection.

Injury not sustained in the course of employment

It may be argued that the injury was not sustained in the course of employment. This could be because:

- the injury was not sustained at work at all; or
- it was sustained at work and during working hours, but the employee was performing unauthorized acts, which could not be regarded simply as unauthorized ways of performing authorized functions. A defence to liability here will be an express prohibition. Such a prohibition will not however, remove liability as regards unauthorized methods of performing authorized tasks.

Absence of vicarious liability

An employer may try to avoid liability by arguing that they are not vicariously liable. In cases of alleged vicarious liability it has to be established: first, that the employee is liable; and second, that the employer is vicariously liable for the employee's act(s) or omission(s). There may not be liability for the actions of an employee in the following situations.

- Where the employee is 'lent' to another employer and is working for, and under the control of that other employer. Vicarious liability may be transferred in such cases, the question of control being paramount.
- Where the employee knows (or should know) that what they have done is expressly outside the limits of their authority.
- Where the actions of the employee are excessive, for example a security guard who uses excessive violence against an intruder.

Safety Discipline

Three separate aspects of safety discipline are dealt with here. First what is the position if an employee has to be suspended from work (or transferred or dismissed) because continued employment in the original work would constitute a breach of the common law and/or statutory duty of care? Second, what is the position where employees disregard safety rules and procedures? Third, what if employees refuse to perform their duties, claiming that the work is unsafe?

Medical suspension or dismissal

Under the EP (C) A an employee, or someone in Crown employment, who is suspended on medical grounds, has a right to be paid for up to 26 weeks.[32] They must be suspended under one of a limited number of sets of regulations specified in schedule 1 to the Act or under related codes of practice issued or approved under section 16 of HSWA. The qualifying employment and hours requirements are the same as for guarantee pay, as are the rules about short-term and task contracts, alternative work and availability for work (see above, p. 67). An application may be made to an industrial tribunal within the usual three-month period. The employee must be available for work and not incapable of work because of illness or injury.

Where a suspension does not fall under the EP (C) A provisions, the employee may be able to mount a challenge on the grounds of breach of contract, possibly resigning and claiming constructive dismissal. The employee would have much less chance of success in cases where the suspension was with pay. If a dismissal is ultimately effected it will be subject to the usual requirements of unfair dismissal law provided that the employee has two years' qualifying employment. (The qualifying period will be only one month if the dismissal is for a reason which would otherwise give rise to a medical suspension under EP (C) A.) First, is there a fair reason? Breach of statute is one of the reasons laid down. Second, has the employer behaved reasonably? In this respect proper procedure is important as is investigation of the possibilities of a transfer to other work if the organization is sufficiently large.

In cases where the fitness of the employee is in dispute the provisions of the Access to Medical Reports Act 1988 may be of relevance (see chapter 11). A further problem may arise where colleagues refuse to work with a person because of medical factors. AIDS is a particular example. What if, despite medical evidence to the contrary, employees will not work alongside an AIDS virus carrier? In the event of a dismissal a tribunal would have to be convinced that this was a substantial reason for dismissal and that the dismissal was altogether reasonable.

Disregard of safety rules or procedures

Employees who disregard safety rules and procedures may be subject to discipline, including dismissal, in the same way as if there were a breach of some other type of rule. All the usual requirements laid upon employers need to be met – rules must be reasonable, applied consistently and fairly, and communicated to employees and the procedure for handling disciplinary breaches must be reasonable (see chapter 7). A dismissal for a safety breach would need to be defended in the light of the normal requirements of unfair dismissal law.

An employer may seek to change existing safety rules or introduce new rules. If the change is a direct result of new legislation, the requirements automatically become an implied term of contracts of employment. Where the change stems from a policy change rather than a change in legislation an employer will need to consider the existing terms of employment and whether the change can represent a breach of contract (see chapter 3). The procedure for implementation (advance warning, consultation and so on) may be important. For example, employers introducing no smoking policies might justify their actions on the basis of their general duties under HSWA, provide employees with evidence to support this, give advance warning, perhaps survey employee opinion or consult in other ways and provide some facilities for smokers after the rule becomes operative.

Refusal to work on grounds of lack of safety

What is the legal position if an employee refuses to work because what they are being asked to do seems to them to be unsafe? On the one hand the employee has a contractual duty to take reasonable care, so that they may feel that they will be in breach of such a duty. Moreover, they may feel they are in breach of statutory duties also. On the other hand, they are required by their terms of their contract of employment to obey the lawful commands of their employer. The critical question here is whether the employer's command is lawful. This means it must not only be within the terms of the contract, but also must not involve the employee engaging in a criminal act, or indeed being unable to act with due care. The problem is that opinions may well differ and neither party is likely to be able to wait for a legal ruling. The advice of specialists (safety managers, union representatives and perhaps even factory inspectors) is about as far as one can go. If there is a refusal to work the matter may then become a disciplinary one.

As part of their contractual duty to provide their employees with a safe system of work and take reasonable care of their safety, employers must investigate all bona fide complaints about safety brought to their attention by employees (*BAC Ltd* v. *Austin*). Failure to do so could give grounds for an employee to resign and claim unfair constructive dismissal. If the employee chooses to stay but refuses to do the work, the question of whether or not the employer is in breach of a contractual term or a statutory duty will not be conclusive in determining the fairness or otherwise of any consequent dismissal. The test will be reasonableness (*Lindsay* v. *Dunlop Ltd*). Relevant factors may include the attitude of other employees in the same position and what steps the employer is taking to deal with the safety problem. Employers might fare better if they did not treat refusal to work on safety grounds as straightforward disobedience. Dismissing for refusal to work before there has been a proper investigation of the employee's complaint and before the results of that investigation have been communicated to the employee may well be unfair. Any employee with a special condition ought to be treated as sympathetically as possible and alternative duties considered, especially if the condition is likely to be temporary. Pregnant women anxious about the effects of working at VDUs might fall into this category.[33]

In *Piggott Brothers and Co. Ltd* v. *Jackson and ors*, an employer's failure to get a definitive explanation of the cause of the employees' symptoms (experienced as a result of exposure to fumes) was held to amount to unreasonableness. This was so even though ventilation had been improved and the problem had been investigated by HSE inspectors who thought it was a 'one-off' that had ceased to exist. Dismissals for refusal to work were held to be unfair. The Court of Appeal would not disturb these findings – the decision was a permissible option on the facts (see below, p. 315).

Notes

1 The Health and Safety (Training for Employment) Regulations, SI 1990/ 1380.
2 HSWA 1974 *c.*37, s. 2(1)
3 The poster is entitled 'Health and Safety Law: What you should know'. The requirement to display it arises out of *The Health and Safety (Information for Employees) Regulations*, SI 1989/682 (operational from 18 October 1989).
4 HSWA, s. 2(3)
5 Health and Safety Policy Statements (Exception) Regulations 1975.
6 *Guide to Preparing a Safety Policy Statement for a Small Business*, Department of Employment, London: HMSO, 1990.

7 s. 2(1) – general duty, s. 2(2) (a) – safe system of work, and s. 2(2) (c) – information and instruction.

8 HSWA, s. 40.

9 s. 3(1).

10 s. 4(2).

11 SI 1983/943 as amended by SI 1989/319. The Alkali etc. Works Regulation Act 1906 and other provisions require that certain works must be registered with the Secretary of State for the Environment. The registration system was modified recently by SI 1989/318.

12 HSWA, s. 6; Consumer Protection Act 1987, s. 36 and Schedule 3.

13 *Safety Representatives and Safety Committees Regulations* SI 1977/500. (SRSC Regulations).

14 *Ibid.*, Regulation 3 (4).

15 *Ibid.*, Regulation 5.

16 *Code of Practice on Time Off for the Training of Safety Representatives*. This was issued under Regulation 4 (2) (b) of the SRSC Regulations. London: HSC, 1978.

17 HSWA, s. 2 (7).

18 1961 *c.*34. See Redgrave's Factories Acts for comprehensive coverage of the subject.

19 The Pressure Systems and Transportable Gas Containers Regulations, SI 1989/2169.

20 OSRPA, 1963, s. 67.

21 Health and Safety (Enforcing Authority) Regulations, SI 1989/1903. These regulations came into force on 1 April 1990.

22 Another procedural difference is that because the criminal law is involved an appeal against the decision of an industrial tribunal lies with the Divisional Court of the Queen's Bench Division (see above, p. 13) rather than with the EAT.

23 National Health Service (Amendment) Act 1986 as amended by the National Health Service and Community Care Act 1990.

24 HSWA, 1974 s. 37.

25 HSWA, s. 20.

26 HSWA, s. 25.

27 HSWA, s. 47.

28 Unfair Contract Terms Act 1977, s. 2.

29 Occupiers' Liability Act 1957; Occupiers' Liability (Scotland) Act 1960.

30 Limitation Act 1980.

31 Under s. 28 (9) of HSWA.

32 EP (C) A, s. 19.

33 433 IDS Brief 10.

5
Health and Safety: Major Regulations

Introduction

Chapter 4 described the provisions of the main Acts of Parliament governing health and safety at work in Great Britain. The present chapter deals with some of the sets of regulations issued under these Acts, particularly those which have widespread application. In addition, the provisions of the Fire Precautions Act 1971 are described. (The descriptions of legislation in this chapter do not, of necessity, constitute exhaustive accounts.) The final section of this chapter examines the European Community dimension, which will have increasing effects upon health and safety at work in the UK. The question of health and safety documentation is addressed prior to dealing with the matters above.

The occupier of a workplace – usually the employer – is required to keep particular registers and must display certain forms and notices under the various safety statutes. The HSE issues a comprehensive, free catalogue of its publications[1] and a complete list of forms can be obtained free of charge from any HSE enquiry point. The requirements include the following items.

- HSWA poster.
- Notification of accidents form. Employers will probably need a supply of these. Copies of the form can be used as a book.
- Accident book, for DSS purposes.[2]
- An up-to-date certificate of insurance. This must be displayed by virtue of the Employers' Liability (Compulsory Insurance) Act 1969. (See above, p. 112).

In addition, there are specific requirements under particular sets of regulations as well as under the main Acts themselves. The Factories

Act, for instance, requires registers showing the testing, inspection and examination of chains, ropes and lifting tackle. A failure no display notices, submit forms or keep registers is a criminal offence.

Under the Factories Act 1961 and the Offices, Shops and Railway Premises Act 1963 an employer will need to register with the inspectorate using the prescribed form.

Reporting of Injuries, Diseases and Dangerous Occurrences Regulations 1985 (RIDDOR)

These regulations were issued under HSWA and came into force in April 1986.[3] They apply to the reporting of injuries sustained as a result of an accident arising out of or in connection with work. The person injured may be an employee, a self-employed person, a trainee who is not an employee, or anyone else (such as a member of the public or a visitor). The regulations also require the reporting of specified dangerous occurrences and diseases.

Types of injuries to be reported

Over-three-days injuries
Injuries resulting from accidents at work which cause incapacity for more than three days must be reported to the enforcing authority in writing within seven days of the accident.

Specified major injuries (including fatalities)
Any of the following must be notified immediately to the enforcement agency by the quickest practicable means, as well as reported in writing within seven days.

- Death.
- Fracture of skull, spine or pelvis, arm, wrist, leg or ankle (but not hand or foot).
- Serious eye injuries.
- Amputation of a hand or foot; or of a finger, thumb or toe, or part thereof if the joint or bone is completely severed.
- Injuries or loss of consciousness arising from electrical shock.
- Decompression sickness.
- Illness or loss of consciousness as a result of absorbing a substance.
- Illness resulting from exposure to a pathogen or infected material.
- Loss of consciousness due to lack of oxygen.

- Any other injury requiring immediate entry to hospital and detention for in excess of 24 hours.

Death within one year of notification of a reportable injury must also be reported in writing.

Types of dangerous occurrence to be reported

These include;

- collapse or overturning or failure of cranes, excavators etc;
- collapse of scaffolds and buildings;
- accidental release of various substances;
- accidental release of highly flammable liquids;
- accidents involving road tankers;
- fires and explosions.

The full list is to be found in part 1 of schedule 1 to RIDDOR and in the HSE Guide.[4] Dangerous occurrences must be notified immediately and then reported in writing.

Reporting an injury or dangerous occurrence

Written reporting must be carried out within seven days of the injury or dangerous occurrence using the official form F2508. The responsibility for reporting will vary according to the circumstances.

	To be reported by
Injuries to employees	The employer
Injuries to self-employed;	
- working under the control of someone else	The controller of the premises
- working under own control	The self-employed person
Injuries to trainees who are not employees	The provider of the training
Injury to someone else (e.g. visitor; member of public)	The controller of the premises
Dangerous occurrences	The controller of the premises, except in certain circumstances where the responsibility would lie with the owner of a pipe-line or the operator of a vehicle.

Keeping records

A record must be kept of all reportable injuries and dangerous occurrences. The record must contain:

- date, time and place of accident or occurrence;
- name and occupation of persons affected;
- nature of injuries or condition;
- a brief description of what happened.

Copies of form F2508 would suffice as would entries in a Department of Social Security (DSS) accident book.

Reportable diseases[5]

A disease is reportable if it meets the following three requirements.

- It is one of those listed in RIDDOR. These cover poisonings, skin diseases, lung diseases, infections and other conditions.
- There is written diagnosis from a doctor – a medical certificate or a Statutory Sick Pay form – showing that the employee suffers from the disease.
- The employee is in one or more of the work activities specified in the regulations.

Reporting must be done by completion of form F2508A. This needs to be done by the employer in the case of an employee, by the provider of training in the case of a trainee who is not an employee and by the self-employed for themselves. Records must contain details of the occupation of the person affected, the name and nature of the disease and the date of diagnosis. Copies of the official form F2508A would suffice.

Enforcement agencies

Reports must be made to the appropriate enforcement agency. In the case of factories and sites this will be the HSE. In the case of offices and shops it will be the Environmental Health Department of the local authority. Failure to report is a criminal offence punishable by a fine.

Health Provisions

Control of Substances Hazardous to Health (COSHH) Regulations 1988[6]

These regulations, which are issued under the Health and Safety at Work etc. Act 1974, became operative on 1 October 1989. (Various detailed amendments to the COSHH Regulations are made by the COSHH (Amendment) Regulations, SI 1991/2026. These revoke the amendment regulations of 1990 and operate from 1 January 1992.) The starting point of the provisions is the requirement for an employer to carry out an assessment of work tasks which are likely to create risks for the health and safety of employees from exposure to hazardous substances. This should have been done by 1 January 1990. From the assessment should flow decisions about the measures necessary to prevent or control such exposure. The central requirement is the duty to prevent or control exposure to substances hazardous to health. The regulations then go on to require maintenance of control measures, and in certain cases, the monitoring of exposure and health surveillance. Workers exposed to hazardous substances have rights to information, instruction and training. The regulations apply regardless of the type of workplace.

Substances covered by the regulations
The regulations cover virtually all substances hazardous to health. Substance means 'any natural or artificial substance whether in solid or liquid form or in the form of a gas or vapour (including micro-organisms)'[7]. More specifically the regulations cover:

- all substances listed as dangerous under the Classification, Packaging and Labelling of Dangerous Substances Regulations, 1984[8] which are very toxic, toxic, harmful, corrosive or irritant;
- all substances for which a maximum exposure level (MEL) is set out in schedule 1 to the COSHH Regulations;
- all substances where the HSC has approved an occupational exposure standard (OES);
- any dust when present at a substantial concentration in the air;
- any micro-organism which can cause illness;
- any other substances which create hazards comparable with those above.

The regulations prohibit the use of some substances for specific purposes set out in schedule 2. There are few exceptions and in the main these are substances already covered by separate legislation. The exclusions comprise:

- lead;[9]
- asbestos;[10]
- substances which are hazardous solely because of their radioactive, explosive or flammable properties, or solely because they are at a high or low temperature or pressure;
- situations where a substance is administered in the course of medical treatment;
- exposure to substances below ground in any mine within the meaning of the Mines and Quarries Act 1954.[11]

Hazard and risk

The *hazard* presented by a substance is its potential to cause harm. The *risk* from a substance is the likelihood that it will cause harm in the actual circumstances of its use. The degree of risk will therefore depend upon:

- the hazard presented by the substance;
- how it is used;
- how it is controlled;
- who is exposed;
- how much exposure there is;
- how long the exposure lasts;
- what the person is doing, etc.

The main requirements of the regulations

The starting point for compliance with the provisions is regulation 6 which states that

> An employer shall not carry on any work which is liable to expose any employees to any substance hazardous to health unless he has made a suitable and sufficient assessment of the risks created by that work to the health of those employees and of the steps that need to be taken to meet the requirements of these Regulations.

The assessment must be reviewed if it is suspected of being no longer valid or if there has been a significant change in the work. The regulations therefore require an initial assessment to be made and that the assessment be kept up to date.

Flowing from the assessment is the central requirement of the regulations that exposure to substances hazardous to health is either prevented, or if not reasonably practicable, adequately controlled.

Thus, the regulations impose on employers a general duty to protect the health of their employees and others. Employers must ensure, as far as is reasonably practicable, that all control measures, equipment and facilities are properly applied or used and employees must use them fully and properly and report any defects. Such control measures must be maintained in an efficient state and kept in good repair and efficient working order. Where the regulations state that it is necessary, there must be environmental monitoring and health surveillance. Employees exposed to hazardous substances must be provided with information, instruction and training, including that relating to:

- the risks created;
- the precautions which should be taken;
- the results of environmental monitoring;
- the collective results of health surveillance.

Where there are union safety representatives, information will need to be provided under the Safety Representatives and Safety Committees Regulations.

The responsibility of the employer for protection of the health of individuals extends beyond their own employees. So far as is reasonably practicable, assessment, prevention/control and the monitoring of control measures should take into account not only others on the premises but any other person who is likely to be affected by the work. So far as is reasonably practicable, environmental monitoring should be applied to non-employees on the premises, but there is no duty to people not on the premises. The same is true for the provision of information, instruction and training. As far as health surveillance is concerned, the regulations apply only to employees. Contractors, sub-contractors and the self-employed all have the duties of employers.

The essence of the regulations involves a three-stage process:

1 Assessment of risks and the measures needed to comply with the regulations.
2 Introduction of preventive or control measures.
3 Monitoring of the control measures.

This process is shown in figure 5.1.

The employer's defence
It is a defence for any person: 'to prove that he took all reasonable precautions and exercised all due diligence' to avoid committing an offence by contravening these regulations.[12]

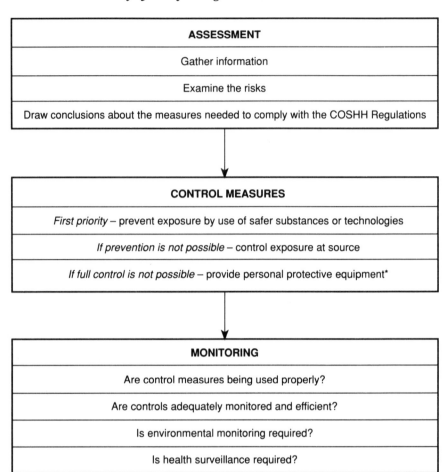

Figure 5.1 The three-stage process involved in meeting the requirements of the COSHH regulations

Environmental monitoring
Monitoring of exposure is required where the failure or deterioration of control measures could result in a serious health effect, where it is necessary to ensure exposure limits are not exceeded, where control measures are inadequate and in the case of certain substances and processes specified in schedule 4 (which also lays down the frequency

of monitoring). Records relating to identifiable individual employees must be kept for at least 30 years, and in other cases at least five years.

Health surveillance

This is required where the employee is exposed to one of the substances and engaged in a process specified in schedule 5, or where an identifiable disease or adverse health effect may be related to the exposure. In the latter case there must be a reasonable likelihood that the disease or effect would occur under the particular conditions of work, and there must be valid techniques for detecting indications of the disease or effect. Records must be kept for at least 30 years. Cases under schedule 5 require medical examination by a doctor at least every 12 months. There is a right of appeal against the doctor's decision.

The Noise at Work Regulations 1989[13]

General requirements

These regulations operated from the beginning of 1990 and are intended to meet the requirements of EC directive 86/188. The regulations specify three action levels for noise – a first level of 85dB(A), a second level of 90dB(A) and a peak action level. The measure dB(A) indicates loudness in decibels in a way that is adjusted to the character of the human ear. These action levels relate to daily noise exposure – the total exposure over the whole working day – without taking into account the use of ear protectors. The peak action level – a peak sound pressure of 200 pascals – is designed to protect people against explosive noise (for example, from cartridge operated tools and guns). This may be particularly relevant where the environment is generally quiet except for a small number of very loud noises.

Duties are placed upon employers and employees for the protection of everyone at work. Duties are also placed upon designers, manufacturers, importers and suppliers. They must provide information about noise generation if it is likely to reach 85dB(A) or over. The employer has a general duty to reduce risk of hearing damage to employees to the lowest level practicable.

There is a duty placed upon employers to provide information, instruction and training for employees. This should cover noise risks, precautions, employee obligations under the regulations and how to obtain ear protection.

If an employee's exposure is likely to reach any of the action levels the employer must arrange for a noise assessment to be carried out by a competent person. Records of assessments must be kept. Where the noise level is likely to reach 90dB(A) or the peak level, exposure must be reduced, as far as is reasonably practicable, by means other than ear protectors. There can be relaxation of this requirement if the daily personal noise exposure averaged over the whole working week is less than 90dB(A).

Noise levels from 85dB(A) but under 90dB(A)

An employer in such circumstances must provide suitable ear protectors if requested to do so by the employee. The employer is under no legal duty to ensure that the protectors so provided are actually worn, nor is the employee under any legal duty to wear them.

Noise levels from 90dB(A) and sound pressure from 200 pascals

An employer must provide suitable ear protection to reduce the risk of hearing damage and has a duty to ensure so far as practicable that the protectors are worn. An exemption may be provided where protectors would cause greater risk than they would prevent. All noise protection equipment must be properly maintained and properly used. The employee is under a legal duty to wear the protection. Employees must co-operate with any of the employer's actions that are taken to satisfy the regulations and must report any defects in equipment.

Ear protection zones

Where noise reaches 90dB(A) or peak level, the area must be designated an ear protection zone, and have warning signs conforming to BS5378.

Safety Provisions

The Electricity at Work Regulations 1989[14]

These regulations came into force in April 1990. In the main they are concerned with prevention of danger from electric burn, electric shock, electrical explosion or arcing or from fire or explosion stemming from electrical energy. The regulations cover all workplaces to which the Health and Safety at Work Act 1974 applies. They relate to any electrical equipment even if manufactured and installed prior to April 1990, and any work activity. Some of the regulations impose absolute duties – ones which must be fulfilled irrespective of costs and other factors.

The regulations cover the following:

- systems, work activities and protective equipment;
- the strength and capability of electrical equipment;
- adverse or hazardous environments;
- insulation, protection and placing of conductors;
- earthing or other suitable precautions;
- integrity of referenced conductors;
- connections;
- means for protecting from excess of current;
- means for cutting off the supply and for isolation;
- precautions for work on equipment made dead;
- work on or near live conductors;
- working space, access and lighting;
- competence to prevent danger and injury.

The onus is upon the employer to assess the work activities which use electricity or which may be affected by it. Employers must have regard to all foreseeable risks. Duties are also placed on the self-employed and employees. Where matters are within their control, persons in each category become duty-holders. In criminal proceedings a duty-holder has the defence that all reasonable steps were taken and all due diligence exercised in an attempt to avoid committing the offence. However, this may not provide an adequate defence where the regulations lay down absolute standards. Firms without electrically competent personnel will probably need to secure the services of an electrical contractor to help them meet the requirements of the legislation.

The Health and Safety (First-Aid) Regulations 1981[15]

These regulations place a general duty upon employers to make adequate first-aid provision for their employees if they are injured or become ill at work. Employers must provide, or ensure that there are provided, adequate and appropriate equipment and facilities for enabling first-aid to be rendered (regulation 3). First-aid is defined (in regulation 2) to mean:

- treatment for the purpose of preserving life and minimizing the consequences of injury and illness until the help of a medical practitioner or nurse is obtained; and
- the treatment of minor injuries which would otherwise receive no treatment or which do not need treatment by a medical practitioner or nurse.

The treatment of minor illnesses, as distinct from injuries, falls outside this definition. Therefore, the administration of tablets or medicines is not covered.

An employer is under a duty to inform his employees of the arrangements made in connection with first-aid. A self-employed person has a duty to make adequate first-aid provision for himself. The regulations have widespread application but do not apply in the circumstances specified under regulation 7, for example in coal mines.

The legislation is accompanied by an approved code of practice. Where first-aid arrangements are made by a registered medical practitioner or qualified occupational health nurse, they can be different from those in the code, providing that they are at least equivalent. An occupational health service should provide suitable cover for all employees during working hours. In other cases, the arrangements should comply with the code.

There must be first-aid boxes and kits, and in high-risk establishments there should be a suitably equipped and staffed first-aid room. In all cases there must be suitable persons available to render first-aid. Where the suitable person is absent 'in temporary and exceptional circumstances' the employer must appoint a person to take charge of treatment, equipment and facilities.

The code was revised in 1990. The main changes arising out of the revision are as follows.

- Employers should make an assessment of the hazards in their workplace, and in deciding the type of first-aid provision and the number of first-aiders, they should take into account this assessment and not just the number of employees.
- First-aiders should be trained to deal with the specific hazards of their workplace rather than having a more general training.
- When deciding on the provision, an employer should take into account the regular and foreseeable absences of first-aiders (for instance, annual holidays).
- Where special first-aid techniques require specified items of equipmement, these should be available in addition to standard first-aid equipment.

Various changes have been made to the HSE guidance notes accompanying the code, including in respect of the training of first-aiders and the list of items to be included in first-aid boxes and kits.

There has been a separate code of practice published recently which covers first-aid arrangements for off-shore installations and pipeline works.[16]

The Fire Precautions Act 1971

The Fire Precautions Act 1971 places duties on occupiers or controllers of premises in respect of:

- measures for providing warning of fire;
- means of escape in case of fire.

A fire certificate is required for any building where:

- more than twenty people are employed; or
- more than ten are employed on any floor other than the ground floor; or
- flammable materials are stored in or under the building.

The local fire authority is responsible for the operation of the Act, including issuing fire certificates. (The HSE and other enforcement agencies remain responsible for dealing with fire risks arising out of the production process itself.) The certificate will lay down conditions which must be complied with, including the provision and maintenance of:

- the means of escape in case of fire;
- fire doors;
- fire alarms and fire fighting equipment;
- emergency lighting and exit signs.

Moreover, the certificate will require that employees be instructed in the:

- fire drill (which is to be held at least once a year);
- locations and use of fire fighting equipment and fire alarm points;
- use of fire doors;
- stopping and isolation of machinery;
- arrangements for evacuation.

Factory premises certificated prior to the 1971 Act (which became operational in 1976) are certificated under the Factories Act. Premises certificated under the Offices, Shops and Railway Premises Act 1963 are deemed to be certificated under the 1971 Act.

The Pressure Systems and Transportable Gas Containers Regulations 1989[17]

These regulations impose safety requirements in relation to pressure systems and transportable gas containers which are used or intended for use at work. The terms are defined in detail in regulation 2. There are also requirements preventing certain vessels from becoming pressurized as a result of outlets being obstructed. Duties are placed upon designers, manufacturers, importers and suppliers in relation to design and construction, and upon installers and those who carry out repairs or modifications.

In relation to transportable gas containers, the regulations lay down that they must be verified as conforming to certain approved design standards or specifications. Checks must be made when containers are filled, and non-refillable containers must not be refilled. There are requirements in relation to modification and repairs. Various records must be kept.

As regards pressure systems, duties to provide information are placed upon designers, suppliers, importers, repairers and those who modify systems. The installer is under a duty to ensure that nothing in the manner of the installation gives rise to danger and the user is required to establish the system's safe operating limits. Various records must be kept.

Major provisions relating to pressure systems, contained in regulations 8–12, do not become operative until 1 July 1994. These include the requirement for a pressure system user to have a written scheme for the periodic examination of specified parts of the system by a competent person. This scheme must be drawn up (or be certified as being suitable) by a competent person and must be reviewed and modified at appropriate intervals. The competent person must make a report containing information which includes the date by which any repairs, modifications or changes in safe operating limits should be made. The user is prohibited from operating the system after that date unless the required changes have been made or a postponement agreed within the terms of the regulations. Where the competent person believes there is imminent danger unless certain repairs, modifications or changes in safe operating limits are carried out, he must make a written report to that effect, and use of the system is prohibited until the amendments are effected. There must be adequate and suitable instruction, in terms of safe operation and emergency action, for persons operating the system. The system must not be operated except in accordance with these instructions. A system must be properly maintained.

The defence for a person accused of being in breach of the regulations is that:

> . . . the commission of the offence was due to the act or default of another person not being one of his employees. . . . and that he took all reasonable precautions and exercised all due diligence to avoid the commission of the offence. *(Regulation 23)*

However, the accused must provide the prosecutor with as much information as he has in his possession to identify or help identity the other person. This must be provided at least seven clear days before the hearing.

Construction Regulations

These apply where there are 'building operations' and 'works of engineering construction'. (These terms are to be found in the Factories Act 1961, section 176 as extended.) In addition, various other sets of regulations may apply (for example, in respect of first-aid or eye protection) as may HSWA and other statutes (such as OSRPA in respect of site offices).

Building operations include the following in relation to buildings: construction, structural alteration, repair, maintenance, re-pointing, re-decorating, external cleaning, demolition and preparatory work (including the laying of foundations). Works of engineering construction include construction of a railway line or siding (except on an existing railway) and the construction, structural alteration or repair of docks, harbours, tunnels, canals, bridges, reservoirs, roads, sewers and pipe-lines. Demolition is also included.

The main regulations

There are four main sets of regulations, *viz*:

- The Construction (General Provisions) Regulations 1961.
- The Construction (Lifting Operations) Regulations 1961.
- The Construction (Health and Welfare) Regulations 1966.
- The Construction (Working Places) Regulations 1966.

Taken together, these regulations include provisions in respect of the following:

- the handling of materials;
- vehicles on sites;
- ladders;
- gangways and runs;
- stairs;
- excavations, shafts and tunnels;
- scaffolding;
- dangerous locations (for example, roofs);
- hoists;
- lifting appliances;
- demolition.

They cover the whole range of construction activities from ground works to working at heights and specify precautions to be taken at each stage; for example, shoring of excavations, provision of access to workplaces and specifications of precautions at a workplace over two metres from ground level. In addition, they require statutory inspections of workplaces, plant and equipment and specify the time intervals between such inspections.

The Construction (Head Protection) Regulations 1989[18]

These regulations operated from 30 March 1990. They apply to building operations and works of engineering construction, which in practice means most construction activities.

The person in control of a site can make rules governing when and where head protection should be worn. Employees must wear such protection when instructed to do so by their employer or to comply with rules made by the person in control of the site. Self-employed workers must similarly wear head protection when instructed by a person in control, or when required by rules drawn up by that person.

Employers must provide suitable head protection for their employees and the self-employed must provide it for themselves. The protection must be maintained, and replaced whenever necessary. Employers must ensure that their employees wear suitable head protection whenever there is any foreseeable risk of head injury. Anyone in control of workers, employers, the self-employed or employees with control over others must ensure that those workers wear head protection whenever there is any foreseeable risk of head injury. These requirements must be met so far as is reasonably practicable.

By virtue of the Employment Act 1989[19] Sikhs are exempt from the legal requirement to wear a safety helmet on a construction site if they wear a turban. Neither the Sikh nor the employer will be liable in tort for injury, loss or damage caused by the failure to meet the normal legal requirement. Injuries suffered by the Sikh will be compensated for only to the extent that the injuries would have been caused even if a helmet had been worn. An employer requiring a Sikh to wear a crash helmet will be indirectly discriminating against him under the Race Relations Act 1976 unless it can be shown that the requirement was justifiable. It will be presumed to be unjustifiable unless there are reasonable grounds for believing that the Sikh would not wear a turban.

The European Dimension

The purpose of this section is to deal with proposals which have been adopted by the EC but which have not yet resulted in UK legislation. The legislative process of the EC is described briefly in chapter 1.

Recent developments

Because of changes introduced by the Single European Act (SEA) 1986 which became operative in July 1987, health and safety has become an important area of European legislation. Two aspects of the SEA are of particular significance. First, the introduction of article 118A into the Treaty of Rome gives health and safety a particular prominence in the objectives of the European Community. Article 118A states that particular attention shall be paid to encouraging improvements in the working environment as regards the health and safety of workers in order to harmonize conditions within the community. To help achieve this, the qualified majority voting procedure introduced by SEA can be used to adopt directives. This means that health and safety matters are less likely to get held up in the EC legislative machine since unanimity is no longer required. The vehicle of a 'framework' directive (see below) has been used to give effect to the objectives of article 118A.

The second aspect of the SEA that is particularly relevant to health and safety is the new article 100A. This allows the Council to adopt by a qualified majority, in co-operation with the European Parliament, measures to further the establishment and functioning of the internal market. While article 100A excludes matters of taxation, free movement of people and provisions relating to the rights and interests of employed people, it has been held to *include* technical standards and safety requirements for specific products. This has given rise to a series of 'new approach' directives, for example on machinery safety.

In addition to developments arising out of the introduction of articles 100A and 118A which use the qualified majority voting procedure, there are health and safety provisions in the Charter of Fundamental Social Rights (The 'Social Charter' – see below) and in the EC's environmental protection programme.

Directive on the introduction of measures to encourage improvement in the safety and health of workers at work (the 'framework directive')

The 'framework' directive adopted in 1989 can be seen as an EC equivalent of HSWA.[20] It lays down broad duties akin to those contained in Section 2 of HSWA and embodies the principle (found in British law, in, for example, the COSHH and Noise Regulations) that the risks inherent in work activities should be assessed, and appropriate control (including preventive) measures introduced.

The framework directive has so far given rise to nine 'daughter' directives. Two of them have implementation dates in 1993: Asbestos (1 January 1993) and Biological Agents (26 November 1993). The remainder, described below, have to be implemented by 31 December 1992. It must be stressed that:

- these directives have to be given effect through domestic legislation;
- existing domestic legislation may or may not be adequate to meet the requirements of the directives.

The HSC has recently published draft regulations to give effect to the 'framework' directive and the 'daughter' directives described below.

Workplace health and safety[21]
This directive lays down minimum standards in respect of a number of areas including:

- the keeping clear of escape routes and emergency exits;
- workplace cleanliness;
- maintenance of machinery and equipment and the rectification of faults;
- structural stability;
- electrical installations;

- fire detection and fighting equipment;
- room ventilation, temperature and lighting;
- rest room and sanitary facilities.

Use of work equipment[22]
The areas to which this directive relates include:

- the suitability and safe use of work equipment;
- minimum standards for the prevention of fires, discharges of gas or dust, and contact with electricity;
- safety standards during maintenance work;
- requirements in respect of control devices, guards and so on.

Use of personal, protective equipment (PPE)[23]
This directive lays down that PPE should be used when risks cannot be prevented. Employers must assess the risks, select PPE which gives protection and is suitable and provide it free of charge. Technical standards for PPE are determined by a separate directive.

Manual handling of loads[24]
This directive lays down minimum standards for the handling of loads, particularly where there is a danger that a worker may suffer a back injury. The emphasis is upon avoiding manual handling but where it is necessary an employer will need to assess the operation. This means taking into account factors including the size of the load, the physical effort required, the nature of the job and the working environment. On the basis of the assessment an employer must then introduce appropriate measures for avoiding or reducing the risk.

Display screen equipment (VDUs)[25]
This directive must be the subject of domestic legislation to be in force by 31 December 1992. Employers will be responsible for ensuring that all equipment installed from that date onwards meets the legal requirements. Existing equipment must be brought up to standard by the end of 1996. The legislation is likely to apply to most VDUs in commercial use.

The directive provides for:

- mandatory inspections of computer equipment and associated furniture;
- training in health and safety;
- the restructuring of job functions to allow periodic breaks from screen work;

- regular free eye tests and special glasses where necessary;
- minimum standards in relation to computer screens, keyboards, desks, chairs, lighting, noise, humidity and software.

Employers will need to carry out an assessment of work stations.

Carcinogens[26]

This directive lays down that employers must carry out an assessment of the risks related to exposure to carcinogens at work and use substitute substances or processes where possible. Where substitution is not possible, work should be conducted in a controlled environment. Otherwise, exposure should be reduced to as low a level as possible. Emergency procedures must be established. Workers' health will have to be monitored and the results of surveillance made available to them.

Temporary workers[27]

This directive applies to those working under fixed-term contracts and those workers supplied by agencies. (The draft regulations intended to give effect to the framework directive are also intended to provide for the implementation of this directive.) An employer will be responsible for the health, safety and welfare of staff supplied by agencies, and must provide information, training and medical surveillance for temporary workers on the same basis as for those who are permanent.

In addition, there are a number of proposals for directives for example, limit values to protect workers from chemical agents, including health and safety proposals derived from the EC Charter of Fundamental Social Rights of Workers (The Social Charter).

Health and safety directives proposed under the Charter of Fundamental Social Rights

Ten directives are proposed here. In addition, the directive on working time can be said to have health and safety implications since draft proposals contain provision for statutory daily and weekly rest periods for shift workers and a ban on overtime for night workers. A directive on the health and safety at work of pregnant women is near adoption. (Legislation to enable the UK to conform to this is likely to require an employer to conduct an assessment of the risks to the health and safety at work of pregnant women and to take measures in the light of that assessment.) Other directives may impinge on health and safety e.g. the proposed directive on young workers. The proposed health and safety directives will lay down minimum standards:

- for medical assistance on board vessels;
- for work at temporary or mobile construction sites (for example health care provision);
- for the drilling industries;
- in quarrying and open-cast mining;
- on fishing vessels;
- on information about certain dangerous industrial agents;
- on exposure to risks from certain physical agents (such as vibration; electro-magnetic radiation);
- on the use of asbestos, reviewing the existing provisions;
- on activities in transport, including the handling of loads;
- for safety signs at the workplace.
- Proposals for the extractive industries seem likely to be combined in one directive.

Only the proposals relating to asbestos have so far been adopted. It should be noted, however, that the other nine health and safety directives are similarly subject only to qualified majority voting in the Council of Ministers. By contrast, 'Social Charter' directives other than those relating to health and safety will require unanimity because they concern the rights and interests of employed people.

Notes

1 *Publications in Series*, London: Health and Safety Executive, 1990.
2 Social Security (Claims and Payments) Regulations, SI 1979/628.
3 RIDDOR, SI 1985/2023, as amended.
4 *Reporting an Injury or a Dangerous Occurrence*, London: Health and Safety Executive, 1990.
5 *Reporting a case of Disease*, London: HSE, 1990.
6 SI 1988/1657 as amended. On dangerous substances see: Dangerous Substances (Notification and Marking of Sites) Regulations, SI 1990/304; Control of Industrial Major Accident Hazards Regulations, SI 1984/1902, as amended; Classification, Packaging and Labelling of Dangerous Substances Regulations, SI 1984/1244, as amended.
7 COSHH, Regulation 2, para 1.
8 SI 1984/1244, as amended.
9 Control of Lead at Work Regulations, SI 1980/1248.
10 Control of Asbestos at Work Regulations, SI 1987/2115.
11 Mines and Quarries Act 1954 *c*.70, as amended.
12 COSHH, Regulation 16.

13 SI 1989/1790.

14 SI 1989/635.

15 SI 1981/917. See also: *First-Aid at Work*, COP No. 42, London: HMSO, 1990.

16 *First-Aid on Offshore Installations and in Pipeworks*, COP No. 32, London: HMSO, 1990.

17 The Pressure Systems and Transportable Gas Containers Regulations, SI 1989/2169.

18 SI 1989/2209.

19 EA, 1989, s. 11.

20 89/391/EEC.

21 89/654/EEC.

22 89/655/EEC.

23 89/656/EEC. Technical standards are determined by 89/686/EEC which has to be operative in Member States by 1 July 1992.

24 90/269/EEC.

25 90/270/EEC.

26 90/394/EEC.

27 91/383/EEC.

6

Pensions and Social Security

Pensions

The legal framework

Like other areas of employment, pensions has elements of both statute and common law. However, the statutory framework for pensions comprises more than just statutory regulation of private arrangements, because the State is also a direct provider of benefits. The State scheme comprises a basic pension and an additional, earnings-related element. The latter is known as the State Earnings-Related Pension Scheme (SERPS). Alongside the State scheme are private arrangements in the form of employer-run pension schemes and personal pensions. Employer schemes have their legal basis in trust law because they work through a system of trustees and trust deeds, although they may also create contractual relationships between employers and employees through the contract of employment. By contrast, personal pensions are contractual but involve a contract for services between the individual and the provider.

The Social Security Act 1986 introduced fundamental changes in respect of pensions and the Social Security Act of 1990 has continued the process. The overriding purpose of the 1986 Act, the main provisions of which began to operate in 1988, was to offset the growing cost of the State pension scheme by a combination of stick and carrot. The stick was a reduction in future benefits payable under SERPS (as described below); the carrot was an incentive to encourage investment in personal pensions. Employees may now contract out of SERPS and have a personal pension instead, subject to a minimum level of contribution.

The 1986 Social Security Act also made other changes. First, anyone may now opt out of a company scheme. That is, it can no longer be a condition of employment that an employee must be a member of a company pension scheme. Such clauses are now unenforceable at law. Second, employers operating money-purchase schemes (described below, see p. 147) may now contract their employees out of SERPS, subject to a minimum contribution level equal to the National Insurance (NI) contracting out rebate. This is the amount of the combined employer and employee reduction in NI where there is contracting-out under an employer's scheme (see below, p. 146). Third, occupational schemes must now provide minimum pensions for widowers if they are to contract out of SERPS. Fourth, occupational pension schemes must now provide facilities for in-house additional voluntary contributions (AVCs) and for free standing additional voluntary contributions (FSAVCs) bought from outside. Finally, the period after which a pension must be preserved has been reduced from five years to two. Once two years has elapsed, therefore, no refund of pension contributions is payable.[1]

The pensions revolution has been continued by the provisions of the Social Security Act 1990. This deals primarily with four areas:

- Protection against inflation for the accrued rights of early leavers.
- Increase to pensions in payment to protect against inflation.
- Restrictions upon the use of fund surpluses.
- New and strengthened institutions.

For early leavers, all preserved rights will be revalued according to the rate of inflation (but to a maximum of 5 per cent) whereas previously only rights acquired from 1985 were revalued.[2] The period for revaluation is that between leaving and retirement and this provision of the Act operates from 1 January 1991. The Social Security Act 1985 required for the first time that an employee leaving a company before retirement age should have an alternative to deferred benefits, that is, their pension being frozen. The Act laid down that the pension scheme must offer the employee a transfer value – an actuary's assessment of the value of the deferred pension. As already noted, the Social Security Act of 1986 has reduced the length of time after which refunds of contributions may be claimed, so the options available on early leaving are of increased interest. These options are now as follows:

1 a deferred pension which remains with the former employer's scheme until the benefits are payable, or

2 a transfer value which may be:
  (a) transferred to a new employer's scheme, if the scheme will accept it; or
  (b) be used to purchase an approved annuity from an insurance company; or
  (c) be transferred to a personal pension plan.

The actuarial reviews of deferred pensions under the Social Security Act 1990 may lead to an increase in transfer values.

All pensions in payment will be index-linked (again up to 5 per cent) but only for rights acquired after an (as yet unspecified) appointed day. It was originally expected that the day would be 1 January 1992, but implementation has been deferred beyond this date because of uncertainty about the cost of adjustments to schemes in the light of the *Barber* judgment (see below, pp. 151–2).

As regards surpluses, the Finance Act 1986 laid a duty on trustees to arrange for an actuarial valuation of their scheme to show the extent of any surplus. (An actuarial valuation of a scheme involves producing a long-term budget forecast which ultimately shows whether there is a surplus or a deficit. The forecast takes into account not only existing assets and liabilities but also projected flows of income and expenditure over a long period, based upon a variety of assumptions.) The basis for valuation is set out in Inland Revenue regulations. Where a fund is shown to have a surplus, the actuary must present the full range of options to the trustees, who must decide what should be done to dispose of it. The surplus must be limited to 5 per cent of the scheme's assets, as actuarily calculated. Tax relief is lost from the investment income from amounts in excess of this. Contribution holidays must not exceed five years. The Social Security Act 1990 requires that the first call upon the surplus must be indexation of pensions in respect of rights acquired before the appointed day by pensioners and existing staff. Only then can a contribution holiday or refund be taken.

Finally, the 1990 Act sets up new institutions and strengthens existing ones. The provisions of the Act itself were based largely upon the report of the Occupational Pensions Board (OPB), a quasi-government body which oversees the pensions field and makes proposals for reform. Personal pensions must be OPB-approved and the OPB ensures the accuracy of preserved pensions when there is a job change. The OPB has now established a pensions registry and a tracing service. This helps people to track down frozen pensions when they have lost touch with the scheme through mergers, liquidations and so on. The registry is based in Newcastle upon Tyne.

The second of the institutions is the Occupational Pensions Advisory Service (OPAS). This is a charitable body which was set up to help employees and pensioners with their pensions problems. It now receives grants from the government to sort out various pensions difficulties, including by means of arbitration. This leaves only the most difficult cases for the third of the institutions – the entirely new Pensions Ombudsman.[3]

The Ombudsman has some important legal powers and is effectively judge of disputes of fact or law. He investigates alleged injustices resulting from maladministration in respect of acts or omissions of trustees or managers of employers' schemes or personal pensions. Moreover, the Secretary of State may make regulations extending the Ombudsman's role to the acts or omissions of employers.

The sorts of problems which have been occurring include:

- contributions (AVCs, for example) not being paid into the pension fund;
- those arising from takeovers and mergers, especially in relation to pension fund surpluses (see below, p. 150);
- tracing who is responsible for paying a pension;
- disputes over early retirement benefits;
- those relating to difficulties in obtaining information;
- problems over unequal treatment (see below, pp. 150–2)
- and further legislation is now likely as a result of the Robert Maxwell affair.

The State scheme

State pensions are part of the wider State National Insurance Scheme, contributions to which are, in the main, compulsory. The discriminatory pension ages of 65 for men and 60 for women remain lawful while this is not true for employer schemes (see below, p. 151). A person may reduce their National Insurance contributions by opting out of SERPS. They can do this only if they have a personal pension or are a member of an employer scheme. It is not possible to opt out of SERPS more generally, nor is it possible to opt out of the basic State scheme under any circumstances.

The key legal aspects of the State pension scheme are:

- it is provided by statute;
- it is financed through the State NI scheme;
- deductions of NI contributions from pay are lawful under the terms of the Wages Act 1986 because they are required by statute;
- the appeals mechanism used generally for the social security system is available for handling disputes.

A State pension is payable if a man has reached 65 (or a woman 60) and has retired. Until recently, earning anything more than a small amount after retirement would result in the pension being reduced, although this did not apply from the age of 70 upwards for men and 65 upwards for women. However, this earnings rule has now been abolished, so that pensioners are able to continue working to any extent without their pensions being reduced. The rates of pension payable (from April 1992) are: single person £54.15 per week; married couple £86.70 per week. These figures relate to the basic element of the pension and assume a full contribution record. A person with an incomplete contribution record will suffer a pro rata reduction in the pension. However, a man retiring at 60 or over will have his NI contributions credited for periods during which he is not in work. Extra pension is paid where there are dependants. As already noted, there is, in addition to the basic pension, an earnings-related element (see below).

Benefits cannot be taken before 65 (60 for women), but can be taken later, so that an increased pension is payable at 70 (65 for women). The employee pays no NI contributions beyond 65 (60 for women), but his employer must continue to make contributions at the normal rate. The self-employed do not pay any contributions once they become 65 (60 for women). The State scheme provides no lump sum payment on retirement nor do employees' NI contributions attract tax relief. However, pensions are increased annually in line with the rate of inflation.

The earnings-related addition to the basic pension, SERPS, was introduced in 1978 as a result of the Social Security Pensions Act 1975. It takes into account earnings throughout the person's working life and revalues them to allow for inflation. The best twenty years can be taken for calculation purposes, although this will not actually come into effect until 1998, that is, when SERPS has been operational for twenty years. The maximum earnings-related pension allowable is 25 per cent of earnings – 1.25 per cent of average weekly earnings per year of contribution. Earnings, for the purpose of the calculation, are those in excess of the lower NI limit (currently £54 per week) but below the upper limit (£405). The Social Security Act 1986 reduces the 25 per cent to 20 per cent for those retiring after the tax year 2007–8, from when the calculation will be based on all the years rather than upon the best twenty. The 1986 Act also reduces dependants' benefits from the tax year 2000–1.

Under the Social Security Pensions Act 1975, employees were

allowed to be contracted out of SERPS only where an employer's scheme paid at least as much pension as the person would have obtained under SERPS. More recently, contracting out of SERPS is possible where an employee has a personal pension (see below, pp. 153–4) or is in an employer's money-purchase scheme without any guaranteed level of benefit. Contracting out means that both the employer and the employee pay a reduced NI contribution:

- an employer pays 3.8 per cent less NI in respect of the employee;
- the employee pays 2.0 per cent less NI.

In both cases, the percentage reduction is applied to the band of earnings between the lower and upper NI limits (see above).

Employer schemes

Constitution and structure

Pension scheme contributions are put into a pension fund which is independent of the employer's business and is established under a trust. The trustees are responsible for managing the fund and its investments. A trust deed lays down the purpose of the scheme and its framework for operation. It sets out the trustees' powers and responsibilities, which include ensuring that the scheme can meet its liabilities towards its members in terms of paying pensions and death benefits. There may be several amending deeds. The detailed terms and conditions of a pension scheme are set out in its rules. Some schemes, however, are statutory, the main ones being the Civil Service, the National Health Service, local government and the teachers. In the local government scheme the local authority as a whole acts in the role of trustee although the form of legal appointment is different from that in the private sector, and the benefits are laid down by statute.

The main benefits payable under company schemes are:

- a pension payable at retirement age or earlier;
- lump sum life assurance paid out on death in service;
- dependants' benefits.

Schemes are of two sorts: final earnings and money-purchase. The former pays a pension based on; earnings at or near retirement, the number of years the employee has contributed to the scheme and an accrual rate (a rate of pension per pensionable year, for instance, one sixtieth or one eightieth). A typical pension scheme based on an accrual rate of one eightieth might pay a pension as follows:

$$\text{Pension} = \frac{\text{Earnings}}{80} \times \text{Number of years}$$

Forty is often the maximum number of years giving, in the above example, a pension equal to half of the final salary. The Inland Revenue sets regulations to limit benefits to two-thirds of final salary after ten years' service. Good schemes do offer the two-thirds maximum, but typically after 40 years with an accrual rate of one sixtieth. By contrast, a money-purchase scheme offers no guarantee of the level of pension. The level of pension will depend upon the amount of contributions going into the scheme and how successfully those contributions are invested. On retirement, a pension is bought with whatever amount of money is available to purchase it.

Investment of pension funds may be carried out in a number of ways:

- by insurance companies on behalf of the trustees;
- by the trustees themselves, but with specialist functions, such as actuarial advice or investment advice, bought in;
- by specialist fund managers on behalf of the trustees.

No tax is paid upon the investment income just as there is no tax payable on employer and employee income which is used for contributions.

Despite the revolution in pensions since 1988, trust law continues as the legal basis of pension schemes. What responsibilities do trustees have, therefore, and what remedies are available if trustees do not fulfil their responsibilities? The overriding responsibility is a duty to act in the best interests of scheme members and this applies even to non-contributory schemes. This means, in practice, that they must be prudent and reasonable, including ensuring that there are sufficient funds to meet liabilities. It follows, therefore, that trustees could be sued for damages if they are in breach of trust. Where their actions are in breach of a statutory duty, this also might permit an action. Where behaviour is criminal, for example, fraudulent, it would be subject to the normal rules of criminal law.

The trustees will usually be managers of the company and there are often additional trustees from among the rest of the workforce. Recently, there has been an increase in the appointment of independent trustees. This may be of importance, because while there may be disputes between scheme members and trustees, there may also be disputes between trustees and the company. Trustees who are managers of the company may find themselves in a position where loyalties conflict. In this respect, it is important to note that trustees can seek a declaration from the courts if they are unsure about what they should do. Moreover, a recent case has helped to clarify the responsibilities of companies. In *Imperial Group Pension Trust Ltd* v. *Imperial Tobacco Ltd*, the scheme had a practice of paying pension increases in excess of 5 per cent and the new owner of the company was attempting to stop that practice by altering the rules to limit increases to 5 per cent. The court held that an employer's power under the rules of a scheme to give or withhold consent to the amendment of rules had to be exercised in good faith. This was based on the implied term of mutual trust and confidence in the contract of employment. Deciding in advance that future increases would not exceed 5 per cent, to the detriment of pensioners, would not be acting in good faith. Presumably such a decision would amount to a breach of the term of trust and confidence in the employment contract. Employees who believe that the company is responsible for the trustees paying an increase smaller than the scheme can afford may therefore be able individually to claim a breach of contract.

The contract of employment is thus the other area of common law which may affect pensions. Pensions may form part of the contract so that any attempt by a company to adversely change the scheme might amount to a breach of contract. Currently, a number of issues under consideration by some companies may have this effect, *viz*: changing from a final earnings to a money purchase scheme; increasing the pensionable age for women; altering the accrual rate from one sixtieth to one eightieth. In this context, the decision in *Mihlenstedt* v. *Barclay's Bank International Ltd* is of some interest. Here the Court of Appeal held that where a contract of employment provides for membership of a pension cheme, the employer has an implied duty to act in good faith.

Disclosure of information

The rules on disclosure of pension scheme information are to be found in regulations issued under the Social Security Act 1985.[4] (Different requirements apply in the public sector.) They mean that scheme members and recognized trades unions have a right of access to the basic legal documents (trust deed and rules) and a right to know who the trustees are. Employees joining a scheme on or after 1 November 1987 must be automatically supplied with certain information within 13 weeks of becoming a member. The information includes:

- eligibility and conditions of membership;
- the basis on which the employee's and employer's contributions are calculated;
- tax approval;
- the conditions under which benefits are paid;
- an address for enquiries.

The above information is also available on request and may be sought by members, prospective members, their spouses, beneficiaries and recognized trades unions. Such requests can be made no more frequently than every three years. Material alterations need to be notified to members and beneficiaries within one month of the change.

Various constitutional and other documents must be made available for inspection on request, but no more often than once a year. These must be provided if requested, on payment of a reasonable charge. The documents to be inspected and/or provided are:

- trust deed or other constitutional document;
- pension fund rules;
- annual report (to be provided free of charge when a copy is requested).

Entitlement to the above information is accorded to the same persons as indicated earlier. The annual report must contain the latest audited accounts and an actuarial statement relating to the scheme. (Accounts have to be audited each year; actuarial valuations have to be carried out every 3½ years). A right to inspect annual reports from previous years is given every three years. An annual report must be drawn up and accounts audited even if nobody requests them.

Finally, in the following circumstances members are given rights to obtain information relating to their individual position.

- Where a person has or is about to become entitled to benefit, they must be given information about the amount of entitlement and any conditions for the continued payment of benefit.
- Employees have a right, once a year, to request a statement of acquired benefits and likely entitlement based upon current contributions and salary.
- Employees leaving service must be told of their rights and options including details of cash equivalents and transfer values if they request them.

- Where a scheme is wound up, the employee must be told of their benefit entitlement and where they can obtain information after the scheme has been wound up.
- Where a member dies before retirement, dependants or other beneficiaries must be given details of their benefit entitlement.

Pension fund surpluses

One of the most frequent causes of collective disputes in the pensions field has been the question of surpluses – the amount of money in a pension fund which is in excess of that actuarily required to meet the scheme's liabilities. (Other sources of dispute have included investment policy.) A major issue is ownership. As already noted, there are now some statutory provisions, but these did not come about until after a number of cases had reached the courts. An employer at common law can stop contributions to a pension scheme if it is actuarily overfunded because his or her duty is to pay only the 'balance of the scheme', but this is now subject to the statutory requirements already described.

The statutory provisions do not however, resolve the question of ownership of surpluses. Are they subject to the trust deed, that is, for the benefit of the scheme's members, or are they fortuitous and belong to some extent to the company? In *Davis and anor* v. *Richards and Wallington Industries Ltd and ors*, a pension scheme was wound up and a surplus existed. The court ruled that some of it derived from over-payment of employer's contributions and belonged to the company. The remainder (derived from employees' contributions and transfer values) was not subject to the trust deed and therefore had to pass to the Crown.

In *Mettoy Pension Trustees Ltd* v. *Evans* it was held that the surplus which existed when the fund was wound up had to be used for the benefit of the scheme's members. In *Re. Courage Group's Pension Schemes*, the new owner tried to extract the pension fund surplus for his own use. The agreement of the trustees was needed. The trustees sought a declaration and the High Court ruled that they could not so agree. It would be ultra vires the powers of trustees to agree to changes which could defeat the whole purpose of the scheme.

Pensions and sex discrimination

Occupational pension schemes have found themselves in conflict with EC legislation which outlaws sex discrimination. The first EC Equal Treatment Directive was adopted in 1976 and relates to sex discrimination in the workplace.[5] The second, in 1979, covered statutory social security systems, but allowed as lawful discrimination in pensionable age and survivors' benefits.[6] The third directive, in 1986, covered occupational pension schemes and other employment-related benefit schemes such as sickness and maternity pay.[7] A draft directive on statutory and occupational pension schemes would equalize State pension ages but has been opposed since it was first put forward in October 1987. Therefore, discriminatory State pension ages remain lawful, although other discrimination based upon them may not be. Thus, in *James* v. *Eastleigh Borough Council*, concessionary arrangements for entry to leisure facilities applied to men of 65 or over and women of 60 or over constituted unlawful sex discrimination.

The 1986 Equal Treatment Directive requires that there shall be no discrimination on grounds of sex, marital status or family circumstances as regards:

- who may join a scheme and on what terms;
- the level of employee contributions;
- the level of employer contributions in final earnings schemes, except that positive discrimination is allowable to secure greater equality;
- rights to benefits and the level of benefits.

However, the directive does provide for exceptions, notably:

- discrimination as regards pensionable age until equality is achieved in respect of pensionable age in the State social security system;
- as regards money purchase schemes, including personal pensions and AVCs, where the different life expectancy of men and women can still be taken into account actuarily;
- discrimination in respect of survivors' benefits until achieved in the State scheme.

The directive has to be implemented in EC member countries by 1 January 1993. The vehicle for implementation in Britain is the Social Security Act of 1989. All paid maternity leave must count towards pensionable service by 1993 to meet the requirements of the directive.

Case law, particularly from the European Court of Justice, has already settled a number of important issues in relation to sex discrimination in the pensions field. In *Marshall* v. *Southampton and South West Hampshire Health Authority* the European Court ruled that discriminatory retirement ages were unlawful. The Sex Discrimination Act 1986 subsequently outlawed the practice and provided statutory remedies.[8] In *Barber* v. *Guardian Royal Exchange Assurance Group* the European Court ruled that pensions were pay under article 119 of the

Treaty of Rome and that discrimination in pensions on grounds of sex was unlawful. Thus, pensionable age had to be the same for each sex. The Government has announced that it will give legislative effect to this, although in practice the decision can probably be relied upon anyway. However, while the essence of the *Barber* decision is clear, the implications as regards retrospection are by no means certain.

- Does the decision apply only to pension benefits earned since the date of the decision (17 May 1990)? or
- Do previously accrued entitlements have to be equalized for all persons in a scheme on 17 May 1990? or
- Do all pension payments made after 17 May 1990 have to be equalized including those made to existing pensioners and to early leavers?

It is hoped that the ECJ will resolve the issue through its decisions in respect of the *Coloroll* pension schemes. However, there may be a final settlement of this matter as a result of the pensions agreement reached at the EC 'Summit' meeting in Maastricht in December 1991. This agreement limits pensions equality to benefits earned from and including 17 May 1990 – the date of the *Barber* judgment – except where proceedings had commenced prior to that date.

Another issue is whether pension schemes discriminate against women by discriminating against part-time employees, a very large proportion of whom are women,. In *Bilka-Kaufhaus* v. *Weber von Hartz*, the European Court ruled that refusing to allow part-time employees to join a pension scheme (where a very large proportion of part-timers were women) constituted indirect sex discrimination and was in breach of article 119 of the Treaty of Rome. (A similar decision in relation to statutory sick pay was made in *Rinner-Kühn*, see pp. 155–6). Where the actual terms of a pension scheme are less favourable, the discrimination is a continuing act which is taken as being done at the end of the period of employment (*Barclay's Bank plc* v. *Kapur* – a race relations case).

Because of the different pensionable ages operated by the State scheme, some employers have deducted the amount of the State basic pension from the employer's scheme pension for women aged 60 but under 65. The aim has been to ensure that the total pension received by a woman in that age bracket was the same as that received by a man of the same age. This practice was held to be unlawful by the EAT in *Roberts* v. *Birds Eye Walls Ltd* since the benefits paid under the employer's scheme were discriminatory on grounds of sex. The case is now before the Court of Appeal which has referred it to the ECJ.

Personal pensions

These are private pension arrangements made by individuals, usually through insurance companies. A personal pension allows the holder to opt out of SERPS, or if the person is in a company scheme, to opt out of that. A person starting employment with a company which has a pension scheme may therefore choose between that scheme, a personal pension and staying in SERPS. If they join the employer's scheme or take out a personal pension they may contract-out of SERPS. The legal basis of personal pensions is a contract for services between the pension provider and the individual. Disputes might turn on questions of breach of contract and would be resolved through the normal courts. The OPAS and Pensions Ombudsman are also available as quicker and less expensive routes. A pensions register, in Newcastle upon Tyne, is available to help people locate both personal and company schemes where there are difficulties.

Personal pensions were introduced in 1988 and are money-purchase plans. The level of benefits depends upon the amount of the contributions and the success of investment. At retirement, the amount of money standing to the employee's credit is used to buy a pension for him. Because the level of benefits depends very largely on the amount of money paid in, there is no guaranteed level of benefit. Nor is there any guarantee that the benefits would be better than those of SERPS, out of which the employee has contracted.

The proportion of earnings which may be paid into such a pension increases with age to a maximum of 40 per cent at the age of over 60 years. Various Finance Acts and the Financial Services Act 1986 lay down the tax treatment of pension funds and set out regulations governing the providers of personal pensions, including in relation to investor protection. The incentive to transfer to personal pensions comprises the following two elements.

- A transfer to the pension provider of 5.8 per cent of NI contributions, that is, an amount equal to the reduced NI contribution where there is contracting-out of an employer's scheme. This is payable until 1993 but is subject to review by the Government Actuary as regards payment thereafter.
- An incentive payment from the NI Fund of 2 per cent of earnings, payable until 1993. This applies only to those who prior to 1 January 1986 were not in jobs covered by contracted-out schemes.

Both the resultant amounts must be paid into the personal pension fund and attract tax relief. It is open to a person to transfer back to SERPS at a later date.

The minimun contribution payable by employers is an amount equal to the employer's share of the difference between the full rate of NI and the contracted-out rate – 3.8 per cent of NI. Beyond that, an employer need not pay anything, the matter being subject to management discretion or possible negotiation. The 17.5 per cent combined employer/employee pension contributions limit excludes the above incentives – they are additional. An employee will need separate insurance cover for death in service and ill-health early retirement.

Statutory Sick Pay

Background

The Statutory Sick Pay (SSP) Scheme was first introduced in 1983.[9] It made employers legally responsible for admininstering Statutory Sick Pay for the first eight weeks of sickness. In 1986, SSP was extended so that it covered the first 28 weeks of sickness. Employers act as State agents and are reimbursed by the government through reduced NI contributions (and if necessary, through the PAYE system). Reimbursement is at the rate of 80 per cent of the cost of SSP rather than in full, as formerly. Since 1985, employers have been given compensation for NI contributions on SSP, but this has now been abolished.[10]

A relief scheme exists for small employers.[11] In this context, a small employer is one who has paid (or is liable to pay) combined employer and employee NI contributions of £16,000 or less in the last complete tax year before the days to which the claim relates. The scheme provides that there will be full reimbursement of SSP where the employer's liability exceeds six weeks in aggregate for a period of incapacity for a particular employee. However, full reimbursement applies only to the period after the six weeks has passed – prior to that reimbursement is at the normal, 80 per cent rate.

Eligibility

There has to be a period of four or more consecutive days of incapacity for work before there is entitlement to SSP. Incapacity for work means that the employee is incapable through 'disease or bodily or mental disablement of doing work which he can reasonably be expected to do under (his) contract'.[12] Two periods of incapacity are linked and treated as one if the gap between them is less than eight weeks. SSP applies only to employees, who are defined as those working under a contract of service or holding an office where emoluments are chargeable for income tax schedule E purposes. There are no qualifying periods of employment or hours requirements.

There are a number of people who fall within the above definition but who are nonetheless excluded from entitlement to SSP. These are:

- people who have reached State pensionable age;
- those on contracts for three months or less (but there are some exceptions);
- anyone below the SSP minimum earnings level (see below);
- people who were ill prior to starting work;
- those becoming ill after the commencement of a strike;
- people in legal custody;
- anyone who has used up his full entitlement to SSP;
- people abroad outside the EC;
- pregnant women who are within the disqualification period (see section on statutory maternity pay below, p. 159).
- people who have recently had other State benefits e.g. Maternity Allowance.

A person excluded from entitlement to SSP may be able to claim State Sickness Benefit.

SSP stops after 28 weeks. Anyone who is still incapacitated in the twenty-ninth week will transfer to Invalidity Benefit. Employers must issue transfer forms to employees after 22 weeks. An employee changing employers after receiving SSP has a right to a record of SSP from their former employer. This is known as a leaver's statement (form SSP 1(L), although employers may use their own computerized version of the form if they wish).

Rates of SSP

SSP is payable for 28 weeks for each single period of incapacity. The rates per week from 6 April 1992 are:[13]

- for those earning £190 or more per week – £52.50
- for those earning between £54 and £189.99 per week – £45.30

Those earning less than £54 have no entitlement to SSP. In *Rinner-Kühn* v. *FWW Spezial-Gebäudereinigung GmbH & Co KG*, the European Court decided that excluding part-timers from (German)

SSP amounted to unlawful sex discrimination where the part-timers were almost all women, unless the exclusion could be objectively justified by factors unrelated to sex. The UK legislation may therefore be unlawful, although the High Court recently held that the need to preserve jobs was such a factor in relation to the exclusion of part-time employees from unfair dismissal and RP rights. It was accepted that giving these rights to part-time employees would reduce the number of part-time jobs (*R.* v. *Secretary of State for Employment ex parte Equal Opportunities Commission*).

The earnings figures are gross and cover any payments to the employee on which NI contributions are due. They are not, therefore, restricted to basic pay. An average is taken over the eight weeks prior to the commencement of the period of incapacity. Any contractual payments made to the employee during incapacity may be offset against SSP liability. SSP is payable for each employment contract – an employee may be doubly entitled if they meet NI and other requirements.

SSP is taxable and subject to NI deductions and is usually paid in the same way as wages. It is payable for periods of at least four consecutive days. The days must be ones on which the employee would have worked if they had not been sick. These are known as qualifying days. Employers may designate any number of days per week (from one to seven) as qualifying days, but the more qualifying days per week the lower the daily rate of SSP. Nothing is paid for the first three (waiting) days.

Statutory Sick Pay is a minimum. Nothing in the regulations prevents a scheme being operated with higher levels of payments, although the additional payments would not be recoverable from the government.

Notification and evidence of incapacity

Notification of incapacity

How and when an employer should be notified of an employee's incapacity is not laid down statutorily. Rather, employers are told what they cannot do. They cannot:

- require notification before the end of the first day of incapacity;
- demand notification from the employee personally;
- require notification to be given by means of completion of a particular form;

- require medical evidence (for notification purposes – they may require it later);
- demand notification more frequently than once a week.

Late notification is allowable only if there is 'good cause'[14] and SSP can be withheld if there is no good cause. There is an absolute limit of 91 days after incapacity, beyond which notification is not allowed.

Evidence of incapacity

Employers may seek reasonable evidence of incapacity in order to determine whether or not an employee is entitled to SSP, and if they are so entitled, to determine duration.[15] Since self-certification was introduced in 1982, employees have not required a doctor's certificate to support their absence from work for the first seven days. Those absent for four to seven days are normally required to fill in a self-certification form. There is no strict legal requirement for this, it is simply part of the process by which an employer gathers evidence. Employers may design their own forms for this purpose. Since no SSP is payable for the first three days of incapacity, there is no legal basis whatsoever for self-certification for these days.

As noted, the regulations[16] say little more than that an employer should obtain reasonable evidence of incapacity and leave them to design their own form. Not surprisingly there have been cases where trades unions have objected to the forms used. For example, some forms require the following:

- completion in the presence of a foreman or supervisor;
- details of illness;
- doctor's name and address;
- the information on the form to be correct if there is to be a payment;
- agreement to the doctor providing medical information;
- the form to be completed accurately, otherwise disciplinary action may be taken.

Trades unions argue that such forms are not reasonable and that the only information needed is name, employment identification, first and last days of absence and brief reasons for absence. They say that requiring details of illness gives rise to problems of diagnosis by unqualified people and of breach of confidentiality. Ultimately, a failure to pay SSP because the employer felt insufficient or incorrect information had been given could be challenged through the social security appeals process (see below). Any disciplinary action might be open to challenge through normal legal channels (for example claims for damages for breach of contract or for compensation for unfair dismissal).

Certain rules are laid down in relation to evidence from doctors. Regulations prescribe the form of statement to be issued by a doctor.[17] The statement must advise whether the employee should or should not refrain from work. Any period during which the employee should refrain from work – up to six months, or longer in certain circumstances – must be stated. Such medical evidence cannot be required in relation to the employee's first seven days in any period of incapacity.

Disputes

If an employer refuses to pay SSP, an employee has the right to ask for a statement showing:

- for which day(s) the employer intends to pay SSP;
- how much the employer intends to pay per day;
- why the employer thinks SSP is not payable for other days.

Where the reason for non-payment is that the employee is excluded from SSP or has exhausted their entitlement, the employer should inform the employee using the appropriate DSS form – the 'change-over' form, SSP 1. Other reasons for non-payment are; late notification, doubts about the genuineness of the incapacity and a refusal to do lighter (contractual) duties.

It is normal practice for employees to use the established grievance procedure where there are disputes over SSP. If an employee is not satisfied with the outcome of this, however, they may appeal to a DSS adjudication officer, providing this occurs within six months of the first day of disputed SSP liability. Thereafter there are rights of appeal to a Social Security Appeals Tribunal (SSAT) and a social security commissioner, after which appeals on points of law lie with the Court of Appeal (Court of Session in Scotland). (Some decisions can be made only by the Secretary of State for Social Services. See below, p. 163.) A failure to pay SSP when payment is required by the decision of an adjudication officer, SSAT or commissioner will not only be a criminal offence punishable by fine but will allow the employee to enforce payment through the county court. If an employer is insolvent or defaults on payment, an employee may claim SSP from the NI Fund.

Criminal offences

The following are criminal offences, punishable by fine except where otherwise indicated.

- Failure to pay SSP within the time allowed following the formal decision of an adjudication officer, SSAT or commissioner.
- Failure to provide information required by one of the above.
- Failure to keep the required records.
- Failure to provide the employee with a change-over form – form SSP 1.
- Failure to provide the employee with a leaver's statement – form SSP 1(L);
- Providing false information in connection with recovery of SSP. There is the possibility of a maximum fine of £2000 here, or imprisonment for up to three months, or both.

Statutory Maternity Pay[18]

Background

Statutory maternity pay arrangements were completely remodelled in the Spring of 1987 along the lines of the Statutory Sick Pay scheme.[19] From 6 April 1987 employers were given responsibility for paying Statutory Maternity Pay (SMP) to their employees. An employer can recover SMP payments in full by deductions from NI contributions. He or she can also reclaim the NI contributions paid in respect of SMP, the rate having been reduced to 4.5 per cent of the SMP bill.[20]

During the 13-week core period of payment of SMP – starting six weeks before the expected week of confinement (EWC) – a woman is excluded from any right to receive SSP regardless of whether or not entitled to SMP. More generally, SSP and SMP cannot be paid at the same time. Statutory Sick Pay is regarded as terminated the day before entitlement to SMP begins or, where there is no entitlement, would have begun if the woman was qualified.

Eligibility

To qualify for SMP, a woman, who has ceased to work for her employer because of pregnancy or confinement, must:

- have been continuously employed by the same (or an associated) employer for 26 weeks. The continuous employment must extend into the qualifying week – the 15th week before EWC;

- have had normal weekly earnings during the last eight of the 26 weeks at a level not less than the lower earnings limit for NI contributions;
- have reached, or been confined before reaching, the start of the eleventh week before EWC.

It should be noted that employers must pay SMP to an employee who qualifies regardless of whether she will be returning to work with them after the baby is born. An employee is a person whose earnings attract a liability for employee's class 1 NI contributions, or would do if they were high enough. (Social security and tax institutions do not necessarily adopt the same criteria for defining employee as might be adopted by an industrial tribunal). Whoever is liable to pay the employer's share of the class I contribution is to be treated as the employer.

A woman will not be entitled to SMP if:

- she was not employed by her employer (or an associated employer) during the qualifying week;
- she does not have 26 weeks' continuous employment;
- her earnings are below the NI minimum;
- her notice is late and it was reasonably practicable for her to give it in time;
- she does not provide medical evidence;
- she is abroad outside the EC;
- she is a foreign-going mariner whose employer pays NI contributions at a special rate;
- she is in legal custody;
- she is serving as a member of HM Forces.

An employee is not entitled to SMP at all if at the start of the SMP payment period there is no entitlement. Even where there is an entitlement, SMP may not be payable for certain weeks – such as after the woman's death, or if she is in legal custody. Where a woman works for her employer beyond the sixth week before EWC she will lose SMP for those weeks (at the lower rate, providing that at least six weeks of entitlement remain). This will not apply if she works for some other employer before EWC. Any work post-EWC – whether for the same or some other employer – will result in SMP not being payable for that particular week. Once SMP is paid, an employee must notify her employer of any changes, *viz*: starting to work for another employer, being in legal custody, or going abroad outside the EC.

Where an employee is fairly dismissed because of pregnancy the period of continuous employment is treated as not having been terminated. Such circumstances are; where it is impossible for the employee to do her job properly because of pregnancy, or it would be a breach of law (for example, HSWA) for her to continue working. There must be no alternative work available on terms which are not substantially less favourable than those relating to the original work. A fair dismissal does not, therefore, prevent qualification for SMP.

Where a dismissal is unfair and the employer has failed to establish a reason, SMP will still be payable if the dismissal was solely or mainly for the purpose of avoiding the payment of SMP. If an employer demonstrates some other reason for the dismissal, but the dismissal is nonetheless unfair, the compensation awarded is likely to take into account the loss of SMP. (The law on unfair dismissal is described in chapter 7).

If pregnancy ends other than by a live birth before the twenty-eighth week of pregnancy, no SMP is payable, although SSP might be. However, if this happens after the start of the twelfth week before EWC, SMP is payable.

For those who do not qualify for SMP there is a residual State Maternity Allowance.

Payment of SMP

Maternity pay is payable for up to 18 weeks. It cannot start earlier than the eleventh week before confinement, nor later than the sixth week. There is thus a fixed period of 13 weeks, and a period of five weeks which can be taken earlier, later or a combination of the two. A woman will need to cease work at least six weeks before EWC if she is to obtain the full 18 weeks' maternity pay. There are two rates of pay, the higher of which is nine-tenths of normal weekly earnings in the last eight of the 26 weeks mentioned earlier. A woman with two years' continuous employment (or five years' if hours are at least eight, but under 16 per week) is entitled to six weeks on the higher rate, followed by 12 weeks at the lower rate (a flat amount, £46.30 from 6 April 1992).[21] A woman with less than two years' qualifying employment is paid 18 weeks at the lower rate. Wages during maternity leave, company maternity pay and company sick pay can be offset against SMP, but these are the only payments that can be.

Like SSP, Statutory Maternity Pay applies to earnings rather than basic pay, and applies to each employment contract. SMP could be paid twice to one employee, therefore, if that employee worked for two employers or under two contracts (i.e. with two sets of NI contributions) for one employer. SMP is subject to tax and NI contributions. Unlike SSP, however, it is payable only for full weeks – there is no daily rate. Thus, where entitlement is lost for part of a week, the whole week's entitlement is lost.

Payment can be made in the same way as wages, or by means of a lump sum. It can also be paid through a third party (such as an insurance company) although the liability remains with the employer. A woman may claim SMP from the NI Fund if the employer is insolvent or defaults on payment.

Notification and evidence of maternity[22]

A woman must give her employer at least 21 days' notice, in writing if so requested, that she will be absent because of pregnancy or confinement, unless it is not reasonably practicable to give such an amount of notice. Evidence of birth or confinement will be necessary, usually in the form of a maternity certificate (form MAT B1). This is not normally issued earlier than 14 weeks before EWC. The evidence should be provided no later than the end of the third week of payment of SMP, although this can be extended by a further ten weeks if an employer accepts the reason for delay. Where notification is outside the 21 day period and it was reasonably practicable to notify in time, SMP may be withheld.

Disputes

Refusal to pay SMP may be challenged. An employer refusing to pay SMP should, if asked for a written statement, complete form SMP 1 and in doing so state the reason(s) for the refusal. The statement must show the weeks for which SMP is payable, how much SMP is payable per week and why no SMP is payable for other weeks. The form should be given to he employee within seven days of the decision being made. The maternity evidence should be returned to the employee. Some disputes might be avoided if employers make clear to their employees:

- when the employee must notify her intention to stop work;
- the flexibility of the SMP payment period and the employer's need to know the period chosen;
- what evidence of birth or confinement is required and when it is required.

If there is a dispute, the employee should process it through the normal grievance procedure. However, if the employee is still dissatisfied an appeal may be made to a DSS adjudication officer. Thereafter, appeal may be made to an SSAT, a social security commissioner and (on a point of law only) to the Court of Appeal (Court of Session in Scotland).[23] Some decisions, however, can be made only by the Secretary of State for Social Services. These are, whether:

- employment is continuous;
- amounts under separate contracts with the same employer can be added;
- an employee is entitled to compensation for National Insurance contributions on SMP;
- one person is an employer/employee of another and over what period (this also applies in the case of SSP);
- an employer is entitled to recover SMP payments and if so, how much (this also applies to recovery of SSP);
- two or more employers should be treated as one for SMP purposes (this also applies to SSP);

There is a right of appeal against the Secretary of State's decision on a point of law only. An appeal lies to the High Court.

Criminal offences

The following are criminal offences.

- Failure to pay SMP in time following a decision of an adjudication officer, SSAT, social security commissioner or the Secretary of State for Social Services.
- Failure to provide information to the statutory agencies.
- Failure to keep the required records *viz.* dates of maternity absences, copies of maternity certificates and records of weeks during the SMP payment period when no SMP was paid, and the reasons for non-payment. Records must be kept for three years.
- Falsifying documents for the recovery of SMP or NI contributions on SMP.

Notes

1 Social Security Act 1986, s. 10.
2 The Social Security Act 1985 had introduced this limited revaluing.
3 Social Security Act 1990, s. 12.
4 The Occupational Pension Schemes (Disclosure of Information) Regulations, SI 1986/1046.
5 76/207/EEC.
6 79/7/EEC.

7 86/378/EEC.

8 SDA 1986, s. 2.

9 Social Security and Housing Benefit Act 1982 (SSHBA); Statutory Sick Pay (General) Regulations, SI 1982/894 as amended.

10 Statutory Sick Pay Act 1991.

11 SSPA 1991 and SSP (Small Employers' Relief) Regulations, SI 1991/428 as amended by SI 1992/797.

12 SSHBA 1982, s. 1(3).

13 Social Security Contributions and Benefits Act 1992 c 4 s. 157. This Act consolidates and amends certain enactments relating to social security contributors and benefits.

14 SSP (General) Regulations 1982, Regulation 7(2).

15 SSHBA 1982, s. 17(2).

16 SSP (General) Regulations 1982.

17 SSP (Medical Evidence) Regulations, SI 1985/1604.

18 Changes are likely in this area if the EC Directive on the Protection of Pregnant Women at work is adopted in its present form.

19 Social Security Act 1986, Statutory Maternity Pay (General) Regulations, SI 1986/1960 as amended.

20 SMP (Compensation of Employers) (Amendment) Regulations, SI 1991/641.

21 Social Security Contributors and Benefits Act 1992, s. 166.

22 Statutory Maternity Pay (Medical Evidence) Regulations, SI 1987/235.

23 Social Security (Adjudication) Regulations, SI 1986/2218.

7

Discipline and Dismissal

The Legal Context

The legal context within which questions of discipline and dismissal arise is one where the common law contract of employment and the statutory provisions on unfair dismissal inter-relate. An important term of the contract in this respect is the requirement for the employee to obey the lawful commands of the employer. The contract therefore provides a legal basis for discipline by giving the employer authority over the employee. Thus, because serious acts of insubordination constitute misconduct, they are unlikely to lead to findings of unfair dismissal by industrial tribunals (all other things being equal).

Despite the fact that unfair dismissal is a statutory concept, contractual matters may play an important part in its application. First, the essence of the employment relationship in law is still the contract, written or unwritten, between the employer and the individual employee. Second, the terms of the contract may have an important bearing on matters such as the duties of the employee and the place and hours of work. Thus, although the issue to be decided may be whether or not the dismissal is fair, in practice it may be heavily influenced by the terms of the contract and the respective rights of the employer and employee. Third, the institutions operating the legislation have defined important concepts with ideas based on contract. For example, the test for a constructive dismissal (see below, pp. 184–5) is whether there has been a fundamental breach of contract, and the test for a redundancy is whether fewer employees are needed to do the jobs required under the terms of the contract (rather than to do the particular job being done at the time) (*Cowen* v. *Haden Ltd*).

Clearly, unfair dismissal law involves an interplay of statutory provision and common law. It should not, however, be confused with the common law concept of wrongful dismissal, which means that dismissal has not been in accordance with the terms of the contract (see below, pp. 191–2). By contrast, a dismissal is unfair if it fails to meet the statutory test, even though common law contract influences may be at work.

It must be stressed that while contractual matters are often paramount in unfair dismissal cases they are not the ultimate criterion by which decisions as to the fairness or unfairness of dismissals are to be taken. The statutory test can override any contractual considerations (see below, pp. 171–2). These contractual considerations may still form the basis of a case to be pursued elsewhere, however.

To assist employers in achieving good practice in this area and to help them stay clear of tribunals, there is an ACAS Code of Practice on disciplinary practice and procedures in employment.[1] This code has the same status as those mentioned in chapter 2 in relation to race and sex discrimination. A breach creates no liability, but the code is admissible in evidence in a case under the Act and must be taken into account by a tribunal where relevant. This means, for example, that a hiccup in a disciplinary procedure (such as a failure to investigate properly) does not in itself render the employer liable. However if the employee is dismissed and applies to a tribunal claiming that he or she was unfairly dismissed, the breach of code is admissible and must be considered by the tribunal if relevant.

ACAS has more recently produced an advisory handbook on discipline and this contains a full reproduction of the code.[2] The advice proferred by ACAS in its handbook has no legal status, whereas the code has the quasi-legal status already described. However, the handbook offers consistently good advice. To be adequately informed in the area of discipline and dismissal an employer should be familiar with the ACAS Code of Practice and handbook, have a good grasp of unfair dismissal law, and be aware of the terms of the employment contract of the employee being disciplined.

As noted in chapter 2, details of disciplinary rules and procedures for handling breaches of rule must be given to employees within thirteen weeks of commencing employment. As a result of the Employment Act 1989 there is an exception for employers with fewer than twenty employees.[3] In arriving at the total numbers of employees, those employed by any associated employer must be included.

It should be noted that there is no legal definition of gross misconduct. In practice, the following offences are normally included:

- theft, fraud or deliberate falsification of records;
- fighting or assault on another person;
- deliberate damage to company property;
- serious incapability through alcohol or being under the influence of illegal drugs;
- serious negligence which causes unacceptable loss, damage or injury;
- serious acts of insubordination;
- working for a competitor or otherwise damaging the company's commercial interests.

Unfair Dismissal

Meaning of dismissal and effective date of termination (EDT)

Deciding whether or not there has been a dismissal is a matter of fact for tribunals (*Martin* v. *MBS Fastenings (Glynwed) Distribution Ltd*). Where the words used are unambiguously those of dismissal or resignation they alone may be sufficient to determine the issue. The same may be true of acts. Thus, a personnel manager going to work and finding that his boss has put his desk in the car park, with a farewell note, may perhaps (on dates other than 1 April) be taken to have been dismissed. However, the context may also need to be taken into account. Even words which are unambiguous may not represent real intentions when spoken (or shouted) during a heated exchange (*Sovereign House Security Services Ltd* v. *Savage*). Thus some short period of cooling off might be reasonable before the decision becomes final. This gives the parties an opportunity to communicate with each other.

Agreements to exclude unfair dismissal rights are void (but see the ACAS conciliation officer exception on p. 169). A mutual termination by consent, to avoid the act of dismissal, was such an agreement and was therefore void according to the Court of Appeal in *Igbo* v. *Johnson Matthey (Chemicals) Ltd*. However, if an agreement to terminate is made with proper advice and no duress it is a valid mutual termination and no question of dismissal arises (*Logan Salton* v. *Durham County Council*).

Dismissal is defined as:

- termination of the contract by the employer with or without notice;
- the expiry of a fixed-term contract without renewal;

- constructive dismissal (see below, pp. 184–5);
- failure to permit a woman to return to work after confinement.

The effective date of termination (EDT) is when any notice expires or, if there is no notice, the actual date of termination. Oral notice starts on the day after it is given (*West* v. *Kneels Ltd*). A distinction can be drawn between wages in lieu of notice and situations where notice is given but the employee is not required to work it. In the latter case termination is on the expiry of the (unworked) notice (*Adams* v. *GKN Sankey Ltd*). Even when an appeals procedure has been followed the termination will normally conform to the above rules (*Savage* v. *J. Sainsbury Ltd*) unless the contract of employment provides for continuation until the procedure is exhausted, in which case the dismissal prior to appeal is conditional (*Greenall Whitley Plc* v. *Carr*). The EDT was on conclusion of the (unsuccessful) appeal in *Lang* v. *Devon General Ltd* because the right of appeal was contractual. In *Batchelor* v. *British Railways Board* the appeals procedure was part of the contract of employment, but the words 'dismissal with immediate effect' meant that the EDT was prior to the appeal, even though the dismissal might have involved a breach of contract. The remedy in such circumstances would be to sue for damages.

Where notice given by the employer is less than the statutory minimum, the EDT (for the purposes of qualifying employment for unfair dismissal and written reasons claims, and the calculation of the basic award) becomes the date on which the statutory minimum notice would have expired. In constructive dismissals the EDT is at the end of whatever period of notice the employer would have had to give if he had dismissed on the date of the employee giving notice or terminating (whichever applied).

None of the above removes the employer's right to dismiss summarily (that is, without notice or wages in lieu of notice) for gross misconduct. Summary dismissal is not 'undone' by the payment of wages in lieu of notice at a later date (*Octavius Atkinson* v. *Morris*). For the woman refused her right to return to work the dismissal is taken as having effect on the notified day of return.

It should be noted that sometimes the contract of employment can end because one party is no longer capable of performing it in the way the parties envisaged. This is called frustration. The circumstances are likely to be external, unforeseen and not the fault of either party (*Paal Wilson & Co* v. *Partenreederei*). Long-term illness is an example. A borstal sentence was frustration in *F. C. Shepherd & Co. Ltd* v. *Jerrom*.

The contract may be said to be frustrated after the passage of time. The significance of frustration is that it is not a dismissal, therefore no question of unfair dismissal or redundancy would arise.

The expiry of a fixed-term contract is itself a dismissal. Such a contract must have definite starting and finishing dates, although there may be provision for termination by notice within its period (*BBC* v. *Dixon*). This contrasts with a 'task' contract which is discharged by performance. Its expiry does not constitute a dismissal (*Wiltshire County Council* v. *NATFHE and Guy*).

Exclusions

The coverage of the legislation is much more limited than many people believe. The following are excluded.

- Anyone who is not an employee (see above, pp. 54–6).
- Anyone who is employed for fewer than 16 hours a week (but see below).
- Anyone who has reached normal retiring age. Where there is a normal retiring age and it is the same for men and women, that age applies even if it is different from 65. In any other case 65 will apply.[4]
- Anyone with less than two years' employment with their present employer if that employment started on or after 1 June 1985. (Anyone who started their employment on 31 May 1985 or earlier will already have sufficient qualifying employment).
- Anyone who is the subject of a certificate excepting them from the legislation in the interests of national security or confirming that they have been dismissed for that same reason.
- Anyone in a number of specified occupations, namely share fishermen/women, the police, and the Armed Forces.
- Those who ordinarily work outside Great Britain.
- Those with contracts for a fixed term of one year or more who have agreed in writing to waive their rights.
- Those covered by a dismissal procedure which is exempted from the legislation by ministerial order.
- Anyone who has made an agreement to refrain from complaining to a tribunal 'where a conciliation officer has taken action'.[5]
- Anyone whose employment contract has an illegal purpose (to defraud the Inland Revenue for instance). An unknowingly illegal contract may not restrict statutory rights.[6]

It should be noted that the legislation does apply to Crown servants, and to House of Commons staff.

The hours qualification arises out of the legal definition of continuous employment.[7] An employee must either be employed for

16 hours or more per week, or work under a contract which normally involves employment for 16 hours or more. Those with five years' continuous employment enjoy continuity if the contract is for eight or more hours per week. Continuity is also preserved where there are gaps in the employment contract because of incapacity, a temporary cessation of work (*Ford* v. *Warwickshire County Council*), custom or arrangement and pregnancy or confinement. However, separate contracts with the same employer cannot be aggregated to obtain sufficient hours and therefore sufficient continuous qualifying employment (*Surrey County Council* v. *Lewis*). However, there could be one 'global' contract providing for work to be carried out simultaneously for one employer at several different sites. The hours could then be aggregated. There is no continuous employment qualification if the dismissal is for reason of race, sex, trades unionism or non-unionism, although race and sex discrimination cases would have to be taken under the Race Relations Act 1976 and Sex Discrimination Act 1975 rather than the unfair dismissal provisions of the Employment Protection (Consolidation) Act of 1978 (EP(C)A) in the absence of two years' continuous employment. The qualification is one month where the dismissal is on medical grounds specified in schedule 1 of the EP(C)A. It should be noted that continuous employment begins on the date specified in the contract of employment, even if this is not a working day, rather than when the employee actually starts to do the work (*General of the Salvation Army* v. *Dewsbury*).

Normal retiring age (NRA) means contractual retiring age where there is one which is strictly applied. A contractual retiring age which is not strictly applied creates a presumption that the NRA is the same. In such circumstances, and also where there is no contractual retiring age at all, the overall test is the reasonable expectation of employees (*Waite* v. *GCHQ*). The reference group for establishing NRA will be determined by the 'position' held by the employee. Position means the following taken as a whole; status as an employee, nature of the work and terms and conditions[8] (*Hughes* v. *DHSS*). It should be noted that an NRA in excess of 65 will allow unfair dismissal claims up to that NRA. This contrasts with redundancy where eligibility for RPs is restricted to those who have not reached 65 years even if the NRA is in excess of 65.

The essence of the law on unfair dismissal

The essence of the law on unfair dismissal is the right of the employee not to be unfairly dismissed by their employer. The employee has this right regardless of whether or not they are in a union. In deciding cases, industrial tribunals go through a two-stage process. They ask: Has the employer established a fair reason for the dismissal? Did the employer act reasonably or unreasonably?

The starting point is to ask when a dismissal is fair, rather than when it is unfair. This is because the statute defines fairness rather than unfairness. The fair reasons for dismissal – the first stage of the process – are:

- the capability or qualifications of the employee;
- the conduct of the employee;
- the employee was redundant;
- the employee could not continue in their work without contravention of a statutory duty or restriction;
- some other substantial reason (SOSR).

A dismissal will also be fair if it can be shown that its purpose was to safeguard national security.[9] If an employer cannot establish a fair reason the case will fall. On the other hand, if a tribunal is satisfied that one of these reasons has been shown, it must then decide whether the employer acted reasonably or unreasonably in treating it as a sufficient reason for dismissal. The second stage of the process therefore, is a test of reasonableness. The statute says little about reasonableness except that tribunals must take into account, 'the size and administrative resources of the employer's undertaking', and decide the issue, 'in accordance with equity and the substantial merits of the case'.[10] In practice reasonableness comes down to proper procedure, consistency and the appropriateness of dismissal as the form of disciplinary action to be taken. The last of these involves consideration of the severity of the employee's offence as well as any mitigating factors such as length of employment, good record, provocation and domestic or personal difficulties.

The onus of proof for establishing a fair reason lies with the employer. The employee may, however, wish to bring evidence and put arguments in order to challenge the reason put forward. On reasonableness the onus of proof is neutral. Both parties will need to present arguments and evidence on this point. If the act of dismissal itself is denied the employee will be responsible for establishing dismissal within the meaning of the Act. The employee will also be responsible for proof of loss for compensation purposes. If the dismissal is alleged to be on grounds of sex or race discrimination an employee with two years' continuous employment will be able to use unfair dismissal law where the onus of proof of the reason for dismissal is upon the employer. Those without the qualifying employment will be restricted to use of the discrimination legislation where the onus of proof is on the complainant. If the dismissal is alleged to be on union or non-union grounds the unfair dismissal legislation can be used irrespective of whether or not there is qualifying employment. However, where the applicant has less than two years' continuous employment, the onus of proof of reason will lie with them rather than with the employer.

Fair reasons

Capability

It is fair to dismiss an employee on the grounds of capability or qualifications, but subject to the test of reasonableness. Capability refers to 'skill, aptitude, health or any other physical or mental quality'. Qualifications mean any 'degree, diploma or other academic, technical or professional qualification'[11]. In practice, dismissals on the grounds of capability fall into two categories: those involving incompetence and those involving ill-health. Where incompetence reflects the fact that the employee is working below capacity rather than a lack of ability the issue is to be treated as one of misconduct rather than one of capability (*Sutton and Gates (Luton) Ltd* v. *Boxall*). Evidence of the employee's incompetence will be needed, although quantitative measures will not always be possible. Loss of confidence in an employee, more likely in a management position, can amount to incompetence.

Where there is alleged incompetence, tribunals will want to be satisfied that the employer has provided the measure of supervision and training that a reasonable employer would provide (*Mansfield Hosiery Mills Ltd* v. *Bromley*). There should be warnings and a chance to improve (*James* v. *Waltham Holy Cross Urban District Council*).

Dismissal of a probationary employee is likely to come before the tribunals only infrequently because of the two-year qualifying period for claimants. The employer will generally find they have a greater freedom to dismiss in such cases, although warnings and evidence will still be required. An employer can reasonably expect a higher standard from a probationer, since they are 'on trial'. However, the employer should fulfil the following duties:

- maintain appraisal;
- provide guidance through advice and/or warning;
- make an honest assessment at the end of the probationary period, based on an adequaate investigation;
- provide warnings if the probationer is likely to fail;
- provide a chance to improve if likely to fail;
  (*Post Office* v. *Mughal*).

In ill-heath dismissals much depends on the context. A dismissal in a small firm will often be fair, while in a larger firm, where the work can be 'covered', it may well be unfair. The nature of the job will be a consideration too: is it a relatively low level job which can be covered, or a senior position which is difficult to fill except by permanent replacement? At some stage, provided a proper procedure has been followed, an ill-health dismissal is likely to be fair. The procedural necessities were set out in *East Lindsey District Council* v. *Daubney*. These include ascertaining the medical position and consulting with the employee. See also *Egg Stores* (above, p. 87).

Conduct
This is probably the most common reason put forward for dismissal, and ranges from the mundane (clocking offences, theft, drunkenness and fighting) to the more unusual (having long hair, not wearing a tie properly, and even losing the company cat). The EAT has set out what it considers is the correct approach for tribunals to take. Known as the *British Home Stores* v. *Burchell* test and endorsed by the Court of Appeal in *W. Weddell & Co Ltd* v. *Tepper*, it requires the tribunal to ask the following questions.

- Did the employer have 'a reasonable suspicion amounting to a belief' that the employee had committed the misconduct, at the time the dismissal decision was taken?
- Did the employer have reasonable grounds for this belief?
- Did the employer carry out a reasonable investigation?

These three requirements – belief, reasonable grounds and reasonable investigation – are widely applied by tribunals. As a result there is a duty imposed upon employers to handle misconduct cases with some care, although they will not be expected to establish an employee's guilt beyond all reasonable doubt as would be necessary in the Crown Court.

Certain offences normally attract the label 'gross misconduct'. As already noted, these include theft, physical violence, drunkenness, breach of confidence and refusal to carry out a legitimate order. What constitutes gross misconduct is a matter of fact for tribunals to decide (*Dalton* v. *Burton's Gold Medal Biscuits Ltd*). Gross negligence, in the absence of any element of intention, does not amount to gross misconduct (*Dietmann* v. *London Borough of Brent*).

Sometimes misconduct can be traced to a group of employees but the individual culprit(s) cannot be identified. Subject to the following rules the dismissal of the whole group – a 'blanket' dismissal – may be fair.

1 The act would justify dismissal if committed by an individual.
2 A reasonable investigation and a reasonable procedure have been carried out.
3 There is more than one suspect.
4 There has been a reasonable identification of the group and every one in the group could have been responsible for the misconduct.
5 It is not possible to identify the individual culprit.

All the above must be views formed at the time on reasonable grounds (*Parr* v. *Whitbread plc*). Where there is a group, *all* of whom it is reasonably believed are guilty of misconduct, each case should be investigated separately (*Cowton* v. *British Railways Board*).

Special care needs to be taken in dealing with misconduct by apprentices. In general, the standard of justification for dismissal for misconduct may be set higher because of the career repercussions of dismissal and the tender age of the person. The contractual terms, such as provision for notice and provision for summary dismissal for misconduct, will have an influence. Employers should consider discussing any possible dismissal with the apprentice's parents. Dismissal for poor performance should occur only if the apprentice will not 'make the grade' (*Hill* v. *Mallinson Denny (NW) Ltd*), and all the usual rules about dismissal for incompetence apply. Redundancy should be avoided during the term of the apprenticeship if at all possible. An apprenticeship contract may be frustrated, for example, by absence caused by a borstal sentence (*F. C. Shepherd and Co Ltd* v. *Jerrom*). Any unfair dismissal compensation or wrongful dismissal damages will include something for loss of future prospects. Where there is no provision for termination by notice during the term, pay for the remainder of the term will be included. Expiry of the apprenticeship constitutes dismissal, but failure to appoint to a post will most likely be a fair dismissal for SOSR. Such a situation is not a redundancy and there is no obligation to offer a post (*North East Coast Shiprepairers* v. *Secretary of State for Employment*).

Redundancy

The essential characteristic of redundancy is that the employer requires fewer employees (see below, pp. 196–8). A properly carried out dismissal by reason of redundancy will be a fair dismissal, although the employee, if qualified, may be entitled to a statutory redundancy payment. Properly carried out in this context means that the dismissal passes the general test of reasonableness, and in addition satisfies the selection requirements laid down in the statute (see below, p. 211). The expiry of a fixed-term contract could be dismissal for redundancy if redundancy was the reason for non-renewal.

Redundancy is a management decision and unless there is bad faith or illegality it is unlikely to be susceptible to legal challenge. The fact of needing fewer employees is what matters; once this has been established few tribunals will put the reasons under a microscope. The statutory rights of unions in this field are limited to advance warning and consultation; there is no legal right to a share in decision-making.

Contravention of statutory duty or restriction

This reason is likely to apply, for example, to people who drive on the public road as part or the whole of their job. Loss of licence means that they cannot do this job without a breach of law. More generally the employer should check that there would in fact be a breach of statute if the employee continued to do their normal job and seek expert advice if there is any doubt. Second, could the job be done by that person in any other way, for example, by using public transport? If driving were only a small part of the job this may be feasible. Moreover, the general stage 2 test of reasonableness applies: has the employee been warned of the risks of losing their job if they lose their licence? Has the employer looked at the possibility of alternative work? Has proper procedure been invoked? Are there mitigating factors such as a good record and long service?

Some other substantial reason (SOSR)

The dismissal of a temporary replacement for someone on maternity leave or someone suspended on medical grounds specified in schedule 1 of the EP(C)A would be a dismissal for SOSR if the replacement was informed in writing at the outset that they would be dismissed on the return of the absent employee. A dismissal for economic, technical or organizational reasons arising out of the transfer of an undertaking is also a dismissal for SOSR.

The main application of SOSR, however, is where the employer seeks to change employees' terms and conditions of employment unilaterally as a result of some form or reorganization. The justification for doing this, which is usually accepted by tribunals, is the need for business efficiency or financial saving (*Hollister* v. *National Farmers' Union*). The financial problems facing firms in recent years have greatly influenced tribunals in this respect but management will need to show a sound business reason for introducing the change, and evidence of some advance consultation with employees. Moreover, anyone dismissed for not agreeing to the change will need to be given due procedural rights – investigation of their circumstances, warnings, right to put their case, right of appeal and so on. In other words, the test of reasonableness will have to be satisfied. It is possible that an employee may justifiably resign as a result of the employer's actions, and claim constructive dismissal. A finding of constructive dismissal may result, but it will not necessarily give rise to an unfair dismissal (see below, p. 185). Where the reorganization leads to a requirement for fewer employees this will be a redundancy. The employee who is confronted by an imposed change in terms and conditions of employment (a wage reduction, for instance) may of course invoke common law procedures in order to obtain remedy. In the light of the employer's repudiation of contract the employee may continue working and sue for damages for the breach (*Ferodo Ltd* v. *Rigby*). Changing terms by terminating existing contracts and offering re-engagement on new terms removes the threat of common law actions but may open the door to unfair dismissal claims as in *Gilham and ors* v. *Kent County Council*.

The expiry of a fixed-term contract can be SOSR. The employer will need to show that they had a genuine need for a fixed-term contract in the first place, and why that reason has ceased to operate. The dismissal would then have to stand the test of reasonableness. As noted earlier, a dismissal as a result of the expiry of a fixed-term contract could be for reason of redundancy rather than SOSR.

SOSR could include the dismissal of people with personal characteristics that are unconventional or socially unacceptable. Such people have little protection unless the characteristics have no bearing at all on the work situation. In fact, employers can nearly always argue that such factors do have a bearing because, for example, of the effect on relationships with other employees and/or customers. Because of this it remains to be seen whether the dismissal of AIDS virus carriers will be unfair. The dilemma for people with something to hide is that hiding it will help them obtain a job, but after discovery by the employer the deceit will count against them in any unfair dismissal claim. The Rehabilitation of Offenders Act 1974 offers protection in certain employments to some of those who have criminal records (see above, pp. 31–3). Another issue assuming prominence is the introduction of rules prohibiting smoking at the workplace. Such rules will need to be introduced in a reasonable way, including the provision of adequate notice. One tribunal found that an employee's resignation, because such a rule was to be introduced, did not constitute constructive dismissal (*Rogers* v. *Wicks and Wilson Ltd*). There was no implied contractual term giving a right to smoke. The company was carrying out its duties under the Health and Safety at Work Act 1974. The consequences of breaking a non-smoking rule will have to be made clear to employees, and any dismissal will be subject to the general test of reasonableness.

Reasonableness

The ACAS Code on Disciplinary Practice and Procedures in Employment, and a wealth, if not a surfeit of case law, provide a clear indication of what is meant by reasonable. In short it means:

- following proper disciplinary procedure, including carrying out a reasonable investigation;
- being consistent in the application of discipline;
- that the disciplinary action taken needs to be appropriate for the particular case or, to borrow a phrase from criminal law, the punishment must fit the crime;
- taking into account any mitigating circumstances (including long service, good record, provocation and domestic or personal problems).

The standard of proof required is that facts need to be established on the balance of probabilities.

The ACAS code
The code deals with both rules and procedures. The former set standards of conduct at work, the latter provide means of dealing with a failure to meet those standards. On rules the code states that: they should be reasonable; they should be readily available; management

should do all it can to ensure that employees know and understand them; management should make employees aware of the likely consequence of breaking any particular rule. Faced with an industrial tribunal, management will want to be able to give positive answers on these points. From the employee's point of view, however, each of the above provides a potential mitigating factor to be offset against the breach of discipline.

Management should be in a position to provide a tribunal with a copy of the disciplinary rules, as well as with evidence that the dismissed employee had the rules drawn to their attention. If rules are not communicated properly the employee will have the defence that they did not know of a particular rule. That argument will be difficult to sustain if the employer has evidence (for example a signature for receipt) that a rule book was given to the employee. The assumption in law is that the employee will have read the rules. Possibly, if the rules are unclear, they can argue that they knew of the rule, but had not been told that they could be dismissed for breaking it. An employer should be ready to demonstrate that the rules are fully applied in practice and are applied in a consistent and non-discriminatory manner. Establishing this should form part of the disciplinary investigation (*West Midlands Travel Ltd* v. *Milke and Poole*). If it can be shown that management often turned a blind eye to breaches of rule there may be doubts about the reasonableness of dismissing.

Where there is gross misconduct an employer may dismiss summarily. However, this does not mean that proper procedure can be dispensed with; an opportunity to explain will be necessary in most cases (*W. & J. Wass Ltd* v. *Binns*). There should always be a full investigation and a chance for the employee to put their case. Typically, the employee will have been sent home following their misconduct. A period of suspension, therefore, can be used to gather the facts, hear the employee's side of the story and arrive at a decision. That decision would not be at risk, if the employee's misconduct is criminal, simply by virtue of an acquittal in the Crown Court. The Court and the tribunal are deciding different issues, and different degrees of proof are necessary. An employee may be not guilty, but the employer may still have dismissed fairly.

The code states that procedures should be speedy and in writing. They should indicate the range of disciplinary action and specify which levels of management have authority to take particular action. Immediate superiors should not have power to dismiss without reference to senior management. The code envisages a system of warnings which is typically in four stages:

1 A formal oral warning for minor offences.
2 A written warning for subsequent minor offences or a more serious offence.
3 A final written warning (or a disciplinary suspension) for further misconduct, making clear that dismissal may follow if there is not adequate improvement.
4 Dismissal if there is not adequate improvement.

Sometimes the procedure may be entered at the second or third stage if there is serious misconduct, and of course the right exists to dismiss summarily for gross misconduct. Previous warnings may be relevant to dismissal even if they were for different reasons. An employer can take into account:

• the substance of previous warnings;
• the number of previous warnings there have been;
• the date(s) of previous warning(s);
• the period of time between warnings;
(*Auguste Noel Ltd* v. *Curtis*).

The code goes on to detail a number of requirements which have become quite prominent in the deliberations of industrial tribunals.

• The employee has a right to know the charges against them, and to have an opportunity to state his or her case – principles derived from the concept of natural justice. See *Pritchett and Dyjasek* v. *J. McIntyre Ltd*, however, in which these requirements were not met but the dismissal was nevertheless judged to be fair.
• The employee has a right to be accompanied by a union representative or some other person.
• Except for gross misconduct there should be no dismissal for a first offence. Instead, a system of oral and written warnings should be used. A warning, however, is not just a general exhortation to improve. It spells out the offence and indicates what will or may happen if it recurs, or if there is no improvement.
• There should be a careful investigation before any disciplinary action is taken.
• The reasons for the choice of disciplinary penalty should be explained to the employee.
• The employee should be given a right of appeal, and told of this right, and how to exercise it.

The code distinguishes between suspension with pay while an alleged breach is being investigated, and the use of suspension without pay as a disciplinary penalty. Criminal offences outside employment should not be taken as automatic reasons for dismissal The main consideration is whether it makes the employee unsuitable or unacceptable in their employment. Records of disciplinary breaches should be kept, as should details of warnings (including oral ones) and disciplinary penalties. Although records may be kept, the slate ought to be wiped clean after a period of satisfactory conduct. The length of the period is not specified in the code.

Case law

Tribunals have added the chance to 'make good' or improve to the questions they are likely to ask of an employer. They have also been influenced by the principles of natural justice (see above). These include the requirement that nobody should be a judge in their own interest. This is significant particularly in relation to appeals. It prevents those taking the original decision from being involved in any subsequent appeal against that decision. An appeals body should act in good faith (*Khanum* v. *Mid-Glamorgan Area Health Authority*). Refusal to grant a right of appeal which is part of the contract of employment may lead to a finding of unfair dismissal (*West Midlands Co-operative Society Ltd* v. *Tipton*; but see *Batchelor* v. *British Railways Board*). The reference in the statute to 'equity' has been taken as the basis for the need for consistency of treatment as part of reasonableness. Where comparisons are drawn with how other people have been treated in the past, including elsewhere in the organization, consistency is to be applied to the organization and not to individual managers (*Post Office* v. *Fennell*). If more than one person is being dismissed as a result of an incident:

● Are they being dismissed for the same offence?
● Are there any differences between the cases such as past records or mitigating factors? (*Eagle Star Insurance Co Ltd* v. *Hayward*).

In practice, some degree of inconsistency may be reasonable if the facts of different individual cases can be distinguished, as in *British Steel Corporation* v. *Griffin*. Taking into account the 'size and administrative resources of the . . . undertaking' may affect such factors as the offering of alternative work, but is not an excuse for the absence of a proper investigation.

In the early days of the legislation the maxim applied in some cases was that a breach of disciplinary procedure made an otherwise fair dismissal automatically unfair. Since then appeals have produced the doctrine that breach of procedure is an important factor to be taken into account, but does not necessarily make an otherwise fair dismissal unfair. It may or may not do (*West Midlands Co-operative Society Ltd* v. *Tipton*). The approach to be adopted, as laid down by the appellate courts is as follows.

- The tribunal should not put itself in place of the respondent and say what it would have done if it, the tribunal, had been the employer.
- Rather, it should note that for any disciplinary offence there will be, among employers, a range of reasonable responses (*British Leyland (UK) Ltd* v. *Swift*).
- The tribunal should ask itself if the response of the employer before it falls within that range. If it does, the employer has behaved reasonably. If, on the other hand, no reasonable employer would have behaved in that way, the employer before it has behaved unreasonably.

Until recently, a further complication in the approach to the question of reasonableness had been the operation of the 'any difference' test (*British Labour Pump Co Ltd* v. *Byrne; W. & J. Wass Ltd* v. *Binns*). If there has been a breach of procedure this test asks whether the proper application of procedure would have made any difference to the outcome. For example, would dismissal have been averted if the applicant had had an opportunity to state their case, or if a warning had been given? Often the answer has been that it would have made no difference, or, at best, that it would have delayed the dismissal (for example pending fuller investigation). As a result of the House of Lords ruling in *Polkey* v. *A. E. Dayton (Services) Ltd*, however, the application of the any difference test is normally likely to be restricted to questions of compensation. A reduction can be made to reflect the chance that a dismissal would still have occurred even if the correct procedure had been followed. This 'Polkey reduction' is separate and distinct from any reduction for contributory fault. The substantive matter of the fairness or otherwise of the dismissal will be decided according to what the employer did rather than what they might have done. The correct statutory tests are fair reason and reasonableness. Exceptionally, perhaps, an employer may be able to dispense with the procedural niceties on no difference grounds and still be reasonable.

The *Polkey* decision should restore to procedural propriety some of its former importance. As the Court of Appeal noted in one of the cases arising out of the 1984–5 Miners' strike, not even a heated industrial dispute is an excuse for serious procedural flaws (*McLaren* v.

National Coal Board). However, the *Polkey* decision is also a reminder that a lack of proper procedure does not mean that a dismissal is automatically unfair. The correct test is reasonableness. The effects of *Polkey* appear to be that procedural lapses are more likely to result in findings of unfair dismissal, but that unfair dismissal compensation will sometimes have a Polkey reduction. It should be noted that a procedural deficiency cannot be remedied on internal appeal merely by a review of the case. What is needed is a rehearing (*Whitbread & Co. plc* v. *Mills*).

In *W. Devis & Sons Ltd* v. *Atkins* it was decided that post-dismissal evidence not connected with the reason which the employer gave for the dismissal could not be admitted except in the determination of compensation. Similarly, the test of reasonableness is to be applied to the employer's behaviour at the time of the dismissal, on the basis of the facts that they had at their disposal, or should have had if a reasonable investigation had been carried out. However, post-dismissal facts which emerge during any internal appeal can be taken into account in deciding reasonableness (*West Midlands Co-operative Society Ltd* v. *Tipton*). Ultimately, reasonableness is a question of fact for the tribunal to determine (*Union of Construction, Allied Trades and Technicians* v. *Brain*).

Reasonableness in redundancies
There has developed, in addition to the case law already mentioned, some case law specific to dismissal by redundancy. This is discussed below, see pp. 211–18.

Special cases

The two-stage process of unfair dismissal law involves the establishing of a fair reason, and the satisfying of the test of reasonableness. It now has to be added that some dismissals are not subject to this process because the statute provides specifically for them.

Automatically unfair dismissals
In certain cases the statute instructs that dismissals are to be regarded as automatically unfair once the reason for dismissal is established. This applies to:

- dismissals on grounds of proposed or actual trades union membership or activity, or proposed or actual non-membership. (Prior to the operation of

the Employment Act 1988, the dismissal of a non-unionist in a 'closed shop' could sometimes be fair.);[12]
- unfair selection for redundancy (see below, pp. 211–17).;
- dismissals on grounds of pregnancy.

Dismissals on grounds of union activity or membership or non-union membership are not subject to the requirement for qualifying employment nor to the usual age limits. If the applicant has the normal qualifying employment the onus of proof lies with the respondent (*Shannon* v. *Michelin (Belfast) Ltd*). Otherwise it lies with the applicant (*Smith* v. *The Chairman and other councillors of Hayle Town Council*). Even in the former circumstances however the applicant will have to adduce evidence that the reason for dismissal was trades unionism, as well as rebutting the employer's reason. The courts have tended to interpret trades union activity narrowly (see *Chant* v. *Aquaboats Ltd*). However, in a recent case, dismissal for past union activities elsewhere was interpreted by the Court of Appeal as being dismissal because of a fear that such activities might be repeated in the present employment. Thus the dismissal was on grounds of trade union activity and was automatically unfair under EP(C)A s. 58 (i) (b) (*Fitzpatrick* v. *British Railways Board*). The statute says that union activities must be at the 'appropriate time' if they are to be protected – namely, outside working hours, or in working hours with the employer's agreement or consent – but does not say what constitutes such activities. The courts have ruled, for example, that these activities do not include the actions of the union itself (*Therm-A-Stor Ltd* v. *Atkins and others*) or the acts of a union member not done formally within the union's responsibility (*Drew* v. *St Edmundsbury Borough Council*). A non-unionist has the right not to be dismissed for refusing to make a payment (to a charity, for instance) in lieu of a union subscription.

In pregnancy dismissals the employer has the following defences.

- At the date of termination of employment the employee could no longer do her work adequately.
- She could not have continued working after termination of employment without contravening a statute (such as the Health and Safety at Work etc. Act 1974).

Even if one of the above applies, the employer or successor must still offer suitable alternative employment, if there is any, on terms which 'are not substantially less favourable to her'. The onus of proof will be upon the employer to show that a suitable offer was made, or that there was no suitable available vacancy. Selection for redundancy on grounds of pregnancy will automatically be unfair dismissal following the House of Lords ruling in *Brown* v. *Stockton on Tees Borough Council*, and in any case opens up the prospect of a claim on grounds of sex discrimination (*Hayes* v. *Malleable Working Men's Club*). It should be noted, however, that dismissal because of pregnancy is not automatically sex discrimination. Much depends upon how a man would have been treated if he had had a similar absence record (*Webb* v. *Emo Cargo (UK) Ltd*). However a recent decision of the ECJ suggests that in European law, pregnancy dismissals may automatically be sex discrimination (*Dekker* v. *Stichting Vormingscentrum voor Jong Volwassenen (VJV Centrum) Plus*).[13] The right not to be unfairly dismissed because of pregnancy is subject to the normal qualifying employment and hours requirement for unfair dismissal claims. Where these qualifications and requirements are not met the claim may be pursued as sex discrimination under the Sex Discrimination Act. (The requirement for a period of qualifying employment is likely to be removed to allow the UK to conform with the EC's proposed Directive on the Protection of Pregnant Women at Work.)

In addition to the automatically unfair dismissals mentioned above there are some further special cases. These are: dismissal of strikers; constructive dismissals; failure to permit a woman to return to work after confinement; dismissals associated with transfers of undertakings.

Dismissal in connection with industrial action
Dismissal in connection with a lock-out, strike or other industrial action is largely excluded from unfair dismissal law (see below, pp. 244–6).

Constructive dismissals
A constructive dismissal is termination by the employee, with or without notice, in circumstances where the employee is entitled to terminate the contract without notice because of the employer's conduct. These are circumstances where the employer is guilty of gross misconduct as a result of which the employee has a right to resign and claim that they have been unfairly dismissed. It is important to note not only that the onus of proof will be upon the applicant, but also that the two-stage process does not apply. Instead, the test is whether there has been a breach of contract (*Western Excavating (ECC) Ltd* v. *Sharp*). This, however, establishes only the fact of dismissal, and not its fairness or otherwise.

It has to be stated that, perhaps surprisingly, constructive dismissals are not automatically unfair (*Savoia* v. *Chiltern Herb Farms Ltd*; see also *Vose* v. *South Sefton Health Authority*). The employer may argue that it was necessary to change the contract of employment unilaterally in the interests of the business. This would have special weight if the business was in trouble or had to make specified savings. Other breaches would be less easy to defend, for example, breach of trust – an implied contractual term; *Woods* v. *W. M. Car Services (Peterborough) Ltd* – abusive language, failure to provide proper safety arrangements or reducing an employee's pay and/or status. Of course (as noted earlier, p. 176) the employee does not have to resign and claim constructive dismissal (that is, accept the employer's repudiation of contract). They can affirm the contract, either accepting the change, or rejecting it but carrying on working and suing for damages (*Ferodo Ltd* v. *Rigby*).

Refusal of right to return to work after confinement

Next, there is the position of the woman who is refused her right to return to work after confinement. It was noted earlier that this was part of the statutory definition of dismissal. It will not be treated as dismissal, however, if the employer has five or fewer employees and it was not reasonably practicable to allow her to return to work or offer her alternative employment on 'terms not substantially less favourable to her'. Nor will it be a dismissal, irrespective of the size of the firm, if it is not reasonably practicable to take her back, but she is offered alternative employment which she unreasonably refuses. The onus is upon the employer to show that there was no dismissal.

Dismissals in connection with transfers of undertakings

Finally, there is the question of dismissals in connection with the transfer of undertakings. Regulations issued under the European Communities Act 1972 apply where there is a transfer but not where there is simply a change in the ownership of share capital. Undertaking includes 'any trade or business . . . in the nature of a commercial venture'.[14] Contracts of employment automatically transfer with the business, as do rights and duties under the contract, including continuity of employment. Dismissals arising out of the transfer are automatically unfair, unless there is some economic, technical or organizational reason for them 'entailing changes in the workforce'. Such a reason, including redundancy, would constitute SOSR. Thus, the mere change of identity of the employer does not give an employee the right to resign and claim unfair dismissal or redundancy. However, a detrimental and substantial change to the employee's working conditions will give a right to claim unfair dismissal. (The subject of dismissal in connection with the transfer of an undertaking is explored more fully below, see pp. 221–2.)

Remedies

Reinstatement and re-engagement

Reinstatement, re-engagement and compensation are the remedies laid down in the statute, in that order of priority. Reinstatement means the complainant is treated in all respects as if they had not been dismissed. Re-engagement can be with the employer, an associated employer or with a successor of the employer, and must be in comparable or other suitable employment. Unless there has been contributory fault on the part of the applicant re-engagement should be on terms as favourable as reinstatement. In making an order for reinstatement or re-engagement the tribunal must consider:

- the complainant's wishes;
- whether it is practicable for the employer to comply with the order – only exceptionally will engagement of a permanent replacement prior to the hearing be admissible as a defence;
- if there was contributory fault, whether it is 'just' to make the order.

Compensation is the remedy in the vast majority of cases.

Compensation

There are three types of award.

1 Basic award.
2 Compensatory award.
3 Additional award ('special' award in cases involving dismissal for union or non-union reasons).

Interest is payable on industrial tribunal awards (see below, pp. 315–16). The basic award uses a formula which takes into account the employee's age, length of employment and gross weekly pay. A week's pay for those whose pay does not vary with output means the amount payable under the contract of employment. Non-contractual overtime is thus excluded. For those whose pay varies with output, those who work shifts and those with no normal hours, a twelve-week average is taken. The concept of a week's pay is dealt with more fully below, see pp. 205–6). The basic award formula is the same as that used to calculate a statutory redundancy payment except that employment below the age of 18 years counts for the basic award but not for RP purposes. There is entitlement to half a week's pay for every year of employment under the age of 22, one week's pay from 22 but under 41, and 1½ weeks' pay from 41 years on. The maximum number of years which can be counted is 20, making the maximum number of weeks' pay 30. The limit on weekly earnings to be taken into account is currently £205 – this is increased annually – so the maximum basic award is £6150. The award can be reduced because of the employee's conduct before dismissal, or because the employee unreasonably refused an offer of reinstatement. If the employer is insolvent, the basic award (but not the compensatory, additional or special awards) may be paid out of the National Insurance Fund. In an unfair dismissal where the reason for dismissal is redundancy the employee will not be entitled to both a statutory redundancy payment and the unfair dismissal basic award. If the employee unreasonably refused suitable alternative employment or accepted renewal of contract and has no entitlement to a redundancy payment because of this, the basic award of unfair dismissal will be equal to two weeks' pay.

By contrast the compensatory award draws more on the principles used in common law damages claims than any statutory formula. The amount depends on the loss suffered and any projected future loss that the tribunal is prepared to take into account. The main heads were set out in *Norton Tool Co.* v. *Tewson*.

- Actual loss of wages and benefits up to the hearing.
- Future loss of wages and benefits.
- Loss arising from manner of dismissal (such as damaged job prospects arising out of damaged reputation).
- Loss of statutory protection because qualifying employment for employment protection will have been lost. EAT has said that a sum of £100 is appropriate.
- Loss of pension rights – the industrial tribunal chairmen (in consultation with the Government Actuary) produced guidelines in 1990 on how to calculate compensation under this head.[15]

The tribunal must raise these heads but the onus of proof of loss lies with the applicant (*Tidman* v. *Aveling Marshall Ltd*).

The applicant must mitigate their loss, for example by looking for another job and by not preventing the employer from complying with a tribunal reinstatement or re-engagement order. If the employer wishes to allege a failure on the part of the employee to mitigate loss the onus is on the employer to prove such failure (*Bessenden Properties Ltd* v. *Corness*). In practice the onus is often put on the employee to show mitigation, as was done by the EAT in *Scottish and Newcastle Breweries Ltd* v. *Halliday*. The compensatory award can be reduced if there has been contributory fault or to reflect the Polkey factor. The maximum award is currently £10,000. (See below, pp. 316–18) for a worked example of unfair dismissal compensation).

Where the applicant is re-engaged or reinstated but the terms of the order are not fully complied with there may be an award according to loss sustained. Where the reinstatement or re-engagement is not effected this award is additional to the basic and compensatory payments, and is at the tribunal's discretion:

- 26–52 weeks' pay in dismissals on ground of race or sex;
- 13–26 weeks' pay in all other cases, except dismissals for unionism or non-unionism which are treated differently (see below).

Such extra compensation is payable only where an employer's compliance with the tribunal order is practicable. The maximum earnings limit applies here so the additional award cannot exceed £10,660 (52 weeks × £205 per week). Thus, in unfair dismissals other than those arising out of unionism or non-unionism the maximum compensation payable – all three awards together – is £26,810.

There is no provision for an employer to be compelled to reinstate or re-engage a dismissed employee. Nor can an industrial tribunal order for reinstatement or re-engagement be the basis of an ordinary damages claim in the courts (which would not be subject to unfair dismissal compensation limits). The only compensation payable for failure to comply with a tribunal order is an additional award by the tribunal itself (*O'Laoire* v. *Jackel International Ltd*).

Where the dismissal is for union or non-union reasons (including selection for redundancy on these grounds) there is a minimum basic award of £2700. The compensatory award is again based on loss, but there is a special rather than an additional award. The special award is calculated as follows.

- Where the tribunal refuses to order re-employment, 104 weeks' pay subject to a minimum of £13,400 and a maximum of £26,800.
- Where the tribunal makes an order for re-employment but the employer fails to comply without showing that it was not practicable to comply, 156 weeks' pay or £20,100, whichever is the greater, with no maximum.

- In both of the above cases a week's pay is not subject to the statutory earnings limit of £205.

The special award may be reduced because:

- of the employee's conduct before dismissal;
- the employee refused an offer of reinstatement;
- the employee prevented the employer complying with an order for reinstatement or re-engagement.

Either the applicant or respondent may claim that the respondent was induced to dismiss by trades union industrial action or the threat of it. If such pressure was put upon the respondent employer because the applicant would not join a union that union may be included as a party in the proceedings. This process, known as joinder, may result in the union being ordered to pay part or all of the compensation.

Interim relief
This is a rarely sought remedy which was devised to take the heat out of dismissals for union reasons, and to give recognition to the fact that such dismissals involved a breach of the right to freedom of association. It was thought that these dismissals were particularly likely to lead to industrial disputes. More recently, dismissals for non-unionism have been included in the provisions.

An employee dismissed for proposed or actual union membership or activity, or non-unionism, may apply to an industrial tribunal no later than seven days after the effective date of termination. In the case of dismissal for union reasons the relevant union must provide a certificate confirming that the applicant was a member of, or proposed to join that union, and must state that in their view the reason for the dismissal was as alleged. The tribunal, must decide whether it is 'likely' that it would find it an unfair dismissal at the full hearing. 'Likely' means more than a reasonable chance – it means a 'pretty good' chance (*Taplin* v. *C. Shippam Ltd*). If this is the tribunal's assessment it must say so, and explain its powers. It will then ask the employer if he will agree to reinstate or re-engage the applicant and if there is agreement it will make an order to that effect. If the employer fails to attend, or refuses to reinstate or re-engage, the tribunal 'shall make an order for the continuation of the employee's contract of employment'. This will include all remuneration, benefits and continuity, but will exclude the requirement to work. It will last until a full hearing of the case takes place.

Remedies Other Than an Unfair Dismissal Claim

Apart from an unfair dismissal claim there are two other types of legal action which may be taken by a person who is dismissed. These are, first, the use of public law, and second, suing for remedies for breach of contract. Where that breach of contract relates to dismissal it is known as wrongful dismissal. In addition: dismissal of a reservist absent on active service would probably be a breach of the Reserve Forces (Safeguard of Employment) Act 1985; dismissal of a registered disabled person could be a breach of the Disabled Persons (Employment) Act 1944.

Public law remedies

These derive from the fact that the jurisdiction of the High Court includes the exercise of supervision over inferior courts, tribunals and public officials (see above, p. 13, for a fuller description). Where a person's rights are affected by a decision made by 'someone empowered by public law' judges may enforce duties or quash decisions if they are, for example, illegal, irrational or procedurally deficient (*Associated Provincial Picture Houses Ltd* v. *Wednesbury Corporation*; *Council of Civil Service Unions and others* v. *The Minister for the Civil Service*). Such judicial review has an advantage over unfair dismissal law for the dismissed person in that it allows the dismissal to be permanently reversed. The general rule is that this remedy is available only where there is no other means of challenging the decision in question. Exceptionally, however, courts will depart from this rule, as in *Calveley and ors* v. *Merseyside Police*, where decisions to dismiss were quashed by the Court of Appeal, despite the fact that the complainants had a right of appeal to the Secretary of State under their disciplinary procedure and were exercising it. The High Court had refused to order that the dismissal be quashed because all other available remedies had not been exhausted, but the Court of Appeal thought that the serious breach of disciplinary procedure involved in the case justified an exception.

The availability of public law remedies in the employment field is not restricted to employees (people working under contracts of employment). Thus, a self-employed contractor or a public office holder, such as a magistrate or a member of a health authority, would be able to seek such remedies if they were dismissed from their positions. For judicial review to be used by a public sector employee they will have to show that their terms and conditions were in some way statutorily controlled, and that the dismissal was in conflict with the public body's statutory restrictions on dismissal. Thus in *R.* v. *Liverpool City Corporation ex parte Ferguson and Smith* the applicants were teachers whose pay and conditions were statutorily underpinned, and the decision to dismiss was in conflict with the fact that a local authority cannot dismiss when the reason is grounded in illegality (in this case the setting of an illegal rate).

Remedies for wrongful dismissal

These remedies can be sought by anyone who is employed under a contract of employment. There are no qualifying rules in relation to, for example, age, number of hours worked or length of employment. The remedies are sought from the employer. The basis of the case would be that the employee has been dismissed, and that the dismissal is in breach of one or more of the terms of the contract. Thus, a dismissal with less than the required contractual notice would be wrongful (as would be one with less than the statutory minimum notice if greater – see next section) unless the employee agrees to wages in lieu. (The law tends to regard wages in lieu as damages for breach of contract.) A dismissal during the term of a fixed-term contract which had no provision for termination by notice during its term would also be wrongful dismissal. So too would be a dismissal without the employer going through contractual appeals machinery, or through the disciplinary procedure as a whole if that were contractual (see *Dietmann* v. *London Borough of Brent*). The manner of the dismissal may involve a breach of the term of trust: for example, dismissal in a blaze of publicity amidst unsubstantiated allegations of dishonesty.

Damages are the principal remedy available for wrongful dismissal, but where the employer had the right under the contract to terminate it with notice the damages will be limited to wages for the contractual notice period (or minimum statutory notice period if longer). Where the employer had no such right of termination – such as under a fixed-term contract with no provision for termination by notice during its term – the damages will not be so limited. In this case they will relate to the unexpired part of the term.

A second remedy sometimes sought in wrongful dismissal cases is an injunction, that is, an order temporarily preventing the dismissal from being effected. The courts will only exceptionally grant such injunctions because it is not thought desirable to order even temporary performance of a contract of employment against the wishes of one of the parties. Special circumstances need to apply, as they did in *Hill* v. *C. A. Parsons & Co.* in 1971. Recently, there is some evidence that the courts may be more willing to grant such injunctions. In *Irani* v. *Southampton and South West Hampshire Area Health Authority* there were again special grounds: there was still confidence between employer and employee, a disputes procedure was available, and damages would not have been adequate as a remedy. An injunction was also granted in *Powell* v. *London Borough of Brent*. The injunctions in *Hill*, *Irani* and *Powell* were all temporary. There are established rules for how courts will deal with applications for temporary injunctions. The test is known as the 'balance of convenience' test (see above, p. 83) Briefly, this involves establishing whether there is a serious issue to be tried and which of the parties would be worse affected by an adverse interim ruling of the court if they were ultimately successful in an action for damages. The court is not required to look, at this stage, at the relative strength of the parties' cases (*American Cynamid* v. *Ethicon Ltd*).

Contract law provides a third remedy – an order for specific performance of the contract other than on the temporary basis described above. In relation to the employment field this is of only theoretical interest.

Use of ACAS arbitration

Employers and employees may prefer, however, to settle their differences through voluntary third party adjudication, although the statutory provisions are not abrogated by them doing so. In particular, they may wish to use ACAS arbitrators. The advantages of this method include the following.

- Speed – an on-site arbitration hearing and decision can be achieved more quickly than an industrial tribunal hearing and decision.
- Informality – arbitration procedures involve the presentation of cases but legal procedure is not used and the arbitrators are often not lawyers.
- Flexibility – the terms of reference can be drawn to take into account local industrial relations circumstances, for example, rules, custom and practice.
- Greater emphasis on reinstatement or re-engagement where the dismissal is held to be unfair. This is because the parties have agreed in advance to accept the arbitrator's decision. The decision of an industrial tribunal is

seen as being imposed from outside. Moreover, he speedier handling of the case makes such remedies easier to achieve.

Personnel managers, employees and any union officials may feel more at home with this system and may prefer a private hearing to a public tribunal. On the other hand, some employees may positively welcome the chance that a tribunal gives them to air their grievances in public.

Written Statement of Reasons for Dismissal

This right is given to those who had two years or more continuous employment with their employer prior to termination.[16] An employee cannot complain of a failure to provide written reasons without having requested them. A complaint can be made only if there has been an unreasonable refusal to comply with a request or if particulars of reasons were inadequate or untrue. The right is triggered by the employee's request, so there can be no infringement without the employee having first made a request (see below, pp. 297–8).

Notice Periods

The EP(C)A lays down minimum notice periods.[17] The right is given to those employees with one month or more of continuous employment, and is as follows.

- If the continuous employment is less than two years – one week's notice.
- One week's notice per year of continuous employment from two years to 12.

The minimum legal notice to be given where length of employment exceeds 12 years is still 12 weeks. The minimum notice which has to be given by the employee to the employer is one week. This does not increase with length of employment. Contractual arrangements may add to the statutory minimum on either side. (For the purposes of notice, a week does not have to be a 'pay' week as defined in section 153(1) of EP(C)A.)

Fixed-term contracts of one month or less will attract the legal minimum notice only if the employee has already worked continuously for three months. Task contracts expected to last three months or less will be excluded unless there is already three months' continuous employment. Notice may be waived and payment in lieu accepted. The right to terminate without notice because of the other party's repudiation is not affected. The employer must pay the employee during the notice period even if the employee is sick, or there is no work.

For infringement of notice rights the remedy is to sue through the courts for wrongful dismissal – dismissal not in accordance with the terms of the contract. However, there may soon be implementation of statutory provision for industrial tribunals to hear certain breach of contract cases (see above, p. 60). The notice rights apply to those fixed-term contracts with provision for termination by notice within the fixed-term, but do not apply to Crown servants.

Notes

1 ACAS, Code of Practice, *Disciplinary Practice and Procedures in Employment*, London: HMSO, 1977.
2 ACAS, *Discipline at Work*, London: Advisory, Conciliation and Arbitration Service, 1987.
3 EA 1989, s. 13.
4 Sex Discrimination Act 1986 *c*.59, s. 3.
5 EP(C)A, s. 140(2) (e).
6 Wedderburn, Lord *The Worker and the Law*, 3rd edition (1986), Penguin Books, Harmondsworth, p. 235.
7 EP(C)A, Schedule 13.
8 EP(C)A, s. 153.
9 EP(C)A, Schedule 9, para 2(1).
10 EP(C)A, s. 57(3).
11 EP(C)A, s. 57(4).
12 Employment Act 1988 *c*.19, s. 11.
13 The same approach was taken in *Handels-OG Kontorfunktionaerernes Forbund i Danmark (acting for Hertz)* v. *Dansk Arbejdsgiverforening (acting for Aldi Marked K/S)*. A failure to recruit because of pregnancy would also be direct sex discrimination. As regards illness arising from pregnancy, an employer must not dismiss during statutory maternity leave. Thereafter, the relevant test (for sex discrimination rather than unfair dismissal purposes) is how a man with a similar absence record would be treated.
14 The Transfer of Undertakings (Protection of Employment) Regulations 1981, SI 1981/1794, Regulation 2.
15 *Industrial Tribunals: Compensation for Loss of Pension Rights*, London: HMSO, 1990.

16 Increased from six months by EA 1989, s. 15. The two years' qualification applies to any employment commencing on or after 26 February 1990. (Employment Act 1989 (Commencement and Transitional Provisions) Order, SI 1990/189).

17 EP(C)A, s. 49.

8
Reorganization and Redundancy

Reorganization, Redundancy and Changes in Work Practices

Reorganization

Reorganization is a common occurrence in industry but is not a concept to be found in employment law. The legal implications of reorganization, if there are any, will depend upon the facts of the particular case. Thus, reorganization may involve redundancy, which is governed by legal rules, but equally, it may not. It may involve changes of ownership – where there is a substantial amount of law – but equally it may not. It may involve changes in terms and conditions of employment. As noted in chapter 3, a key consideration here is what is permitted under the terms of the contract of employment. Where reorganization results in short-time working or lay-offs there are separate statutory provisions.

Redundancy

In contrast to reorganization, redundancy is precisely defined in law. It is a dismissal which is 'attributable wholly or mainly to':

1 an actual or intended cessation of business, either generally or in the place in which the employee is employed, or
2 an actual or expected diminution in the requirements of the business for employees to carry out 'work of a particular kind', either generally or in the place in which the employee is employed.[1]

'Work of a particular kind' has been interpreted broadly so that a change to techniques and/or materials does not constitute redundancy (*Hindle* v. *Percival Boats*).

Three important preliminary points need to be made about the position of redundancy in employment law. First, it should be noted that redundancy is a form of dismissal. In industrial life a distinction is often drawn between dismissal (that is, 'the sack', for, say, misconduct) and redundancy, which by implication is not seen as dismissal. In law, dismissal is the umbrella concept covering termination by the employer. Redundancy is one form of dismissal. The fact that a redundancy is voluntary will not prevent it from being a redundancy in law as long as the termination is by means of dismissal, rather than by mutual agreement (*Burton, Allton and Johnson Ltd* v. *Peck*). Retirement under an early retirement scheme is likely to be a mutual termination (*Birch and Humber* v. *The University of Liverpool*) but termination as a result of volunteering under a redundancy scheme should be a redundancy, even if there is early payment of retirement benefits (see below, pp. 206–7, with respect to the tax position).

Second, the key to the definition of redundancy is not the fact that the amount of work has diminished, but rather that the employer requires fewer workers. The test for redundancy, therefore, is whether fewer workers are needed. Three types of situation were specified by the Court of Appeal in *McCrea* v. *Cullen and Davidson Ltd*:

1 The work has diminished, so fewer employees are needed.
2 The work has not diminished, but new technology has reduced the demand for employees.
3 The work has not diminished, but reorganization leads to fewer employees being wanted (past over-manning).

All of the above situations constitute redundancy. In general, the redundancy test of fewer employees has been applied to the jobs being done by those made redundant. The exception has been the practice of 'bumping' or indirect redundancy, where if a particular job is to go, the occupant might move to another job, and the person so displaced be made redundant (*W. Gimber and Sons Ltd* v. *Spurrett*). The Court of Appeal has ruled, however, that the fewer employees test should be applied to the work that could be done under the contract rather than to the job actually being done (*Cowen* v. *Haden Ltd*). How widely or narrowly work of a particular kind is defined will thus depend upon how widely or narrowly the contract terms are drawn.

A third factor of considerable importance is that the law accepts redundancy as a legitimate management decision. As noted in chapter 7, redundancy is one of the specified fair reasons for dismissal in the statute containing the unfair dismissal provisions. Essentially, the redundancy decision is a management prerogative and in the absence of bad faith there will normally be no challenge to it (*Moon* v. *Homeworthy Furniture (Northern) Ltd*). Altogether this means that there is no check in law on management dismissing for the reason of redundancy, providing that redundancy is the real reason for the dismissal and that the procedure adopted conforms to the legal requirements (see below). An exception to this occurs in the realm of public law. The redundancy decision of a public body may be quashed on judicial review, as was the case when Liverpool City Corporation set an illegal rate in 1985 (*R.* v. *Liverpool City Corporation ex parte Ferguson and Smith*).

Changes in work practices

One of the most common features of a reorganization is a change in work practices. This may involve increased flexibility of tasks, hours of work or locations. What are the legal implications of such changes? First, the contractual test (what changes, if any, does the contract allow? – see chapter 3) needs to be applied. Can any of the changes which are contemplated be made without breaches in employment contracts? If the answer is no, the position is as described above, pp. 80–4. Where a trades union agrees to flexibility, the likelihood is that it will become an incorporated term of the members' contracts of employment, even if some individuals or groups of members do not approve. This assumes that there is express or implied incorporation of collectively-bargained terms and that members do not take the extreme step of withdrawing authority from the union so that it ceases to be their agent in the matter. (It is in any case a matter of conjecture as to whether such withdrawal could unilaterally remove the incorporation process.)

Second, does the reorganization constitute a redundancy? Nothing in the previous paragraph implies that the level of employment will be reduced, but the purpose of changes in work practices is often to reduce unit costs and a major component of the saving is usually employment costs. Two cases illustrate the distinction which needs to be made. Reorganization was not a redundancy in *Johnson and Dutton* v. *Nottinghamshire Combined Police Authority* because although there were changes in terms – hours of work – no fewer employees were required. In contrast, reorganization was a redundancy in *Bromby and Hoare Ltd* v. *Evans and anor* where employees were replaced by self-employed contractors. The employer required fewer employees. Consequently redundancy legislation was brought into play in the latter case. The various requirements are dealt with in the following sections of this chapter.

Redundancy Payments

Eligibility

An employee dismissed by reason of redundancy may be entitled to a statutory redundancy payment (RP). To qualify, the employee must have been continuously employed by the employer or an associated employer for two years or more, be dismissed by reason of redundancy and be below the upper age limit. Where normal retiring age (NRA) does not discriminate on grounds of sex and is 65 years or lower, the NRA will be the limit. In any other circumstances 65 applies (see table 8.).[2] The concept of NRA is explained above, see p. 170.

Table 8.1 Maximum age limit for entitlement to statutory redundancy payments

	Eligibility limit (*must be under*)
Non-discriminatory NRA of 65 or below	NRA
Non-discriminatory NRA above 65	65
No NRA at all	65
Discriminatory NRAs	65

Since employment before the age of eighteen years does not count towards computation of continuous employment, a person has to be at least 20 to obtain a payment.

Some employees are excluded from the legislation, *viz*:

- Part-time workers (those working under a contract for less than 16 hours per week, unless there has been five or more years continuous employment at eight hours or more).
- Sharefishermen.
- Crown servants and most merchant seamen – these are covered by their own separate agreements.

- Employees whose contract requires them to ordinarily work outside Great Britain, unless they are working in Great Britain at the time of the redundancy.
- Employees of foreign governments.
- Domestic servants employed by close relatives.

There are special provisions for former registered dock workers.[3] NHS employees are no longer excluded.[4] It is possible that the exclusion of part-timers amounts to indirect sex discrimination since the vast majority of part-timers are women (see chapter 3 on the European concept of pay and also *R.* v. *Secretary of State for Employment* at p. 156 above.) The scheme does however include those on fixed-term contracts, excluding apprenticeships. Where the contract is for a term of two years or more, and was entered into after the commencement of the original 1965 Act, there will be a right to claim a payment on expiry of the contract unless there has earlier been a written agreement to waive that right. It would then have to be decided whether the non-renewal was for reason of redundancy (see *Nottinghamshire County Council* v. *Lee*; *North Yorkshire County Council* v. *Fay*). The waiver applies only to the time of expiry and not to redundancy within the term of the contract, although there would be no entitlement to an RP unless the two year qualifying period had already been met.

Meaning of dismissal and onus of proof

The onus is upon the employee to establish that there was a dismissal. Dismissal is defined[5] as follows.

- Termination of the contract of employment by the employer with or without notice.
- Expiry of a fixed-term contract without renewal.
- Termination by the employee, with or without notice, in circumstances where the employee is entitled to terminate without notice because of the employer's conduct (constructive dismissal).
- Failure to permit a woman to return to work after confinement.

Once that fact is established the dismissal is to be taken as for reasons of redundancy if not proved otherwise. This means the employer has to show that the reason was not redundancy. Where unfair dismissal is also alleged, the onus is upon the employer to show the reason for dismissal.

Industrial action or misconduct by the employee[6]

If before giving notice of redundancy the employer is entitled to dismiss for misconduct, a redundancy payment will not be payable even if the reason for dismissal is redundancy (*Simmons* v. *Hoover Ltd*). The test is a contractual one – whether the employee is in breach of contract such that dismissal is justified (*Bonner* v. *H. Gilbert Ltd*). An employee will thus lose entitlement to an RP if dismissed for striking prior to their employer giving them the 'obligatory' notice – that required by contract or statute (whichever greater). Where misconduct, other than taking part in a strike, occurs (or is discovered) during the obligatory notice period, and the employer dismisses for that misconduct, the tribunal has discretion to award the whole of the RP or such part as it thinks fit. An employee will retain their right to an RP if dismissed for striking during the obligatory notice period.

Lay-offs and short-time working

A redundancy payment may also be paid when an employee is laid off or put on short-time working. A person is laid off for the purposes of the legislation where in any week there is no work, and under the contract of employment no entitlement to be paid. Short-time is where reduced work leads to at least a 50 per cent reduction in pay. In both cases there must be four consecutive weeks, or six weeks in any 13. Weeks of lay-off or short-time caused by strikes or lock-outs anywhere cannot be counted. The employee has to give notice of termination of employment, and follow a rather complicated procedure set out in sections 88–89 of the EP(C)A.

Alternative employment

An employee will lose any right to a redundancy payment if the employer offers 'suitable' alternative employment and the employee 'unreasonably' refuses it. Where the terms of the new employment differ from those of the old there is a requirement for a 'trial period' of at least four weeks to establish whether the employment is suitable, without loss of entitlement to claim the RP. The agreement, which must be in writing, has to specify the end of the trial period and the terms and conditions which will apply after its expiry.[7] Qualified acceptance of new employment will allow the employee a reasonable period at common law in which to make a decision, after which the statutory trial period will take effect. The common law trial period can be a specific period by agreement.[8]

The alternative work offer can be made by the employer, an associated employer, or where a business changes hands, by the new owner. The offer must be made before the expiry of the old contract, and must take effect no later than four weeks after that contract expires. It need not be in writing. Continuity is preserved by statute.[9] Whether the employee will retain the right to a redundancy payment after refusing an employer's offer of alternative work or terminating the contract during the trial period will depend on it being established that either the new employment was unsuitable or that it was suitable but the employee was not unreasonable in refusing it.

Although in the statute these two questions are to be decided separately, in practice they sometimes become fused. The onus is upon the employer to prove both suitability and unreasonableness (*Jones* v. *Aston Cabinet Co. Ltd*), and these are matters of fact for the tribunal to decide (*Spencer and Griffin* v. *Gloucestershire County Council*). Skills, earnings, nature of previous work, what is traditionally acceptable and geographical location have all been important.[10] In *Smith* v. *R. Briggs and Co. Ltd* a big drop in earnings potential made the work unsuitable in the eyes of the EAT. Other factors include loss of status (*Harris* v. *E. Turner and Sons (Joinery) Ltd*) and cost and/or inconvenience of travel.[11] Clearly, contractual terms will be an influence, particularly in cases of occupational and geographical mobility. Any move not permitted by the contract may well be regarded as either unsuitable or reasonably refused (*O'Brien* v. *Associated Fire Alarms Ltd*). In *United Kingdom Atomic Energy Authority* v. *Claydon* the contract allowed a move, so the offer was suitable and was unreasonably refused. In general suitable means 'reasonably equivalent' (*Taylor* v. *Kent County Council*).

Where there is a change in the ownership of a business, and a new owner agrees to continue the employment of the employee on the same or mutually agreed new terms, the provision for suitable alternative employment and a trial period apply as if it were still the original employer. The Transfer of Undertakings Regulations, 1981 may also apply[12] (see pp. 219–22 below).

Continuity of employment

Employment is assumed to be continuous unless proved to the contrary. Thus the onus here is on the employer. Continuous employment ends on the 'relevant date'. Where there is notice it is the date of expiry of notice. Where there is no notice it is the date of termination. Where it is the expiry of a fixed-term contract, it is the date of expiry of the contract. The trial period delays the relevant date only for the purposes of calculating the time available for making a claim. For RP purposes, employment before the age of 18 years does not count when computing the length of continuous employment.

A strike does not interrupt continuity of employment, but the week in which a strike takes place does not count for the purpose of reckoning service. There is no break in continuity if there is sickness or injury lasting up to six months (or longer if there is no termination by the employer). There is no break if there is a temporary cessation of work, or absence by arrangement or custom. For RP purposes, movement between local government employers does not break continuity of employment.[13]

For a more general discussion of continuity of employment, see above, pp. 85–8.

Computation of payment

The payment is calculated on the basis of age, length of employment and earnings according to the formula in table 8.2. The Department of Employment produces a ready reckoner for RPs which is included on page 204. The European Commission has made it clear that it does not intend to propose a minimum level of RP for the EC and that there are no current proposals for the standardization of RPs.[14]

No employment beyond 20 years is counted, so the maximum payment is $20 \times 1\frac{1}{2} = 30$ weeks' pay. There is a maximum level of

Table 8.2 Formula for computation of redundancy payments

Age	*No of weeks' pay per year of employment in the particular age category*
Under 22 years	½
22–40	1
41 and over	1½

Service (years)	2	3	4	5	6	7	8	9	10	11	12	13	14	15	16	17	18	19	20
Age (years)																			
20	1	1	1	1	—														
21	1	$1\frac{1}{2}$	$1\frac{1}{2}$	$1\frac{1}{2}$	$1\frac{1}{2}$	—													
22	1	$1\frac{1}{2}$	2	2	2	2	—												
23	$1\frac{1}{2}$	2	$2\frac{1}{2}$	3	3	3	3	—											
24	2	$2\frac{1}{2}$	3	$3\frac{1}{2}$	4	4	4	4	—										
25	2	3	$3\frac{1}{2}$	4	$4\frac{1}{2}$	5	5	5	5	—									
26	2	3	4	$4\frac{1}{2}$	5	$5\frac{1}{2}$	6	6	6	6	—								
27	2	3	4	5	$5\frac{1}{2}$	6	$6\frac{1}{2}$	7	7	7	7	—							
28	2	3	4	5	6	$6\frac{1}{2}$	7	$7\frac{1}{2}$	8	8	8	8	—						
29	2	3	4	5	6	7	$7\frac{1}{2}$	8	$8\frac{1}{2}$	9	9	9	9	—					
30	2	3	4	5	6	7	8	$8\frac{1}{2}$	9	$9\frac{1}{2}$	10	10	10	10	—				
31	2	3	4	5	6	7	8	9	$9\frac{1}{2}$	10	$10\frac{1}{2}$	11	11	11	11	—			
32	2	3	4	5	6	7	8	9	10	$10\frac{1}{2}$	11	$11\frac{1}{2}$	12	12	12	12	—		
33	2	3	4	5	6	7	8	9	10	11	$11\frac{1}{2}$	12	$12\frac{1}{2}$	13	13	13	13	—	
34	2	3	4	5	6	7	8	9	10	11	12	$12\frac{1}{2}$	13	$13\frac{1}{2}$	14	14	14	14	—
35	2	3	4	5	6	7	8	9	10	11	12	13	$13\frac{1}{2}$	14	$14\frac{1}{2}$	15	15	15	15
36	2	3	4	5	6	7	8	9	10	11	12	13	14	$14\frac{1}{2}$	15	$15\frac{1}{2}$	16	16	16
37	2	3	4	5	6	7	8	9	10	11	12	13	14	15	$15\frac{1}{2}$	16	$16\frac{1}{2}$	17	17
38	2	3	4	5	6	7	8	9	10	11	12	13	14	15	16	$16\frac{1}{2}$	17	$17\frac{1}{2}$	18
39	2	3	4	5	6	7	8	9	10	11	12	13	14	15	16	17	$17\frac{1}{2}$	18	$18\frac{1}{2}$
40	2	3	4	5	6	7	8	9	10	11	12	13	14	15	16	17	18	$18\frac{1}{2}$	19
41	2	3	4	5	6	7	8	9	10	11	12	13	14	15	16	17	18	19	$19\frac{1}{2}$
42	$2\frac{1}{2}$	$3\frac{1}{2}$	$4\frac{1}{2}$	$5\frac{1}{2}$	$6\frac{1}{2}$	$7\frac{1}{2}$	$8\frac{1}{2}$	$9\frac{1}{2}$	$10\frac{1}{2}$	$11\frac{1}{2}$	$12\frac{1}{2}$	$13\frac{1}{2}$	$14\frac{1}{2}$	$15\frac{1}{2}$	$16\frac{1}{2}$	$17\frac{1}{2}$	$18\frac{1}{2}$	$19\frac{1}{2}$	$20\frac{1}{2}$
43	3	4	5	6	7	8	9	10	11	12	13	14	15	16	17	18	19	20	21
44	3	$4\frac{1}{2}$	$5\frac{1}{2}$	$6\frac{1}{2}$	$7\frac{1}{2}$	$8\frac{1}{2}$	$9\frac{1}{2}$	$10\frac{1}{2}$	$11\frac{1}{2}$	$12\frac{1}{2}$	$13\frac{1}{2}$	$14\frac{1}{2}$	$15\frac{1}{2}$	$16\frac{1}{2}$	$17\frac{1}{2}$	$18\frac{1}{2}$	$19\frac{1}{2}$	$20\frac{1}{2}$	$21\frac{1}{2}$
45	3	$4\frac{1}{2}$	6	7	8	9	10	11	12	13	14	15	16	17	18	19	20	21	22
46	3	$4\frac{1}{2}$	6	$7\frac{1}{2}$	$8\frac{1}{2}$	$9\frac{1}{2}$	$10\frac{1}{2}$	$11\frac{1}{2}$	$12\frac{1}{2}$	$13\frac{1}{2}$	$14\frac{1}{2}$	$15\frac{1}{2}$	$16\frac{1}{2}$	$17\frac{1}{2}$	$18\frac{1}{2}$	$19\frac{1}{2}$	$20\frac{1}{2}$	$21\frac{1}{2}$	$22\frac{1}{2}$
47	3	$4\frac{1}{2}$	6	$7\frac{1}{2}$	9	10	11	12	13	14	15	16	17	18	19	20	21	22	23
48	3	$4\frac{1}{2}$	6	$7\frac{1}{2}$	9	$10\frac{1}{2}$	$11\frac{1}{2}$	$12\frac{1}{2}$	$13\frac{1}{2}$	$14\frac{1}{2}$	$15\frac{1}{2}$	$16\frac{1}{2}$	$17\frac{1}{2}$	$18\frac{1}{2}$	$19\frac{1}{2}$	$20\frac{1}{2}$	$21\frac{1}{2}$	$22\frac{1}{2}$	$23\frac{1}{2}$
49	3	$4\frac{1}{2}$	6	$7\frac{1}{2}$	9	$10\frac{1}{2}$	12	13	14	15	16	17	18	19	20	21	22	23	24
50	3	$4\frac{1}{2}$	6	$7\frac{1}{2}$	9	$10\frac{1}{2}$	12	$13\frac{1}{2}$	$14\frac{1}{2}$	$15\frac{1}{2}$	$16\frac{1}{2}$	$17\frac{1}{2}$	$18\frac{1}{2}$	$19\frac{1}{2}$	$20\frac{1}{2}$	$21\frac{1}{2}$	$22\frac{1}{2}$	$23\frac{1}{2}$	$24\frac{1}{2}$
51	3	$4\frac{1}{2}$	6	$7\frac{1}{2}$	9	$10\frac{1}{2}$	12	$13\frac{1}{2}$	15	16	17	18	19	20	21	22	23	24	25
52	3	$4\frac{1}{2}$	6	$7\frac{1}{2}$	9	$10\frac{1}{2}$	12	$13\frac{1}{2}$	15	$16\frac{1}{2}$	$17\frac{1}{2}$	$18\frac{1}{2}$	$19\frac{1}{2}$	$20\frac{1}{2}$	$21\frac{1}{2}$	$22\frac{1}{2}$	$23\frac{1}{2}$	$24\frac{1}{2}$	$25\frac{1}{2}$
53	3	$4\frac{1}{2}$	6	$7\frac{1}{2}$	9	$10\frac{1}{2}$	12	$13\frac{1}{2}$	15	$16\frac{1}{2}$	18	19	20	21	22	23	24	25	26
54	3	$4\frac{1}{2}$	6	$7\frac{1}{2}$	9	$10\frac{1}{2}$	12	$13\frac{1}{2}$	15	$16\frac{1}{2}$	18	$19\frac{1}{2}$	$20\frac{1}{2}$	$21\frac{1}{2}$	$22\frac{1}{2}$	$23\frac{1}{2}$	$24\frac{1}{2}$	$25\frac{1}{2}$	$26\frac{1}{2}$
55	3	$4\frac{1}{2}$	6	$7\frac{1}{2}$	9	$10\frac{1}{2}$	12	$13\frac{1}{2}$	15	$16\frac{1}{2}$	18	$19\frac{1}{2}$	21	22	23	24	25	26	27
56	3	$4\frac{1}{2}$	6	$7\frac{1}{2}$	9	$10\frac{1}{2}$	12	$13\frac{1}{2}$	15	$16\frac{1}{2}$	18	$19\frac{1}{2}$	21	$22\frac{1}{2}$	$23\frac{1}{2}$	$24\frac{1}{2}$	$25\frac{1}{2}$	$26\frac{1}{2}$	$27\frac{1}{2}$
57	3	$4\frac{1}{2}$	6	$7\frac{1}{2}$	9	$10\frac{1}{2}$	12	$13\frac{1}{2}$	15	$16\frac{1}{2}$	18	$19\frac{1}{2}$	21	$22\frac{1}{2}$	24	25	26	27	28
58	3	$4\frac{1}{2}$	6	$7\frac{1}{2}$	9	$10\frac{1}{2}$	12	$13\frac{1}{2}$	15	$16\frac{1}{2}$	18	$19\frac{1}{2}$	21	$22\frac{1}{2}$	24	$25\frac{1}{2}$	$26\frac{1}{2}$	$27\frac{1}{2}$	$28\frac{1}{2}$
59	3	$4\frac{1}{2}$	6	$7\frac{1}{2}$	9	$10\frac{1}{2}$	12	$13\frac{1}{2}$	15	$16\frac{1}{2}$	18	$19\frac{1}{2}$	21	$22\frac{1}{2}$	24	$25\frac{1}{2}$	27	28	29
60	3	$4\frac{1}{2}$	6	$7\frac{1}{2}$	9	$10\frac{1}{2}$	12	$13\frac{1}{2}$	15	$16\frac{1}{2}$	18	$19\frac{1}{2}$	21	$22\frac{1}{2}$	24	$25\frac{1}{2}$	27	$28\frac{1}{2}$	$29\frac{1}{2}$
61	3	$4\frac{1}{2}$	6	$7\frac{1}{2}$	9	$10\frac{1}{2}$	12	$13\frac{1}{2}$	15	$16\frac{1}{2}$	18	$19\frac{1}{2}$	21	$22\frac{1}{2}$	24	$25\frac{1}{2}$	27	$28\frac{1}{2}$	30
62	3	$4\frac{1}{2}$	6	$7\frac{1}{2}$	9	$10\frac{1}{2}$	12	$13\frac{1}{2}$	15	$16\frac{1}{2}$	18	$19\frac{1}{2}$	21	$22\frac{1}{2}$	24	$25\frac{1}{2}$	27	$28\frac{1}{2}$	30
63	3	$4\frac{1}{2}$	6	$7\frac{1}{2}$	9	$10\frac{1}{2}$	12	$13\frac{1}{2}$	15	$16\frac{1}{2}$	18	$19\frac{1}{2}$	21	$22\frac{1}{2}$	24	$25\frac{1}{2}$	27	$28\frac{1}{2}$	30
64	3	$4\frac{1}{2}$	6	$7\frac{1}{2}$	9	$10\frac{1}{2}$	12	$13\frac{1}{2}$	15	$16\frac{1}{2}$	18	$19\frac{1}{2}$	21	$22\frac{1}{2}$	24	$25\frac{1}{2}$	27	$28\frac{1}{2}$	30

Table 8.3 (opposite) DE ready reckoner for redundancy payments

Read off employee's age and number of complete years' service. Service before the employee reached the age of 18 does not count. The table will then show how many weeks' pay the employee is entitled to. For the definition of a week's pay, see below, pp. 205–6. The redundancy payment due is to be reduced by one-twelfth for every complete month by which the age exceeds 64 years. Entitlement ceases entirely at 65 or at normal retiring age if below 65 and non-discriminatory.

weekly pay which is counted, currently £205. The maximum statutory RP is therefore £6150. After remaining unchanged between 1965 and 1974, the earnings limit is now increased annually as required by the 1978 Employment Protection (Consolidation) Act.[15] Payments are reduced as the age of 65 is approached, by one twelfth for each complete month over 64.[16]

The statutory scheme lays down minimum RPs. Payments must not be below the level provided by the scheme, but may be added to voluntarily. However, the right to make enhanced RPs may not be universal. A district auditor has successfully challenged the authority of local government to make RPs in excess of the amount provided for by statute[17] (*R.* v. *North Tyneside Metropolitan Borough Council ex parte Allsop*).

Rules for calculating a week's pay are laid down in Schedule 14 of the EP(C)A. A week's pay for those whose pay does not vary with the amount of work done will be the pay received for working normal weekly hours. The concept of normal weekly hours is not defined but where there is entitlement to overtime pay it will be the number of hours beyond which overtime becomes payable. Where there is contractual overtime normal weekly hours will include it. Where pay does vary with the amount of work done, hourly pay is averaged over 12 weeks and the result multiplied by normal weekly hours. If there is shift working so that pay varies from week to week according to shift pattern, the total number of hours over 12 weeks is divided by 12 and the result multiplied by average hourly pay. If there are no normal weekly hours a week's pay will be weekly remuneration averaged over 12 weeks.

The treatment of overtime will depend upon the type of case. Where pay does not vary with the amount of work done, overtime is to be excluded unless it is contractual. Where pay varies with the amount of work done or from week to week because of shift patterns, overtime hours are to be included in the calculation of average hourly pay but stripped of the overtime premium. This can give rise to anomalies where an incentive bonus does not increase with overtime working because the effect of working overtime is to reduce hourly pay (*British Coal Corporation* v. *Cheesborough*). The example in table 8.4 illustrates the point.

Table 8.4 Inclusion of overtime in the calculation of average hourly pay for redundancy payment purposes

	Bonus (£)	Pay at £4 per hr (£)	Total pay (£)	Total hours	Average hourly pay (£)
Normal weekly hours (40)	40	160	200	40	5.00
Normal weekly hours plus 10 hours' overtime	40	200	240	50	4.80

Applications to industrial tribunals

If the payment is not agreed and made, the employee who wishes to claim must make a complaint to an industrial tribunal or an application in writing to the employer. If neither of these is done within six months the application is time-barred, although a tribunal can still award a payment if a claim is made within the following six months if it is 'just and equitable' to do so. Where there is no dispute about entitlement and amount the matter is settled, providing the payment is calculated in accordance with the statutory rules. Any statutory RP must be accompanied by a written statement from the employer indicating how the payment was calculated. An employee may claim a payment, or any unpaid part of it, direct from the National Insurance Fund after taking all reasonable steps (other than legal proceedings) to recover the payment from the employer, or when the employer is insolvent.[18] The Secretary of State then tries to pursue a claim against the employer. An employee refused a direct payment by the Secretary of State can take the Secretary of State to an industrial tribunal.

An RP will be taxable under s. 148 of the Income and Corporation Taxes Act 1988 subject to the exemptions in s. 188, under which the first £30,000 will be tax-free. By contrast, ex gratia payments on retirement or death will be subject to the tax rules governing pension schemes, since they are 'a relevant benefit' under s. 612 of ICTA. Thus, a lump sum retirement benefit will be taxable unless it qualifies for exemption under the rules: these allow tax-free payments of up to 150 per cent of final salary. The early payment of retirement benefits should not affect the tax treatment of RPs.[19] Whatever the size of the RP an employee's right to claim NI Unemployment Benefit is not affected. It should be noted, however, that other payments (such as ex gratia payments, or rewards for past service) may affect such entitlement and might best be replaced by an increased RP. To the extent that wages in lieu of notice are technically damages for breach of contract they should be paid net, although in practice are usually paid gross. Since wages in lieu will vary from individual to individual according to notice requirements, a standard wages in lieu payment (for example, 12 weeks' pay) may be regarded as an RP, thus leaving unfulfilled the duty to pay wages in lieu.

Rebates to employers

Prior to the commencement of section 17 of the Employment Act 1989 in January 1990 there had been a system of rebates paid to employers making statutory redundancy payments. Originally these rebates were paid to all such employers but the proportion of the RP refunded was reduced over the years, and then more recently restricted to small firms. The system of rebates has now been completely abolished.

Early leaving

An employee under notice of redundancy may, during the obligatory notice period, give notice to the employer to leave early. The termination will still be held to be a dismissal for redundancy. Notice from the employee earlier than the obligatory period will mean that the employee has resigned. An employer can require an employee to stay and in the event of a dispute a tribunal will determine how much of the RP, if any, is payable.[20]

Statutory exemption orders

Where an employer and one or more trades unions have a redundancy agreement, they may jointly apply to the Secretary of State for

Employment for exemption from the statutory provisions. However, issues in dispute will still have to be dealt with by industrial tribunals.[21]

Exclusion or reduction of RP on account of pension rights

Entitlement to a statutory RP may be excluded because of pension rights. Section 98 of EP(C)A allows the Secretary of State to make regulations for excluding the right to a statutory RP, or reducing the entitlement, where an employee is entitled to an occupational pension at the time of redundancy. The regulations, issued in 1965, specify that an employer may reduce or exclude an RP, should he or she so choose, where a pension is payable within 90 weeks of the termination of employment.[22] The pension must be equal to at least a third of the employee's annual pay and the employee must have a right to payment on the termination of employment. Annual pay is determined by multiplying weekly pay by 52. Weekly pay is subject to the statutory limit, currently £205. There is a statutory formula for reducing the RP and the employer must give the employee notice in writing that he or she is reducing (or excluding) the RP, and explain how it is to be done.

Redundancy Consultation and Other Procedural Aspects

The Industrial Relations Code of Practice 1972[23]

There is no code of practice governing redundancy, the 1972 Industrial Relations Code of Practice having been revoked in 1991. The main procedural requirement of the code had been that management should, in consultation with employee representatives, seek to avoid redundancies. The code stated that where redundancy proved necessary, various matters should be considered, including the following:

- use of voluntary redundancy, retirement and transfer;
- the phasing of the rundown of employment;
- offers of help to employees in finding work with other employers.

It remains to be seen whether, in the absence of the code, industrial tribunals will find any of these matters to be relevant to the question of reasonableness when determining claims in relation to unfair dismissal for redundancy.

Consultation with trades unions

These are rights given to union officials under the Employment Protection Act 1975.[24] The union must be recognized by the particular employer, and be independent. In fact the right is given to the 'trade union representative', which means 'an official or other person authorized to carry on collective bargaining with the employer in question by that trade union'.[25] If the Act is to apply, the employer must actually be proposing redundancy rather than just considering it. Consultation rights extend to non-unionists of the same description as the members represented by the union. Consultation must begin 'at the earliest opportunity'.[26] More specifically:

- Where the employer proposes to make redundant 100 or more employees at one establishment within 90 days or less the consultation must start at least 90 days before the first dismissal.
- where the number is ten employees or more in one establishment within 30 days or less it must start at least 30 days before the first dismissal.

The employer must also notify the Secretary of State for Employment within the above time periods. Failure to do so could result in a fine.

The consultation process itself comprises the employer disclosing in writing to trades union representatives the whole of the following.

- The reason for their proposals.
- The numbers and descriptions of employees whom they propose to dismiss.
- The total numbers of employees of such description(s) employed at that establishment.
- The proposed method of selection.
- The proposed method of carrying out the dismissals, having regard to any agreed procedure, and the period over which they are to take effect.

Industrial tribunals have also said that employers should disclose information necessary to show how severance pay is calculated.[27] The employer must consider any representations made by the union representatives, and reply to them, stating reasons if any of them are rejected. An employer may argue that there were 'special circumstances' for failing to comply with one or more of the statutory provisions, *viz*:

- The time requirements (effectively an advance warning of redundancy).
- The written information requirements.
- The obligation to consider and reply to any representations.

Receivership does not of itself necessarily constitute the 'special circumstances' which justify the absence of consultation. Tribunals will generally ask:

- What are the 'circumstances'?
- Are they 'special'?
- Did they make full consultation not 'reasonably practicable'?
- Did the employer do as much as was 'reasonably practicable'?

Special means 'exceptional or out of the ordinary' (*Bakers' Union* v. *Clark's of Hove Ltd*).

A recognized, independent trades union may make a complaint to an industrial tribunal no later than three months after the dismissals that one or more of the statutory requirements has not been met. An employer arguing special circumstances will have the burden of proof upon them on this point. The tribunal, if it finds an infringement of the statute, must make a declaration to that effect, and may also make a 'protective award'. This is an award that the employer shall pay the employee remuneration for a protected period. The period is at the discretion of the tribunal, but must not exceed 90 days in the 100 or more employees case, 30 days in the ten or more employees case, and 28 days in any other case. The test is what is 'just and equitable'. An employee whose employer fails to pay them during the protected period may apply to a tribunal within three months of the last day of non-payment. A tribunal may order an employer to pay. In practice therefore those employers who fail to consult and pay a protective award are simply buying out the union's right to consultation.

Notification of proposed redundancies to the Secretary of State for Employment

As already mentioned, an employer must notify the Secretary of State of proposed redundancies involving ten or more dismissals in accordance with certain time periods (see p. 209 above).[28] The unit for consideration is the establishment rather than the organization. Compliance with the notification process does not prevent an employer from altering their plans (for instance, abandoning the implementation of redundancies or postponing them) if circumstances change. Failure to comply leaves the employer liable to a fine. Copies of the notification must be sent by the employer to representatives of independent trades unions which organize any of the categories of workers to be made redundant. The DE encourages use of a standard form for notification to the Minister (figure 8.1).

Time off to look for work or to arrange training

An employee given notice of dismissal by reason of redundancy is entitled to a reasonable amount of paid time off before the expiry of their notice.[29] The time off is within working hours in order to look for new employment or make arrangements for training for future employment. There is a two-year qualifying period for this right, as a result of which the familiar 16 hours qualification (or eight or more if there is five years' continuous employment) applies. An employee refused time off or pay for time off may complain to an industrial tribunal within three months. The maximum compensation payable is two-fifths of a week's pay.

Redundancy and Unfair Dismissal

As already noted, a genuine redundancy properly carried out should not give rise to a claim let alone a finding of unfair dismissal. However, various aspects of the handling of redundancy are covered by the legislation and employers do from time to time fall foul of them. The main area which gives rise to problems is selection for redundancy.

Selection for redundancy

Selection must not be on grounds of race or sex. It must not be because of the employee's proposed or actual union membership or activities; because of union non-membership; in contravention of a customary arrangement; in contravention of an agreed procedure. If the selection fails on any of these points the dismissal is automatically unfair, and the stage 2 test of reasonableness is not applied.[30] An employer has no defence to selection on grounds of sex, race, unionism or non-unionism, once established, but may argue that there are 'special reasons' justifying a departure from a customary arrangement or agreed procedure.[31] In practice, employers will have to substantiate any arguments they put forward for special reasons by, for example, reference to the needs of the business. Employees, on the other hand, will need to provide evidence to establish a customary arrangement.

Figure 8.1

Source: Reproduced with kind permission of the Controller of Her Majesty's Stationery Office

Employment Department — Employment Protection Act 1975, Section 100

Advance notification of redundancies

What is this all about?
As an employer, you are required by law to notify proposed redundancies of ten or more employees

When do I have to do that?
If 10 to 99 employees might be dismissed as redundant from one establishment over a period of 30, days or less – **you must give at least 30 days' notice.**

If 100 or more employees might be dismissed as redundant from one establishment over a period of 90 days or less – **you must give at least 90 days' notice.**

The date of notification is the date it is received by the Department of Employment. For more details, please see leaflet PL833 "Redundancy consultation and notification" You can get one from any Jobcentre or Unemployment Benefit Office.

What information do I have to give?
It is the information requested in the form below. You can send a letter instead but you must give the information asked for in the form. Please send a separate notification for each establishment where it is proposed that ten or more employees will be made redundant.

Where do I send the form or letter?
You may have been given an addressed envelope for the return of the form. If so, please use it. If not, please return the form to the Department of Employment, Redundancy Payments Office, 2 Duchess Place, Hagley Road, Birmingham B16 8NS, or to the nearest Employment Department office.

What if I notify you about redundancies and the circumstances change?
The fact that you have notified us about redundancies does not commit you to them. But if the circumstances change, please let us know.

Anything else?
Yes. One or more group of workers to be made redundant may belong to a recognised independent trade union. If so, you must send a copy of your notification to the representatives of each such trade union.

Data Protection Act 1984
We will put the information you give us on to a computer. We will pass it to, selected government agencies who may offer to let you deal with the proposed redundancy. Information will not be given to any non governmental agencies without your consent.

These notes are for guidance only. They are not a full and authoritative statement of the law.

- *Where there are boxes offering a choice of answer, please tick those that apply.*
- *If there is not enough space for your reply, please continue on a separate sheet of paper and attach it to this form.*
- *Use a separate form for each establishment where redundancies will occur.*

1 Name of employer (CAPITALS please)

2 Address

Postcode

3 Telephone number

4 Who should we contact if we have any enquiries about this form?
Name (CAPITALS please)

5 Please give this person's business address and telephone number if either is not the same as given above:
Address

Postcode

6 Telephone number

7 What is the address of the establishment at which the employees are employed
- as given at 2
- as given at 5

or give details below:

8 What is the nature of the main business at that establishment?

9 Please tick one or more boxes to show the main reason(s) for the redundancies:
- lower demand for products or services **A**
- completion of all or part of contract **B**
- transfer of activities to another workplace following a merger **C**
- transfer of activities to another workplace for other reasons ***D**
- introduction of new plant or machinery **E**
- changes in work methods or organisation ***F**
- introduction of new technology **G**
- something else ***H**

please give details below

Trade union involvement

19 Are any of the groups of employees who may be made redundant represented by a recognised trade union?

Yes ☐

No ☐ ▲ *go to 'Declaration' below*

20 Please give below the name and address of each such trade union:

21 When did consultation with the trade union(s) start?

day	month	year

22 Has full agreement with the trade union(s) been reached?

---

10 How many people do you currently employ at this establishment?

employees

11 How many employees at this establishment do you think **might** be made redundant?

employees

12 If you have the information available, please give figures below to show the numbers employed/to be made redundant

Occupational group	Number employed now	Number to be made redundant
Manual		
I skilled		
I semi-skilled		
I unskilled		
Clerical		
Managerial/technical		

13 How many apprentices and long term trainees may be made redundant?

apprentices/trainees

14 How many employees under 20 years old (including apprentices and trainees), may become redundant?

_____ employees

15 Do you propose to close down the establishment?

Yes ☐   No ☐

16 When will the first proposed redundancy take effect?

day	month	year

17 When will the last proposed redundancy take effect?

day	month	year

18 Briefly, how do you propose to choose which employees should be made redundant?

please enclose a copy of the agreement or give brief details below:

Yes ☐ ▶

No ☐

Declaration

I certify that the information given in this form is, so far as I know, correct and complete.

Signed _____

Date _____

Position held _____

For our use

Agreed procedures will normally apply only in unionized workplaces. Voluntary redundancy was not an agreed procedure for selection in *Rogers* v. *Vosper Thorneycroft* because it merely threw up a pool of people from whom selection had to be made, rather than determining who would be selected.

As a result of the House of Lords decision in *Brown* v. *Stockton on Tees Borough Council* it is clear that selecting a woman for redundancy because she is pregnant constitutes unfair dismissal. Employers must disregard the inconvenience of having to grant maternity leave. Care must be taken to avoid indirect sex discrimination (defined on p. 33 above). Selecting temporary staff for redundancy might amount to unlawful sex discrimination if these employees were predominantly female.

Other than in the above types of case, reasonableness must be judged,[32] and this can include selection criteria (*Bessenden Properties Ltd* v. *Corness*). Some recognition of length of employment is likely to be regarded as reasonable, but so too would be its tempering with business requirements such as the need to keep employees with particular skills, good records or flexible attitudes. Tribunals will want to identify the candidates for redundancy and to know the criteria used for selection between them. They will also want to know how the selection was operated, and by whom. In general, they will look for an objective approach, which includes taking into account length of employment.

Employers may find that performance appraisal schemes provide a useful structure for establishing fair and objective selection criteria and that the use of appraisal data can help to ensure that the act of selection is not itself unfair. Such aspects as skills and qualifications, standards of work, aptitude and attendance and disciplinary record may be considered alongside the traditional factor of length of employment. If such an approach is administered fairly it should protect an employer from a tribunal finding of unfair dismissal for redundancy. Above all, an employer must be able to defend the criteria chosen and the manner of application.

It follows from the above that an employee may be able to mount two separate challenges to the employer's selection decision: one on specific grounds (for example, sex discrimination), the other on the basis of unreasonableness (for example, the criteria adopted).

Where an employee does not have the necessary two years of qualifying employment a case of unfair selection on grounds of race or sex will be possible under the Race Relations Act 1976 or the Sex

Discrimination Act 1975, but not under the law of unfair dismissal. The qualifying period does not apply to dismissals for redundancy where selection is on union or non-union grounds.

Other aspects

The reasonableness factor extends beyond selection to any other relevant issues. A main one in practice is lack of consultation. If redundancy becomes necessary there should be consultation with employees or their representatives (see *Graham* v. *ABF Ltd*). In non-union workplaces, it may be deemed unreasonable if the employee is not consulted and given some advance warning. An employee called into the manager's office at 9.20 am, told for the first time of their redundancy, and departing at 9.30 am the same morning may be being unreasonably treated. Reasonableness will also include an investigation of the possibility of alternative work. The larger the organization the more demanding will be the tribunal's requirements on this point, but ultimately there is no obligation to provide alternative employment (*Merseyside and North Wales Electricity Board* v. *Taylor*). If a redundancy is not reasonable it becomes an unfair dismissal.

In 1982 the EAT laid down some guidelines in *Williams and ors* v. *Comp Air Maxam Ltd*. These comprised the need for advance warning, consultation, objective selection process and examination of possible alternative work. Subsequent decisions make it clear that the absence of one or more of these will not necessarily lead to a finding of unfair dismissal, but they do provide useful guidance.

The effect of a procedural slip-up

For many years industrial tribunals, when faced with an employer who had failed on some point of procedure (for instance a failure to consult the employee) applied what came to be known as the 'any difference' test (*British United Shoe Machinery Co. Ltd* v. *Clarke*). They asked whether, if the employer had adopted the correct procedure, it would have affected the outcome – would it have made any difference? Often the answer arrived at was no and many tribunals concluded on this basis that the dismissal was therefore fair, despite the statutory test being one of reasonableness. The position was changed fundamentally in 1987 by a ruling of the House of Lords in *Polkey* v. *A. E. Dayton (Services) Ltd*. Here it was held that the previous approach was wrong. The correct test was reasonableness, and the any difference test had no part to play in this. However, while the any difference test could not be applied to the question of whether or not the dismissal was fair, it could be applied perfectly properly to the issue of compensation. Therefore, the chances that a redundancy would have occurred even if proper procedure had been followed can be reflected in what has come to be known as a 'Polkey reduction' in the compensation. If a redundancy would merely have been delayed (because of consultation for example) the compensation may be restricted to the period of delay.

Remedies for unfair dismissal by reason of redundancy

The remedies are not different simply because the reason for the unfair dismissal is redundancy. However, the employee will not be entitled to both the basic award of unfair dismissal and a statutory redundancy payment. Reinstatement and re-engagement are not ruled out as remedies but clearly the employer is in a better position to argue that they are not practicable in the first place, or that it was not practicable to comply with a tribunal order if one was made.

Change of Ownership of the Business

Legal context

This is a complex area of law which contains a combination of legislation, some pre-dating Britain's membership of the EC and some deriving from it. The first issue which needs to be established is whether the change of ownership falls within the coverage of the legislation. Both sets of provisions apply to situations where a business is sold or transferred in some other way as a going concern. Changes of ownership which occur through the transfer and accumulation of shares do not fall within the legislation: nor, often, do transfers of organizations which are not businesses.

Provisions of the Employment Protection (Consolidation) Act 1978

Schedule 13 of the 1978 Act deals with how to compute a period of employment. Paragraph 17 is concerned with changes of employer. It states that where a trade, business or undertaking is transferred from one person to another, the period of employment of someone employed at the time of transfer will count as employment with the transferee. The transfer does not break the continuity. However, the transfer must involve the business and not just the physical assets (*Woodhouse and Staton* v. *Peter Brotherhood Ltd*). The EP(C)A does not define trade or undertaking but defines business to include 'a trade or profession . . . and any activity carried on by a body of persons, whether corporate or incorporate'.[33] Reference was made earlier (p. 202) to the provision for offers of alternative work in a redundancy to be made by the new owners as if they were the original owners. This provision relates to the change of ownership of a business 'whether by virtue of a sale or other disposition or by operation of law'.[34] Moreover, change of ownership does not rule out the possibility of one or more owners being both an original and a new owner. As noted below, the term undertaking is defined in the Transfer of Undertakings Regulations.

The Transfer of Undertakings Regulations 1981

Application

These are regulations issued under the European Communities Act 1972 to give effect to the 1977 EC directive on acquired rights. The regulations apply where there is a transfer 'effected by sale or as a result of a sale, by some other disposition, or by operation of law,'[35] but this does not include changes in control which arise simply from changes in share ownership. They apply to undertakings. An undertaking is 'any trade or business . . . in the nature of a commercial venture'. Deciding what is a commercial venture is a matter of first impression for the industrial tribunal (*Woodcock and ors* v. *(1) The Committee for the time being of the Friends School, Wigton (2) Genwise Ltd*). Where there is 'hiving down' of a business by a receiver – that is, the separation of the employees from the business in order to make the latter more attractive to potential buyers – the initial transfer to a subsidiary is not covered by the regulations, so that contracts of employment do not transfer. The transfer of leases, involving a double transfer (back to the lessor and then from lessor to new lessee) can count as a transfer under the Regulations (*Foreningen af Arbejdsledere i Danmark* v. *Daddy's Dance Hall A/S*). So too can the transfer of a lease back to the lessor followed by the sale of the business to a new owner, and the rescission of a lease followed by the owner taking over the running of the business (*P. Bork International A/S (in liquidation)* v.

Foreningen af Arbejdsledere i Danmark; Landsorganisationen i Danmark v. *Ny Molle Kro*). The general principle appears to be that the application of the EC directive (to which the regulations purport to give effect) is not precluded provided that the undertaking retains its identity as an economic unit. The EAT later upheld this principle in relation to franchises in *(1) LMC Drains Ltd (2) Metro Rod Services Ltd* v. *Waugh*.

The regulations are complex and a certain amount of difficulty has been encountered in operating them. For example, in *Banking, Insurance & Finance Union* v. *Barclay's Bank plc* a union complaint that the company failed to consult them about a transfer was dismissed because transfer of the staff and the business separately meant that no transfer had occurred for the purposes of the regulations. Also, the various rights conferred by the regulations depend on the employee being employed at the time of the transfer. Dismissals prior to transfer have sometimes resulted in these rights being lost. This problem has now been settled by the decision of the House of Lords in *Litster* v. *Forth Dry Dock and Engineering Co. Ltd*. Where dismissal arises out of a transfer and there is an economic, technical or organizational reason (ETO) to justify it, any liability is determined according to the principle in *Secretary of State for Employment* v. *Spence and others*. The *Spence* principle makes it clear that responsibility would lie with the transferor if the EDT or relevant date preceded transfer and with the transferee if it came after it. (Relevant date is defined on p. 203 above; EDT on p. 168 above.) There might still be difficulty in establishing the timing of the transfer. The *Spence* principle would also apply to dismissals not arising out of the transfer. By contrast, where the dismissal arises out of a transfer, but there is no ETO, the rule in *Litster* applies. This holds that where an employee has been dismissed prior to the transfer, they are to be treated as if they had not been dismissed. Any liability thus passes to the transferee.

Rights and duties transferred

The regulations reverse the normal common law position that a change in ownership automatically terminates the contract of employment. Instead, the regulations state expressly that the contract of employment will continue, as will rights and duties under it, including continuity of employment. Thus, the mere change of identity of the employer does not give an employee the right to claim a redundancy payment. As already noted, the employee's statutory rights are transferred by virtue of the Employment Protection (Consolidation)

Act 1978. Maternity rights are also transferred. Liability for tortious acts (such as negligence) committed in relation to an employee also appear to transfer (see *Secretary of State for Employment* v. *Spence and ors* on this general question). Criminal liabilities do not transfer, and occupational pension schemes are expressly excluded from automatic transfer. Protective awards do not transfer according to the EAT in *Angus Jowett & Co.* v. *The National Union of Tailors and Garment Workers*, although the failure to pay, being a matter of contract, perhaps might.

Dismissal
A dismissal before or after the transfer will be automatically unfair if the reason is the transfer itself or something connected with it. Automatic means that the second stage test of reasonableness does not apply. There is, however, an exception. The dismissal can be justified as fair if it is for an economic, technical or organizational reason (ETO) entailing changes in the workforce. The Court of Appeal has ruled, in *Berriman* v. *Delabole Slate Ltd*, that changes in the workforce mean a deliberate change in the numbers and functions of employees. Straightforward changes in terms and conditions will, it seems not constitute ETO. In *Wheeler* v. *(1) Patel (2) J. Golding Group of Companies* the EAT held that an ETO must relate to the conduct of the business.

An ETO constitutes SOSR under dismissal law, and requires the normal second stage (the test of reasonableness) to be entered. The onus of proof for ETO lies with the employer (*Litster*). *Gorictree Ltd* v. *Jenkinson* showed that dismissal for an ETO prior to a transfer can simultaneously be dismissal for redundancy giving rise to entitlement to a redundancy payment. This would be true even if the applicant was re-engaged subsequently, including immediately after the transfer, by the transferee. Where the dismissal is post-transfer because the transferee requires fewer employees this can also be due to an ETO (*Meikle* v. *McPhail (Charleston Arms)*). Where redundancy is the reason for dismissal, the statutory provisions relating to unfair selection will apply.

Nothing in the regulations removes the individual's right to resign and claim a fundamental breach of contract, either for unfair dismissal or common law damages purposes. However this right is circumscribed to a degree by the wording of the regulations which says that either 'a substantial change is made in his working conditions to his detriment' or the change in identity of the employer itself is 'significant' and 'to his detriment'.

Trades unions

Collective agreements also transfer automatically, but unless specifically provided otherwise in the agreement these will not be legally enforceable. However the collective agreement terms may be incorporated into individual contracts, which can be enforced (*Marley* v. *Forward Trust Group Ltd*). Occupational pension schemes are again excluded from automatic transfer. Trades-union recognition transfers automatically if the union is independent. Any redundancy agreement will have been transferred automatically so in the event of a redundancy this will be relevant to the question of unfair selection.

The employer has a duty to inform and consult union representatives. These are the representatives of independent trades unions recognized by the employer. Consultation concerns employees who may be affected by a projected transfer. The information to be divulged, in writing, comprises:

- the fact of the transfer, the date and reasons;
- the legal, economic and social implications;
- measures the transferor and the transferee propose to take regarding the employees. If there are no measures this must be stated.

Consultation involves considering union representations and replying to them, giving reasons for the rejection of any of them. As with redundancy consultation the employer may argue 'special circumstances'. Unions may complain to an industrial tribunal within three months. Compensation of up to two weeks' pay may be awarded to each affected employee on the basis of what is 'just and equitable' taking into account the seriousness of the employer's breach of duty.

Rights of Employees on Insolvency[36]

Insolvency rights fall into two categories:

- some debts are given priority (up to a statutory maximum which may be changed from time to time by the Secretary of State);
- some debts (including any unmet priority debts) can be paid out of the NI Fund.

Priority debts

These include the following:

- Statutory guarantee payments.
- Remuneration payable on suspension on medical grounds.
- Payment for time off for union duties or to look for work or arrange training on being made redundant.
- Remuneration payable under a protective award.
- Payment for time off for antenatal care.
- Statutory sick pay.
- Up to four months' wages or salary.
- Accrued holiday pay.
- Contractual sick pay and holiday pay.

Debts which may be claimed from the NI Fund

These are listed below:

- Arrears of pay for up to and including eight weeks. Pay includes wages, salaries, bonuses, commission, overtime pay and the statutory items which make up the priority debts above. The maximum earnings limit, currently £205 per week, applies.
- Holiday pay for up to and including six weeks – again the maximum earnings limit applies. The entitlement must have occurred within the previous 12 months.
- Pay for the statutory notice period or compensation for the employer's failure to give proper statutory notice (again the earnings limit applies).
- Unpaid basic award of unfair dismissal compensation.
- Reasonable reimbursement of apprentices' or articled clerks' fees.
- Statutory Maternity Pay.
- Statutory Redundancy Pay.

(Statutory Redundancy and Maternity pay may also be met from the NI Fund in certain cases where there is no insolvency – see p. 206 above).[37]

Claims

Claims in the first instance should go to the employer's representative on prescribed forms. Debts in addition to those above will be considered by that representative, but will not be paid from public funds. The legislation does however safeguard pension contributions left unpaid by an insolvent employer. The pension scheme administrator applies to the employer's representative in the first instance, but ultimately the NI Fund may pay. As regards any of the debts claimed from the NI Fund, a complaint may be made to a tribunal that the Secretary of State has failed to make a payment, or that the payment is less than the amount it should be. The Employment Protection (Consolidation) Act 1978 provided that the Secretary of State must await a statement from the receiver or liquidator of the amount payable before making such a payment, unless there was likely to be unreasonable delay. Section 18 of the Employment Act 1989 allows the Secretary of State to make payments without a statement if he or she feels that this is not necessary. Moreover, section 19 makes it clear that where payments are made to employees out of the NI Fund the right to a priority claim on the assets of the employer is transferred to the Secretary of State. In the case of unpaid pension contributions an application will be made by an officer of the pension scheme, while in respect of other debts by the ex-employee. The time limit for claims is three months from the Secretary of State's decision. There is no hours qualification for the insolvency rights, nor any qualifying period of employment.

Notes

1 EP(C)A, s. 81.
2 Employment Act 1989.
3 Dock Work Act 1989; Dock Work (Compensation Payments Scheme) Regulations, SI 1989/1111.
4 National Health Service and Community Care Act 1990 *c*.19, s. 66(2) and Schedule 10.
5 EP(C)A, Ss. 83 and 86.
6 EP(C)A, Ss. 82(2) and 92.
7 EP(C)A, s. 84.
8 Grunfeld, C., *Law of Redundancy*, 3rd edition, 1989. London: Sweet and Maxwell.
9 EP(C)A, Schedule 13, para 17.
10 286 IDS Brief 3–5.
11 281 IDS Brief 8.
12 Transfer of Undertakings Regulations, SI 1981/1794.
13 Redundancy Payments (Local Government) (Modification) Order, SI 1983/1160.
14 Written answer no 241/91, OJ, series C, 144/27.
15 EP(C)A, s .148.

16 Employment Act 1989.
17 See *Financial Times*, 9 July 1991. The payments were 3½ times the statutory amount.
18 The Redundancy Fund was merged with the National Insurance Fund by the Employment Act 1990.
19 *Ex Gratia Awards made on Termination of an Office or Employment by Retirement or Death*, Statement of Practice SP13/91, para. 10, London: Inland Revenue, 1991.
20 EP(C)A, s. 85.
21 EP(C)A, s. 96.
22 Redundancy Payments (Pensions) Regulations, SI 1965/1932.
23 Industrial Relations Code of Practice, 1972, issued under s. 1 and Schedule 1 of TULRA 1974. (Originally issued under s. 2 of the Industrial Relations Act, 1971.)
24 EPA, s. 99.
25 EPA, s. 99(2).
26 EPA, s. 99(3).
27 ACAS, *Employment Handbook*, p. 73, London: Advisory, Conciliation and Arbitration Service, 1990.
28 EPA, s. 100.
29 EP(C)A, s. 31.
30 RRA 1976; SDA 1975; EP(C)A, s. 59.
31 EP(C)A, s. 59.
32 EP(C)A, s. 57(3).
33 EP(C)A, s. 153.
34 EP(C)A, s. 94.
35 Transfer of Undertakings Regulations, Regulation 3(2).
36 Insolvency Act 1986. The government has stated that it has no plans for further legislation in respect of employees made redundant by the closure of a business (*Hansard*, HC, 5 June 1991, col. 227).
37 In respect of SMP see: Social Security Act, 1986 and the Statutory Maternity Pay (General) Regulations, SI 1986/1960, as amended.

9
Collective Bargaining and Industrial Action

Trades Union Organization and Collective Bargaining

Freedom of association and non-association

Protection against dismissal on grounds of union membership or activity or non-unionism was dealt with above, see pp. 182–3. The newer right not to be refused access to employment on grounds of union membership or non-membership was described above on p. 42. In addition, employees are given a right not to have action short of dismissal taken against them by their employer:

- because of their actual or proposed membership of an independent trade union;
- because of their actual or proposed union activities; or
- to compel them to join a union (whether independent or not).[1]

Moreover, the non-unionist must not have action short of dismissal taken against them if they refuse to make some other payment (for example to a charity) instead of a union subscription. As far as union activity is concerned, the legal rights apply only if it is at the 'appropriate time':

- outside working hours; or
- within working hours but with the consent or the agreement of the employer.

A complaint may be made to an industrial tribunal within three months. The onus is on the employer to show why the action was taken against the complainant. Any industrial pressure upon the employer is to be ignored. Compensation will be what the tribunal considers 'just and equitable' given the infringement of rights and any loss sustained by the applicant and there does not appear to be a maximum. The applicant must mitigate their loss, and compensation will be reduced if there is contributory fault. The union may be joined in any proceedings involving a non-unionist, and may be required to pay some or all of the compensation. It appears that paying a wage increase to members of one union while not paying it to members of another union can constitute action short of dismissal because of union membership (*National Coal Board* v. *Ridgway and Fairbrother*).

Recognition of trades unions by employers

Recognition means that a trade union is accepted by an employer (or associated employers) for the purposes of collective bargaining – that is, for the purpose of negotiations related to or connected with the matters listed in section 29(1) of TULRA.[2] These are, in essence, matters connected with employment (a-g on pp. 231–2 below). A collective agreement is an agreement between union(s) and employer(s) on one or more of these matters.[3] It should be noted that, in this context, the term 'associated employers' does not refer to membership of an employers' association. Rather, it refers to employers where one is a company controlled by the other, or where both are companies controlled by some third person.[4] Normally, non-unionists will obtain the benefits of collective bargaining along with union members. Indeed, if this were not the case an employer might be taking action short of dismissal against employees on grounds of their non-unionism (as in *Ridgway and Fairbrother*, above).

Some employers are not prepared to go as far as recognizing trades unions for collective bargaining, but will accord them representational rights. That is, they will allow the union to represent individual members who have grievances or are subject to disciplinary action, through the appropriate procedures. There is no legal requirement for an employer to recognize or even give representational rights to a trades union. This true regardless of the extent of union membership among the workforce and the view of the workforce on the question of union recognition. There has been legislation in this area which involved ACAS conducting enquiries among the workforce to establish the extent of union membership and the degree of support for union recognition. It gave rise to a number of difficult cases, among which *Grunwick Processing Laboratories Ltd* v. *ACAS* was the cause celebre. APEX sought recognition from Grunwick Ltd and a strike ensued. ACAS conducted its statutory enquiry but was unable to contact those employees who remained at work. It had no power to obtain the necessary details from the company, and the company would not divulge them voluntarily. The ACAS enquiry was inevitably lop-sided and was successfully challenged by the company in the courts. The company thus prevented ACAS from conducting a proper enquiry and then succeeded in getting ACAS's report set aside because the enquiry on which it was based was not properly conducted. The statutory procedure empowered ACAS to recommend recognition. In the event of an employer failing to comply, the Central Arbitration Committee (CAC) could make a legally-enforceable award to the employees for whom recognition had been recommended. The legislation was repealed in 1980 and has not been replaced. The Labour Party, however, is committed to new legislation, and the TUC has drawn up some proposals. These seem to be based upon the principle that there will be a number of steps towards full recognition, depending on the extent of worker support for it.

The case law confirms that recognition means direct recognition by the employer. It is not sufficient that the employer is a member of an employers' association which recognizes various unions on an industry-wide basis (*NUGSAT* v. *Albury Bros*). Representation of an employee by a full-time union official in respect of a disciplinary matter is not recognition for bargaining purposes (*TGWU* v. *Courtenham Products*) nor is the granting of general representational (as opposed to bargaining) rights (*USDAW* v. *Sketchley Ltd*). There must be an express or implied agreement to recognize, and if implied, there must be clear and unequivocal conduct consistent with recognition (*NUTGW* v. *Charles Ingram Co. Ltd*). Recognition can be partial, that is granted for some purposes but not for others. The issue of whether or not a union has been recognized is a mixed one of law and fact. The onus of proof appears to lie with the trades union to demonstrate the existence of a recognition agreement (*TGWU* v. *Andrew Dyer*).

Where an employer recognizes an independent trades union the officials of that union have various legal rights on behalf of the union. Official means an officer of the union (a member of the governing body or a trustee) or a person who is not an officer but is elected or appointed in accordance with the rules of the union to represent some or all of the members. This includes someone who is an employee of the employer rather than of the union (such as a shop steward or staff representative).[5] Subject to meeting any legal requirements, the rights of the official are as follows.

- Paid time off for union duties, including training for such duties (see below).
- Consultation in respect of redundancies (see chapter 8).
- Consultation in respect of transfers of undertakings (see chapter 8).
- Information for bargaining purposes (see below, pp. 233–5).
- To be appointed as a safety representative and have consequent legal rights[6] (see chapter 4).
- Information about pensions (see chapter 6).

The law does not require an employer to make available physical facilities such as office accommodation, telephone and filing cabinets but an ACAS Code of Practice does recommend that facilities be provided in the interests of good industrial relations (see p. 233 below). The position in relation to safety representatives is different – they must be provided with the facilities necessary to enable them to carry out their statutory functions (see chapter 4). When requested, an employer must allow use of their premises for union ballots as far as is reasonably practicable.[7]

The status of collective agreements

Other than those made during the brief life of the Industrial Relations Act 1971, a collective agreement is presumed in law to be intended by the parties as not being a legally enforceable contract unless the agreement is in writing and contains an express statement to the contrary.[8] Thus, unless the parties state in writing that they wish their collective agreement to be legally enforceable it will be binding in honour only (*Ford* v. *AUEF and ors*).[9] During the life of the Industrial Relations Act 1971, employers and unions conspired to keep the law out of their relations – the British tradition of 'voluntarism' – by inserting TINALEA clauses into agreements. TINALEA signified that 'this is not a legally enforceable agreement'.

Nevertheless, as was noted in chapter 3, there is a process by which collectively-bargained terms can become incorporated into individual contracts of employment. In the last resort, therefore, an action for breach of a collective agreement can sometimes be pursued indirectly through a breach of the contract of employment between the organization and the individual employee (for example *Ferodo* v. *Rigby*, see above p. 80). In such circumstances the parties might agree that one particular case be regarded as a test to determine the general position.

Regardless of whether or not a collective agreement is legally enforceable, no terms which restrict an individual's right to take industrial action will form part of the employee's contract of employment unless the collective agreement:

- is in writing;
- provides for express incorporation of the relevant term(s);
- is reasonably accessible to the employee and may be consulted during working hours;

Moreover:

- the union (or each union) that is party to the agreement must be independent;
- the individual employee's contract must expressly or impliedly provide for incorporation.[10]

It can be seen that while the recognition of trades unions is not required by law, and agreements with unions are not themselves legally enforceable, the act of recognition does have legal implications. This is primarily because union officials are given legal rights upon recognition and because the contract of employment can sometimes be used as a device for indirectly enforcing the terms of collective agreements.

Finally it should be pointed out that the legal status of collective agreements is not influenced by the level at which they are negotiated (industry-wide, company-wide or plant) or by their degree of sophistication or formality, except to the extent that legally-enforceable ageements must be in writing. The law is less than clear about conflicts between the terms agreed at different levels and offers no consistent approach. In *Clift* v. *West Riding County Council* the terms of a local agreement prevailed over those of a national one because the local agreement was made later. However, a national agreement made prior to a local one, and containing a provision that in cases of conflict the national agreement should prevail, was held by the court of Appeal to take precedence in *Gascol Conversions Ltd* v. *Mercer*.

The closed shop

The term closed shop does not appear in the legislation. What does appear is the concept 'union membership agreement' (UMA). This is defined as an agreement or arrangement made between employer(s) and independent union(s) relating to 'employees of an identifiable class' which has the effect in practice of requiring them to be or become members of the union(s) or some other specified independent trade union.[11]

There is no legislation requiring an employer to accede to requests for a closed shop, nor will it be unlawful if an employer does so accede. The existence of a closed shop agreement is not in itself unlawful. However, because of the rights of non-association already referred to, any action to force a person to join a union, either on entry to the firm or subsequently, or denial of access to employment because of non-membership or refusal to agree to join, is likely to be unlawful. If a person is dismissed for their non-unionism the dismissal is automatically unfair – it is not subject to the second stage test of reasonableness (see chapter 7) as would be the case in an ordinary dismissal. Higher compensation levels are also applied. Thus, while the closed-shop is not itself unlawful, anyone who will not accept it and has action taken against them as a result is likely to have a justifiable claim in law.

Facilities for Trades Union Officials and Members

Time off for union duties and activities

These rights arise not simply out of being an employee, but out of being an employee *and* a union member or official. The rights give a 'reasonable' amount of time off during working hours, and are of two types:

1 Paid time off for union officials for:

- duties concerned with negotiations with the employer over matters for which the union is recognized;
- duties concerned with any other functions on behalf of employees of the employer which the employer has agreed the union may perform;
- training for the duties mentioned above.

The duties must relate to or be connected with any of the following matters:

(a) terms and conditions of employment, or the physical conditions in which any workers are required to work;
(b) engagement or non-engagement, or termination or suspension of employment or the duties of employment, of one or more workers;
(c) allocation of work or the duties of employment as between workers or groups of workers;

(d) matters of discipline;

(e) the membership or non-membership of a trades union on the part of a worker;

(f) facilities for officials of trades unions; and

(g) machinery for negotiation or consultation, and other procedures, relating to any of the foregoing matters, including the recognition by employers or employers' associations of the right of a trades union to represent workers in any such negotiation or consultation or in the carrying out of such procedures'.[12]

2 Time off, with no obligation to pay, for union members for union activity regardless of whether or not it is related to the employer.

The provisions relating to paid time off for union officials (but not unpaid time off for members) were altered by the EA 1989.[13] The effect of this is to limit rights to paid time off so that they no longer cover duties:

● which neither concern negotiations with the employer nor have been agreed by the employer;

● which do not relate to or are not connected with any of the matters listed in (a) to (g) above;

● which relate to any associated employer(s) but not to the employer themselves;

● which concern negotiations with the employer over matters for which the union is not recognized, where the employer has not agreed to the duties being performed.

The term working hours is defined to mean contractual hours, so excluding any non-contractual overtime. To attract paid time off training must be relevant to the official's duties, and approved either by the TUC or the official's own union. The rights of both officials and members in relation to time off are subject to the union being independent, and recognized by the employer. The right to unpaid time off will be relevant to union officials who hold positions in geographically-based branches, or hold higher positions in unions where their duties may not (in the main) relate to their own employer. An ACAS Code of Practice, revised in 1991 following the changes made by the Employment Act 1989, provides detailed guidance.[14] A complaint may be made to an industrial tribunal within three months alleging refusal to give time off or refusal to pay for time off.

Many of the decisions made under the legislation prior to its amendment by the Employment Act 1989 are no longer of relevance. However, the principle adopted in *British Bakeries (Northern) Ltd* v. *Adlington and ors* may well be applied to the new provisions. The Court of Appeal decided that attendance at a course on the implications of the repeal of the Baking Industry (Hours of Work) Act 1954 was close enough to the duties defined in section 27 of the EP(C)A to warrant paid time off. The test – that of proximity – is a matter of fact for tribunals to decide.

For a union official to be carrying out a duty within the meaning of the legislation by attending a meeting, their attendance must be expressly or impliedly required by their union (*Ashley* v. *Ministry of Defence*). Whether it is reasonable to grant paid time off is a question of fact for an industrial tribunal to decide (*Thomas Scott and Sons (Bakers) Ltd* v. *Allen and ors*). The facilities already existing under a collective agreement may be taken into account, and were adequate in *Depledge* v. *Pye Telecommunications Ltd.*

Whether union activity falls under section 28 is a matter of fact and degree for an industrial tribunal, but it must in broad terms be connected with the employment relationship (*Luce* v. *London Borough of Bexley*).

Finally, as already noted, there is no legal requirement for an employer to provide physical facilities (except for ballot purposes and to safety representatives). However, the code of practice on time off for trade union duties and activities states that:

> 'Employers should consider making available to officials the facilities necessary for them to perform their duties efficiently and communicate effectively with their members, fellow lay officials and full-time officers. Where resources permit the facilities could include: accommodation for meetings, access to a telephone and other office equipment, the use of notice boards and, where the volume of the official's work justifies it, the use of dedicated office space.'[15]

Disclosure of information for bargaining purposes[16]

This is another right given to the 'trade union representative', defined in the same way as in the redundancy consultation rights (see chapter 8). Again the union must be independent and recognized. Union representatives have a right to information about the company which is both:

- information without which they would 'be to a material extent impeded' in their bargaining; and is
- information which it is good industrial relations practice to disclose.

An ACAS code of practice[17] sets out good practice as including disclosure of information on:

- pay and benefits, for example, principles and structure of payment systems; various distributions of earnings and hours;
- conditions of service, for example, recruitment policy; promotion policy;
- manpower, for example, manpower distributions; manpower plans;
- performance, for example, productivity data; return on capital;
- financial, for example, cost structures, allocation of profits.

The disclosure rights apply only to matters over which the employer already recognizes that union.

There are a number of restrictions upon the employer's general duty of disclosure. These mean that disclosure does not have to be made if:

- it is against the interests of national security;
- it would contravene a prohibition imposed by or under a statute;
- the information was communicated to the employer in confidence;
- the information relates to an individual (unless he or she consents to its disclosure);
- the information would cause 'substantial injury' to the employer (apart from through collective bargaining);
- the information was obtained for the purpose of any legal proceedings.

The employer does not have to show original documents or their copies, nor be involved in an amount of work or expenditure 'out of reasonable proportion to the value of the information' in bargaining terms.[18]

If a union considers that an employer has failed to disclose the required information it may make a complaint to the Central Arbitration Committee (CAC). The Committee may ask ACAS to conciliate, but if that fails it will hear the complaint. If the complaint is upheld, the Committee will specify the information to be disclosed, and a period of time in which disclosure must take effect. A failure to disclose then gives the union a right to apply again to the Committee, this time for an award of improved terms and conditions. If the committee makes such an award it has effect as part of the individual employees' contracts of employment, and is enforceable. The logic is that such an award:

- is in lieu of information which might have led the union to secure a better deal than it did secure;
- will deter employers from refusal to disclose information, since it removes the determination of labour costs from within an employer's control;

• recognizes that employers cannot be directly forced to actually release information.

Unions have, perhaps surprisingly, not made great use of the disclosure provisions. Consequently, there is little case law. In an early case, however, the CAC decided that 'to a material extent impeded' meant that the information must be important and relevant (*Institute of Journalists* v. *Daily Telegraph*). More recently, the CAC decided that a company should disclose details of the distribution of percentage pay awards across certain categories of staff under a performance-related merit pay system. There was a genuine need for the unions to ensure that the system did not operate unfairly against particular categories (such as women and older workers) (*MSF and APEX Partnership* v. *General Accident Fire and Life Assurance Corporation plc*). Claims can be made about the timing of disclosure. Thus in *MATSA and MSF* v. *Smith's Meters Ltd* the CAC ordered the disclosure of gross and net profits as a percentage of sales prior to negotiations instead of subsequently. By contrast, the CAC made no such order about budgetary information in *NAPO* v. *Merseyside Probation Committee* because there was no evidence that the union was to a material extent impeded by having it after the negotiations rather than prior to them.

Industrial Action

Immunity of trades unions

There is no statutory or common law right to strike as such. A striker, unless due notice of termination of contract is given, will break his contract of employment (*Simmons* v. *Hoover*). The result is that an injured party has a right to seek a remedy – damages or an injunction. A strike will also often break a commercial contract between the employer and some other firm – a customer or supplier – again leaving an injured party with a right to sue. Anyone (such as a union official) inducing breaches of contract is likely to commit a tort – a civil wrong. Under such circumstances almost any industrial action would leave unions legally liable. For example, in *Falconer* v. *NUR and ASLEF* the county court held that the two railworkers' unions were liable for damages to Mr Falconer, a passenger, for expenditure and inconvenience caused to him as a result of a one-day strike called by the unions, on the grounds that they had unlawfully induced interference with British Rail's obligations to its passengers.[19]

To enable trades unions to function, Parliament has allowed them a degree of immunity from normal legal actions.[20] This immunity is granted, however, only in respect of certain types of legal action, *viz*, claims in tort for:

- inducing breaches of contract or interfering with the performance of contracts;
- threatening such breaches or interference;
- threatening to induce such breaches or interference;
- conspiracy, where the act if it was done by one person would be lawful.

Moreover, the union must meet certain legal requirements. First, the action must be 'in contemplation or furtherance of a trade dispute'.[21] A trade dispute is a dispute between workers and their employer which relates wholly or mainly to one or more of the matters listed (a)–(g) on pp. 231–2 above (the same matters as have to be considered in relation to paid time off for union officials).[22] It follows from this that there must be a dispute (see *NUS* v. *Sealink* below); the dispute must be a trade dispute; and the trade dispute must be with the employer of the employees who are in dispute. In relation to the last point, a dispute between a union and an employers' association will not necessarily be a trade dispute unless there is a trade dispute with the individual company by which the employees are employed (see also *Kenny*, below).

Second, any act done by a trade union to induce a person to take part in industrial action must be supported by a ballot conducted in accordance with the legal requirements. A majority of those voting must be in favour of the action if immunity is to be obtained.[23] The detailed requirements are set out below (pp. 240–3).

Third, the ballot result is live for four weeks (see p. 243 below). Action starting later than four weeks after the ballot will not be immune unless there is a second, 'successful' ballot. Next, regardless of the outcome of any ballot, secondary action is not immune except where workers involved in a trade dispute (that is, with their own employer) picket lawfully and in the process succeed in taking action which harms some other employer. An example would be pickets persuading the driver of a firm of suppliers to turn around and go away without delivering. Secondary action is where a person induces someone else to break a contract of employment (or threatens a breach of such a contract) with an employer who is not a party to the dispute.

Secondary action will be lawful only if the picketing satisfies the legal requirements, which include the need for it to be peaceful and at or near the picket's place of work (see p. 239 below).[24] Finally, there is no immunity for action which is in support of dismissed unofficial strikers[25] or which is in support of union membership (that is, to force membership upon an employee, or to force an employer to discriminate against a non-unionist).[26]

All of what has been described above refers to the immunity of trades unions as bodies. However, where industrial action is not endorsed by a union, or is repudiated by it, members will still be protected provided that they are acting 'in contemplation or furtherance of a trade dispute'.[27] This protection applies only against certain actions in tort: members would not be protected from dismissal or from actions seeking remedies for breach of contract (see below pp. 243–6).

Unions' liability for the acts of their officials

The EA 1990 extends the liability of trades unions to include the acts of all their officials, and makes new provisions for repudiation of those acts. An act is taken to be authorized or endorsed by a trades union if it is done, authorized or endorsed by:

1 anyone empowered by rule to do, authorize or endorse such acts;
2 the principal executive committee, president or secretary;
3 any other committee or official of the union. This includes officials *not* employed by the union, such as shop stewards. Committee includes any group of persons constituted in accordance with the rules of the union.

An act will be taken as having been done, authorized or endorsed by an official if it is done, authorized or endorsed by a strike committee to which the official belongs, or by any member of that committee. Authorization etc in accordance with 2 or 3 above overrules anything in the union's rules or in any contracts or rule of law.

An act will not be taken as having being authorized or endorsed by virtue of item 3 only, however, if it is repudiated by persons mentioned in 2 'as soon as reasonably practicable'. Repudiation involves written notice to the committee or official without delay, individual notices to members and notice to the employer(s). The notice to the members must contain the statutory wording:

> 'Your union has repudiated any call for industrial action to which this notice relates and will give no support to such action. If you are

dismissed while taking unofficial industrial action, you will have no right to complain of unfair dismissal.'[28]

There is no repudiation if the union fails to comply with the above or fails to comply with the following. If a request is made within six months of repudiation by someone injured through interference with a commercial contract, and no written notice has already been given to that person, the union must provide confirmation of repudiation forthwith.

Where unions are liable for action which is not immune their funds will be at risk from claims for damages except where those funds are protected by statute. Protected property includes political and provident funds.[29] The maximum damages for each legal action (as opposed to each case of industrial action) vary according to the number of members of the union. Where a union has 100,000 or more members the figure is £250,000. This excludes interest (*Boxfoldia Ltd* v. *NGA (1982)*).

An employer may be more likely to seek an injunction than to press a claim for damages. Where an act is done in contemplation or furtherance of a trade dispute, all reasonable steps must be taken by the court to give the union an opportunity to be heard. In deciding whether or not to grant an injunction the court must assess the likelihood of the union's actions being immune.

Picketing[30]

The right to picket arises only in contemplation or furtherance of a trade dispute. Thus, when Kenny Services took over a British Rail contract with its own – KS – employees after British Rail had terminated a previous contract with another firm, the picketing by ex-employees of the former contractor at the British Rail site was unlawful because there was no trade dispute between these workers and their ex-employer. Rather, the picketing was directed at British Rail or possibly Kenny Services (*Kenny Services* v. *TGWU*). Picketing rights are limited to at or near a person's own place of work. A union official may picket at any workplace where members who they represent work, providing they are accompanied by at least one of them. Where a person works or normally works at more than one place, or where the place of work makes picketing impracticable, they may picket at any of the employer's premises at which they work or from which their work is administered. In *(1) Rayware Ltd (2) Islington Pottery* v. *TGWU*, the Court of Appeal ruled that since 0.7

miles away was the nearest public place for picketing, this was near the workplace. It observed that Parliament could not have intended to remove all picketing rights for any group of workers. Workplace means the principal place of work rather than places which may be visited during the course of work (*Union Traffic Ltd* v. *TGWU*). An employee dismissed from their last employment in connection with a trade dispute, or whose dismissal gave rise to a trade dispute, retains their picketing rights.

Picketing is defined as peacefully obtaining or communicating information, or peacefully persuading any person to work or abstain from working. There are no rights to stop people or vehicles. Thus in *Broome* v. *DPP* the attempt to stop a vehicle was a breach of the Highways Act 1959. Peaceful picketing, as defined, carried out at or near a person's own workplace, is immune. Other picketing would not be. Moreover, there is no protection against actions in respect of interference with business by unlawful means or other torts not covered by section 13 of TULRA (see above, p. 236). These would include private nuisance and trespass, for example being on or inside an employer's premises without permission.

Nor is there any immunity for criminal acts such as obstructing a police officer in the course of their duty, obstructing the highway or creating a public nuisance (*Tynan* v. *Balmer*; *News Group Newspapers Ltd* v. *SOGAT* (*1982*) (*No. 2*)). Criminal acts may result from breach of the common law or statute. Thus, in *Thomas* v. *NUM* (*South Wales Area*) mass picketing was held to be a public nuisance at common law and an offence under the Conspiracy and Protection of Property Act 1875.[31] Among other things, the 1875 Act makes it a a criminal offence to use violence or intimidation or watch or beset any place where the person is. Preventing other workers from entry to their workrooms through the medium of a sit-in has been held to be 'besetting' under the 1875 Act (*Galt* v. *Philp*) and following non-strikers in cars was 'persistent following' (*Elsey* v. *Smith*). Various offences specified in the Public Order Act 1986 may be committed in the course of industrial action, and the Act also lays down rules for marches, processions and so on.

The statutory provisions on picketing are accompanied by a Department of Employment code of practice, which is currently being revised.[32] The code is probably best known for its pronouncements on the number of pickets. In general, the number should 'not exceed six at any entrance to a workplace; frequently a smaller number will be appropriate.'[33] It should be noted that this is a provision of the code –

there is no limit laid down in the statutes themselves. The police, however, have a great deal of discretion in the matter, and can limit numbers if they think a breach of public order is likely. Thus, in *Piddington* v. *Bates*, the Divisional Court upheld a police constable's decision to limit the number of pickets to two. Mass picketing, the code suggests, may constitute a criminal offence in itself, through obstruction or possibly even intimidation.

The code suggests that a union should appoint a picket organizer who would have a letter of authority from the union.[34] The organizer would consult with the police over issues such as numbers and locations. They would distribute badges and armbands to authorized pickets, and make sure arrangements to provide for essential supplies or maintenance were effective. They would ensure that outsiders were not allowed to join the picket. On this point it should be noted that it is not for the police to enforce the civil law. Such matters as identifying unlawful picketing are the responsibility of the employer or any other injured party.

Industrial action ballots

As already noted, a ballot is needed if there is to be immunity.[35] Detailed requirements are laid down in the statutes.[36] These are supplemented by a code of practice which was revised in 1991.[37] An employer may obtain an injunction preventing a ballot from taking place if any ensuing action would be unlawful. This was the case in *NUS* v. *Sealink* where company assurances about the immediate future of NUS members' jobs in the ports meant that there was no trade dispute.

The balloting constituency

There are two issues here. First, if the members have different places of work, will separate ballots be required or can there be a single ballot? If those to be asked to vote comprise all the union's members or all of its members employed by one or more employers, aggregation is permitted. The same will be true if the members share a common, distinguishing factor relating to terms and conditions of employment or occupation. Otherwise, separate ballots will be required. The general rule is that there must be a separate ballot unless there is a common factor shared by everyone entitled to vote and no fellow union member sharing that factor and employed by the same employer as the members who do have a vote is excluded. This prevents a union conducting a ballot at some plants of a company but not at others.[38]

Second, within a workforce, who is entitled to vote? Any member who it is reasonable for the union to believe will be asked to take part in the action must have an opportunity to vote. No other person should have the opportunity. The union may choose whether to include or exclude overseas members. If included, they must be distinguished in the result. As a consequence of amendments made by the Employment Act 1989, members on contracts for services (such as freelance workers) will need to be balloted, as will Northern Ireland members if working in Great Britain, or if the industrial action will involve members in both Great Britain and Northern Ireland. Asking other members (for example, staff employees in a dispute involving manual grades) not to cross picket lines could amount to asking them to take part in the action and might require that they be entitled to vote. Otherwise, they might have to be allowed to cross picket lines. Depriving members of the right to vote makes a ballot invalid irrespective of whether the numbers deprived are greater or fewer than the difference in the ballot result (*British Rail* v. *NUR*). In the same case the Court of Appeal made clear that in a large balloting operation some margin of error was allowable as long as the union had done all that was reasonably practicable.

The balloting method

The code of practice gives preference to a fully postal ballot, but the statutory provisions also allow for a workplace ballot or a ballot which is part postal and part workplace. The 1991 Green Paper proposes (p. 14) that ballots should be required to be fully postal if more than 50 members are entitled to vote. If a union is to claim public funding for the ballot it will have to be at least partly postal.

Independent scrutiny

The statutory provisions do not require unions to use an independent scrutineer (unlike political fund ballots and executive elections) but the code advises it and the 1991 Green Paper proposes (p. 14) that it be made a requirement. More recently, the government has proposed that voting papers should be distributed and stored by an independent body.

Voting papers

Voting must be by means of marking a voting paper.[39] The following statement must appear on every voting paper and must not be qualified or commented upon by anything else on the paper:

'if you take part in a strike or other industrial action, you may be in breach of your contract of employment'.[40]

The voting paper must also contain the name of the person who will be responsible for authorizing industrial action if the ballot result records a majority in favour.[41] It must contain at least one of two questions which ask if the person is prepared to take part in or continue to take part in:

- question 1 – a strike;
- question 2 – action short of a strike;

such as to allow the answer yes or no. In *Post Office* v. *Union of Communication Workers* it was ruled that a union wishing to pursue both a strike and action short of a strike, or at least to keep its options open, must obtain a yes majority in answer to each question. A yes to strike action cannot be taken as implying a yes to action short of a strike. A union will also have to make sure, if it is asking its members to cast one vote on several issues at the same time, that there is a trade dispute about each of the issues if subsequent industrial action is to be lawful (*London Underground* v. *NUR*).

The voting process

So far as is reasonably practicable voting must be in secret. Those voting must be allowed to do so without interference from or any constraints imposed by the union, its members, officials or employees. A person should be able to vote without incurring any direct cost to themselves.

The result

The votes must be fairly and accurately counted. Inaccuracies can be disregarded if accidental and too small to affect the result of the ballot. As soon as reasonably practicable after the holding of the ballot, the union should take reasonable steps to provide the following information to those entitled to vote:

- The number of votes cast.
- The numbers answering yes to the question, or to each question.
- The numbers answering no to the question, or to each question.
- The number of spoiled voting papers.

The ballot result details should be provided to employers whose employees were entitled to vote if those employers so request.[42] This is not a statutory requirement but is advised by the code.[43] A union must not call industrial action, nor authorize or endorse it before the last day of voting in the ballot, and for immunity to be preserved any action called must be called by the person specified on the voting paper. If the ballot result is in favour of action, immunity will be preserved providing the action commences before the expiry of a period of four weeks from the date of the ballot. However, if action during this period is prohibited by legal proceedings, the union may apply to have the period of immunity extended by the length of the prohibition. This will be possible only when the court's prohibition order lapses or is discharged, and is at the court's discretion. An extension will not be granted if the court thinks that the ballot result no longer represents the union members' views, or if there is an event likely to occur which would result in a vote against action if another ballot were to be held. In any event, the right to call industrial action on the basis of the ballot will lapse after a period of 12 weeks commencing with the date of the ballot.

In *Post Office* the employer complained that the discontinuity of industrial action meant that a new ballot was required to obtain immunity. The Court of Appeal thought that one ballot could support continuous industrial action over a long period, but might not support sporadic or irregular action. Moreover, considerable turnover of the workforce (so that a large proportion of current employees were not employees at the time of the ballot) may mean industrial action should be limited to those who were employed at that time and had a chance to vote in the ballot. These last two issues did not have to be decided to dispose of the case in *Post Office*, so were not ruled upon. The drift of opinion, however, is fairly clear.

The position of the individual employee

It should be noted that the whole question of immunity applies only to the committing of torts; it does not apply to breaches of contract. Thus, a person who breaks a contract will not be immune from common law claims nor protected against being dismissed for the breach. The likelihood is that a strike or other industrial action will constitute a breach of the individual's contract of employment. This will certainly be the case if there is a restrictive or no-strike clause in the agreement and it is incorporated into the individual's contract of employment (but see p. 230 above). In general, it is not possible to attempt to disrupt the employer's business in order to apply bargaining pressure *and*, at the same time, give loyal service. Anything concerted and aimed at bringing pressure is likely to be regarded as industrial action (see below). It should be noted that industrial action is not defined only in relation to a trade dispute – it may give rise to a trade dispute or some other form of stoppage (for instance, a protest about government policy). In the circumstances on an employee's breach of contract an employer may sue for damages (which would usually be limited to the employee's notice period) or other remedies.

The dismissal of strikers is explicitly put outside the jurisdiction of industrial tribunals unless certain features apply. These features relate to selectivity of treatment of those taking the action. The unit within which comparisons are to be made is the establishment of the employer at or from which the complainant works. If everyone is treated the same, no complaint of unfair dismissal can be heard by a tribunal. If, however, some are dismissed and others are not, there is a possible unfair dismissal claim. The selectivity must apply, however, at the time of the complainant's dismissal, rather than from the beginning of the strike. Thus, if 100 people go on strike, and all are still on strike a month later, the dismissal of the six strike leaders will give rise to unfair dismissal claims. The dismissal of all 100 will not. Moreover, if 40 people had returned to work after a month, the dismissal of the remaining 60 would not give rise to claims, since there was no selectivity among those on strike at the time of the dismissal. Where strikers are dismissed, but only some are re-engaged, the critical factor will be the time interval between the dismissal of those re-engaged and their re-engagement. If this period is three months or more, none of the people who have not been re-engaged will have a claim.

Where a claim is made alleging that dismissal has been selective, it must be made within three months of the complainant's EDT. Where the claim is that there has been a selective re-engagement, it must be made within six months of the complainant's 'date of dismissal'. Date of dismissal, where notice was given, means the date on which notice was given. In any other case it means the EDT.[44]

Whether there exists a strike or other industrial action is a matter of fact for a tribunal to decide (*Express and Star Ltd* v. *Bunday*; *Faust and ors* v. *Power Packing Casemakers*). The key ingredients seem to be cessation of work (or some other sanction such as a work-to-rule or overtime ban), workers acting in combination or in concert, and an intention to exert pressure or make a protest in order to secure or prevent change (for example, to terms and conditions of employment).

The intention behind the acts done as well as their nature and effect should be taken into account (*Faust* – in which it was ruled that a refusal to work non-contractual overtime could be industrial action if it was used as a bargaining weapon).

What is meant by an employee 'taking part' in industrial action? First, a distinction may need to be drawn between engaging in trades union activity, dismissal for which would be automatically unfair, and taking part in industrial action, where there is likely to be no right to make a claim. The dismissal must be one or the other, and this is a matter of fact for the tribunal to decide (*Drew* v. *St Edmundsbury Borough Council*). Second, what does taking part mean? (*Coates and anor* v. *Modern Methods and Materials Ltd*; *Naylor and ors* v. *Orton and Smith Ltd and anor*). Again this is a matter of fact for tribunals. They should judge the issue by what the employee is doing or omitting to do, rather than by what the employer knew, or should have known, at the time (*Manifold Industries Ltd* v. *Sims and ors*). Where action comprises a series of strikes, one day per week, taking part can be applied only to the actual days on strike. If dismissal is to be outside the jurisdiction of tribunals it will need to take place on a strike day (*Looker's of Bradford Ltd* v. *Mavin and ors*). The same principle applied where there was an overtime ban in *Glenrose (Fish Merchants) Ltd* v. *Chapman and ors*.

Jurisdiction is the first issue for a tribunal to decide. The fact that a relevant employee had not been dismissed must be established at the end of the appropriate tribunal hearing. In *P&O European Ferries* v. *Byrne* that employee was anonymous, but the name had to be disclosed in order to allow the employer to present his case. If jurisdiction is established the normal two-stage unfair dismissal process is undergone. The fair reason for dismissal (or for non re-engagement) will have to be something other than going on strike in order to distinguish the case from those of strikers who were not dismissed (or were re-engaged). Picket line violence, damage to the employer's premises and unofficial continuation of a strike after a settlement are some of the reasons which have been put forward. A breach of contract by an employee will not automatically make any resultant dismissal fair. At the second stage, reasonableness will include proper procedure notwithstanding the tensions of an industrial dispute (*McLaren* v. *National Coal Board*; see pp. 181–2 above).

As a result of the Employment Act 1990 an employee has no right to claim that they were unfairly dismissed if at the time of dismissal they were taking part in unofficial industrial action.[45] Thus the law relating to the dismissal of strikers has two separate sets of provisions. First, where the strike is official, or all the strikers are non-unionists, the tribunal will have a limited jurisdiction based upon selectivity, as already described. Where there are union members and the strike is unofficial, tribunals will have no jurisdiction at all. The status of a strike (whether it is official or unofficial) will have to be judged at the time of the dismissal. This is a matter of fact for tribunals to decide and will depend upon an application of the new statutory test of union responsibility for the actions of officials (see above, pp. 237–8).

In a redundancy, the employee will lose the right to a redundancy payment if the dismissal for industrial action occurs prior to the obligatory notice period (see above, p. 201).

Where industrial action comprises partial performance of duties by employees, the employer may:

- reject partial performance and insist that no pay will be due unless there is full performance (*Miles* v. *Wakefield MDC*); or
- accept partial performance, in which case there can be an appropriate reduction in wages in respect of the duties not performed. Alternatively, but with the same effect, full wages may be paid but an amount set-off against them to cover the partial non-performance of duties (*Sim* v. *Rotherham MBC; Wiluszynski* v. *London Borough of Tower Hamlets*).

Notes

1 EP(C)A, s. 23.
2 EP(C)A, s. 32 and EPA, s. 126.
3 TULRA, s. 30(1).
4 TULRA, s. 30(5).
5 TULRA, s. 30.
6 Safety Representatives and Safety Committees Regulations, SI 1977/500, Regulation 3(1). These are regulations made under s. 15 and in accordance with s. 2(4) of the Health and Safety at Work etc. Act 1974.
7 EA 1980, s. 2
8 TULRA, s. 18.
9 The 1991 Green Paper, *Industrial Relations in the 1990s* proposes (p. 36) a presumption of legal enforceability but in January 1992 the government indicated that it would not proceed with the proposal.
10 TULRA, s. 18.
11 TULRA, s. 30.
12 TULRA, s. 29(1).
13 EA 1989 s. 14. This amended s. 27(1) of EP(C)A 1978.

14 *Time off for Trade Union Duties and Activities*, ACAS Code of Practice 3, revised edition (1991). This became operational on 13 May 1991. London: HMSO, 1991.

15 Time off Code, para 28 (pp. 12–13).

16 EPA, s. 17.

17 *Disclosure of Information to Trades Unions for Collective Bargaining Purposes*, ACAS Code of Practice 2, London: HMSO, 1977.

18 EPA, s. 18(2).

19 The 1991 Green Paper, *Industrial Relations in the 1990s*, proposes (p. 16) that customers of public services within the scope of the Citizen's Charter should have a statutory right to bring proceedings to prevent or restrain unlawful industrial action.

20 TULRA, s. 13.

21 TULRA, s. 13(1).

22 TULRA, s. 29(1).

23 TUA 1984, Ss. 10–11, EA 1988 and EA 90.

24 EA 1990, s. 4.

25 EA 1990, s. 9.

26 EA 1988, s. 10.

27 TULRA, s. 13(1).

28 EA 1990 (s. 6, which amends EA 1982, s. 15).

29 EA 1982, s. 17.

30 TULRA, s. 15 as amended by EA 1980, s. 16 and EA 1982, s. 21 and Schedule 3, para 12.

31 s. 7.

32 *Code of Practice on Picketing*, London: DE, 1980.

33 Picketing Code, para 31 (p. 11).

34 Picketing Code, para 34 (p. 12).

35 The 1991 Green Paper proposes (p. 14) that an employer should be given notice of an intention to ballot.

36 TUA 1984, EA 1988 and EA 1990.

37 *Code of Practice: Trade Union Ballots on Industrial Action*. This was issued under s. 3 of EA 1980, as amended by the Employment Acts of 1988 and 1990. Revised edition, 1991. This became operational on 20 May 1991. London: DE, 1991.

38 EA 1988, s. 17.

39 The 1991 Green Paper proposes (p. 14) that the employer should be provided with a sample copy of the ballot paper.

40 TUA 1984 as amended by EA 1988, Schedule 3, para 5(8) (c).

41 EA, 1990, s. 7.

42 The 1991 Green Paper proposes (p. 14) that employers should have a statutory entitlement to receive details of the result and a copy of the scrutineer's report. It also proposes (p. 13) that unions be required to give

seven days' notice of any action to which the ballot relates. The current code (para 56, p. 27) states that 'sufficient' notice should be given.

43 Industrial Action Ballots Code, para 53 (p. 25).
44 EP(C)A, s. 62(4) (a).
45 EA 1990, s. 9.

10

Trades Unions

Legal Status of Trades Unions

Legal personality

The Trade Union and Labour Relations Act 1974 (TULRA) provides a definition of trades unions and describes their legal personality. A trades union is an organization of workers whose principal purposes include the regulation of relations between workers and employers. Bodies such as union confederations, which are themselves made up of trades unions or representatives of trades unions, are also within the definition.[1]

Some trades unions are 'special register bodies', a designation which derives from the now repealed Industrial Relations Act 1971. These unions are either registered companies or otherwise incorporated (for example by charter). With the exception of these special register bodies, trades unions cannot be, and cannot be treated as, corporate bodies.[2] However:

- a union is capable of making contracts;
- its property is vested in trustees;
- it can sue and be sued in its own name;
- proceedings for offences committed by or on behalf of a trades union can be brought against it in its own name;
- judgments against a union can be enforced against any property held in trust as if it were a body corporate.

In short, trades unions are voluntary bodies but statute gives them some of the characteristics of incorporated organizations. They must not register as a company or as a friendly or provident society.

Listing

The Certification Officer (see chapter 1) is required to maintain a list of trades unions which is open to public inspection.[3] Any union may apply for listing (but is not compelled to do so) and if refused may appeal to the EAT on a point of fact or law. Listing is evidence that the organization is a trades union. Listing is also a prerequisite if the union wishes to receive a certificate of independence from the Certification Officer (see below) and if it wants to avoid paying taxes on its provident funds.

Administrative requirements[4]

Unions, whether listed or not, must keep proper accounting records and establish systems of financial control.[5] They must also send an annual return to the Certification Officer, which must include their audited accounts. Where unions run superannuation schemes for their members, these must be subject to actuarial examination.[6] It is a criminal offence to refuse to perform or wilfully neglect these duties, or to falsify documents. These offences are punishable by fine.

Certification as independent

A listed trades union may apply for a certificate of independence.[7] The significance of a certificate of independence for trades unions is that it qualifies them for various statutory rights which are given to independent trades unions only. These include the right to be consulted in a redundancy and paid time off for officials. Independence means that a trades union:

- is not under the domination or control of an employer; and
- is not liable to interference by an employer (arising out of the provision of financial or material support or by any other means) tending towards such control.[8]

A union refused its certificate of independence may appeal to EAT on a point of fact or law.[9] Essentially, the requirement of a certificate of independence is to ensure that organizations are bona fide trades unions.

The Contract of Membership

As far as the law is concerned, unions may recruit whoever they wish. However, in practice they may be constrained by the TUC's 'Bridlington principles' which attempt to impose some order in respect of inter-union relations. At the present time, unions are also free in law to refuse admission, except in the case of a closed shop, where the Employment Act 1980 provides remedies for those unreasonably refused admission (see below, p. 253–5), or on grounds of race or sex (pp. 266–7 below).[10]

On joining a union the individual (regardless of whether they are an employee, or for example, an unemployed person) enters into a contract of membership with the union. The essence of the contract is a subscription in exchange for the provision of benefits and services. The principal source of express terms is the rule book a copy of which must be supplied to each member (or indeed, any person) on request.[11]

There are also implied terms, particularly the application of the principles of natural justice. Thus a member under discipline has a right to be told what is alleged, a right to state their case and a right to a fair judgment. Custom and/or practice may be implied but this would be unlikely if it conflicted with an express term. Remedies for breach of the contract of membership are declarations, injunctions and damages.

The common law concept of a contract of membership is not something unique to trades unions. The concept is applied to voluntary organizations more generally, such as social and sports clubs and political parties. Much of the case law in this field relates to questions of procedure: for instance, an organization has made a decision but the procedure by which it has been arrived at was flawed. There has been either a breach of the organization's rules (including standing orders) or a breach of the principles of natural justice, or both.

The case of *Iwanuszezak* v. *General Municipal Boilermakers and Allied Trades Union* was unusual in that the member claimed that the union was in breach of contract by not representing him properly. It thus rested upon the substantive issue of whether or not the union was providing the service it was contractually bound to provide. The claim failed because there was no term in the contract on which the action could be based, although it is submitted that representation in good faith might conceivably be an implied term. This would allow for the fact that even the most effective representation would probably not satisfy all the members. A duty of care might also be implied, opening up the possibility of a claim in tort for damages for negligence.

Common law claims would be taken through the normal courts, and following the extension of the role of the Commissioner for the Rights of Trade Union Members (henceforth 'the Commissioner') as a result of the 1990 EA there is now assistance available to the member.

The common law contract of membership is statutorily recognized in TULRA 1974 which says that the contract will have an implied term conferring a right on the member on giving reasonable notice, and complying with any reasonable conditions, to terminate their membership of the union.[12]

The rule book is the cornerstone of the contract of membership and for the most part a union is free to determine its own rules, although rules governing union mergers and political objectives require the approval of the Certification Officer. However, the rules will not reign supreme if they involve a breach of the principles of natural justice, nor if they conflict with statutory provision. There is now a substantial amount of statute law governing the internal functioning of trades unions. Ballots are necessary as laid down by statute if unions are to protect themselves from various adverse consequences in relation to industrial action, national executive committee elections, political objectives and mergers. These are dealt with later in this chapter. Figure 10.1 summarizes the overall legal position.

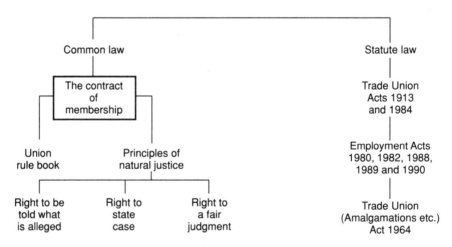

Figure 10.1 Trades unions and their members

Common law actions against unions are dealt with through the normal courts. Complaints of breaches of statute, by contrast, are heard by various specialist employment law institutions. Some are heard by both. Claims that a person has been unreasonably expelled or excluded from a union in a closed shop (under the provisions of the Employment Act 1980) or has been unjustifiably disciplined (Employment Act 1988) are heard by industrial tribunals. (Industrial tribunals are described in chapter 1 and guidance given on handling a case in chapter 12). All the other issues are heard by the Certification Officer (CO). The Commissioner does not decide whether or not rights have been infringed, but has a wide remit to assist union members with their cases.

Trades Unions and their Members: Statutory Provisions

Exclusion or expulsion from a union in a closed shop[13]

Certain rights are given to persons under the Employment Act 1980.[14] A person unreasonably refused admission to or unreasonably expelled from a trades union in a closed shop (that is, in legal terms, where employment is covered by a union membership agreement (UMA)), but not someone who has resigned (*McGhee* v. *TGWU*), may make a complaint to an industrial tribunal within six months of the refusal or expulsion. The right extends to those 'seeking to be in employment' – interpreted by the EAT in *Clark* v. *SOGAT* to mean seeking employment in a particular field of industry rather than in a specific job – as well as covering those already employed. A tribunal will decide the matter 'in accordance with equity and the substantial merits of the case'. Until recently, there was a DE code of practice on closed shops.[15] The matter to be decided is whether the trades union acted reasonably or unreasonably. Acting in accordance with its rules is not conclusive evidence of reasonableness, nor is acting in breach of them conclusive evidence of unreasonableness. The details of the procedure are set out in figure 10.2.

Compensation may be reduced if the applicant fails to mitigate his loss, or if he has contributed to the expulsion/refusal of admission in any way, as in *Saunders* v. *Bakers' Food and Allied Workers' Union*, and *Howard* v. *NGA*. Where unjustifiable discipline under the Employment Act 1988 occurs in respect of someone who is employed or seeking employment where there is a UMA and that unjustifiable

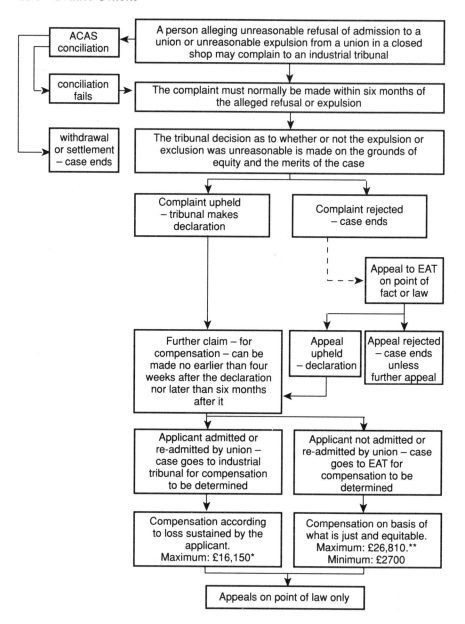

* The sum of the basic and compensatory awards for unfair dismissal
   (see above, pp. 186–8)
** The sum of the basic, compensatory and additional awards for unfair dismissal
   (see above, pp. 186–8)

Figure 10.2 Claims against trades unions for remedies for unreasonable expulsion or refusal of admission

discipline takes the form of exclusion or expulsion, it constitutes unreasonable exclusion or expulsion for the purposes of the Employment Act 1980 section 4. In such circumstances there is no entitlement to claim under the unjustifiable discipline provisions of the 1988 Act.

Union elections[16]

Members of a union's principal executive committee, including non-voting members, and union general secretaries and presidents, must be subject to election at least every five years.[17] Special register bodies (see above, p. 249) are subject only to the original 1984 Act requirements (that is, excluding non-voting members, presidents and general secretaries). Certain general secretaries and presidents who are largely ceremonial are excluded. Elected leaders nearing retirement age may have their period of office extended beyond five years as may some leaders involved in mergers.

The elections must be fully postal, and must meet the following requirements. They must be secret, there must be no interference and there must be no direct cost to the voter. Everyone must have the opportunity to vote by marking a ballot paper. The voting paper must specify the address to which, and date by which it must be returned. Each paper must have a different serial number.[18]

All candidates have the right to prepare an election address and have it sent out with the voting papers at no cost to themselves.[19] They must have the opportunity to prepare the address in their own words. Facilities given to candidates and any restrictions put upon them must be applied equally to all candidates.[20] The minimum length of the address is 100 words. Unions may set deadlines for submission of addresses. A candidate's address must not be changed without their consent except for production reasons. The same method of production must be used for all addresses. Civil or criminal liability for the contents of the address rest solely with the candidate.

There must be independent scrutiny of union elections.[21] The scrutineer has to be named in advance and on the ballot paper so that members can challenge the union's choice if they wish.[22] The qualifications of scrutineers are laid down in a ministerial order.[23] They must be competent and independent of the union and must be one of the following:

- A solicitor with a practising certificate.
- A chartered or certified accountant who is accepted as an auditor.
- The Electoral Reform Society.

- The Industrial Society.
- Unity Security Balloting Services Ltd.

These requirements also apply to political fund ballots. Independent scrutineers have the role of supervising the production and distribution of ballot papers, receiving voting papers returned by voters, reporting on the ballot to the union and retaining custody of the returned voting papers for one year.

The independent scrutineer's report must say whether the ballot appeared to meet the legal requirements, whether the security arrangements were satisfactory and whether the scrutineer was able to carry out their functions without interference. The scrutineer must state the number of voting papers distributed, the number returned, the number of votes for each candidate and the number of spoiled or invalid papers. A union cannot publish the ballot result until it has received the scrutineer's report. Within three months of receiving the report it must provide a copy of the report to each member, as far as is reasonably practicable, or notify the members of the main details through normal channels. The union must also inform members that they can obtain a copy either free of charge or for a reasonable fee, and supply such copies.

Complaints by members about union elections being in breach of statute may be made to the Certification Officer or the High Court. The former, where possible, must give a decision within six months. The Certification Officer can make a declaration: only the courts can make enforcement orders (such as an order to re-run an election). The Commissioner may assist individuals wanting to pursue court actions. Applications to the courts or the Certification Officer relating to elections which have been held must be made within a year of the announcement of the election result. The applicant must have been a member at the time of their application and, if the election has been held, at the time of the election.

Under section 18 of the Employment Act 1988 the Secretary of State may produce codes of practice on the subject of union elections and ballots. A code on Industrial Action Ballots is already in operation (see above, pp. 240–3).

Trade union political activities

The legal framework
The Trade Union Act 1913 (as amended) permits a trades union (regardless of whether or not it is listed under section 8 of TULRA)

to have political objectives as defined by the Act. Activities in furtherance of political objectives must be financed out of a separate fund and members not wishing to contribute to the fund have the right to be exempted (that is, to contract out). To have political objectives a majority of the union's members voting in a ballot must be in favour.

The ballot rules have to be approved by the Certification Officer as do the political rules more generally and any changes in them. A member exempted from paying into the political fund must not be put at a disadvantage (except in relation to the control and management of the political fund) by being exempted. This means that they must not lose any benefits or be put at any disadvantage compared with other members who have not contracted out. Contribution to the political fund must not be a condition of admission to the union. Where a union is liable for damages for committing unlawful industrial action, political funds, like provident funds, are protected.[24]

The Certification Officer issues model political rules for trades unions to use and the actual rules of unions follow these closely if not exactly. The model rules contain an exemption form which members can use to serve notice that they seek exemption. Some other form, to like effect, may also be used. Exempted members must be relieved of payment of the political levy (if separate) or that part of the general subscription which is a contribution to the political fund. In the latter circumstances, the member must be told which part of the subscription is the political element. The exemption means that the member should not pay the political contribution at the time it is due to be levied, rather than having it deducted and later refunded.

Any member who feels that they are the subject of a breach of a union's political rules may complain to the Certification Officer[25] (or alternatively to the courts under common law). If, after a hearing, the Certification Officer believes that a breach has occurred, he may make an order remedying the situation. The Certification Officer's decision is subject to appeal to the Employment Appeal Tribunal on a point of law.

Recent change – membership ballots
The original legislation required a once-for-all ballot if a union was to have political objectives. The Trade Union Act 1984 requires that there be a ballot at intervals of no more than ten years. For most unions, the last ballot was held in the year ending 31 March 1986. The principal ballot requirements are now as follows.[26]

- Voting must be by marking a voting paper.
- The ballot must be fully postal.
- There must be independent scrutiny (of the sort described on pp. 255–6 above) and the name of the scrutineer must be communicated to members and must appear on the ballot paper.
- Secrecy must be secured.
- There must be freedom from interference.
- There must be no direct cost to the voter.

Complaints about ballots may be made to the CO (whose decision should, if possible, be made within six months) or to the High Court, under the statutory provisions. The member complaining must be a member at the time of the complaint and if the ballot has taken place, at the time of the ballot. The Commissioner may assist in court cases. The ballot is required if a union wishes to adopt political objectives. It then follows automatically from statutory requirements that there must be a separate fund from which these objectives are financed. Whether a union subsequently affiliates to a political party is not a matter of law but a matter of union policy.

Definition of political objectives
This definition was altered by the 1984 Act. Anything 'political' must be paid out of the political fund. Everything else can be paid out of general funds. Political means

'the expenditure of money:
(a) on any contribution to the funds, of, or on the payment of any expenses incurred directly or indirectly by, a political party;
(b) on the provision of any service or property for use by or on behalf of any political party;
(c) in connection with the registration of electors, the candidature of any person, the selection of any candidate or the holding of any ballot by the union in connection with any election to a political office;
(d) on the maintenance of any holder of a political office;
(e) on the holding of any conference or meeting by or on behalf of a political party or of any other meeting the main purpose of which is the transaction of business in connection with a political party;
(f) on the production, publication or distribution of any literature, document, film, sound recording or advertisement the main purpose of which is to persuade people to vote for a political party or candidate or to persuade them not to vote for a political party or candidate'.[27]

In (c), 'political office' means an MP, MEP, member of a local authority or any position within a political party.

Although decided prior to the operation of the Trade Union Act (TUA) 1984 the following cases illustrate how the definition is applied in practice. In *Richards* v. *NUM*, the Certification Officer held that a march and lobby organized by the Labour Party, and a contribution to the financing of a new headquarters for the Labour Party, were political within the meaning of the legislation. He thus ordered the transfer of the relevant sums from the political to the general fund (from which they had originally been paid). In broad terms, the legislation refers to party political activities rather than political activities more generally. For example, in *Coleman* v. *POEU* there was a complaint about the union's general fund being used to pay for affiliation to a campaign which was alleged to be party political. The complaint was rejected because, while the campaign was clearly political, it was not political within the meaning of the legislation.

Other changes
Recent legislation makes it clear that political fund debts can be paid off only from the political fund and that no assets can be transferred into the political fund other than political fund contributions and property accruing from managing political fund assets.

There is a duty upon employers not to deduct political fund contributions from contracted-out members who have notified them in writing. An employer refusing to stop political fund deductions or cancelling the whole of the subscription deduction (when not done for others) may be subject to a complaint to a county court. Where a county court order is obtained a member may pursue a case at an industrial tribunal under the Wages Act 1986 to seek repayment of an unlawful deduction.[28]

Unions must inform members of the right to contract out of the political levy and tell them that a standard form is available from the union or the Certification Officer.

Union discipline[29]

As a result of the operation of the Employment Act 1988, there is now a statutory right given to union members and ex-members not to be unjustifiably disciplined. This includes the right not to be disciplined for failing to participate in industrial action and applies even if the majority of members have voted in favour of the action in a ballot. The member may complain to an industrial tribunal. Discipline covers expulsion, fines, deprivation of any benefits or services and any other detriment. It includes advising or encouraging another union not to accept the person as a member. As already noted, where expulsion occurs in a closed shop, unjustifiable discipline will constitute unreasonable expulsion for the purposes of the 1980 Act, and is to be dealt with under those provisions rather than under the 1988 Act. Similarly, where a union advises or encourages another union not to accept the person into membership and where the person is seeking employment in a closed shop, such unjustifiable discipline will be unreasonable exclusion under the 1980 Act and will be dealt with under those provisions.

The decision to discipline, for it to be covered by the legislation, has to be taken by a union in accordance with its rules, by an official, or by a group which includes an official. The legislation confers rights which are additional to any others that the member may have (for example under union rules).

Discipline is unjustifiable if the reason for it is that the member's conduct includes one of the following or something which amounts to one of the following:

1 *Industrial action*
  (a) Failing to participate.
  (b) Indicating opposition or lack of support.
  (c) Failing to refuse to perform certain contractual or other agreed duties.
  (d) Encouraging or assisting anyone else to perform such duties.
2 *Assertions*
  (a) Asserting that the union, or its officials, representatives or trustees, has contravened or is proposing to contravene the union's rules, any agreement or law.
  (b) Attempting to justify any such assertion.
  (c) Consulting or seeking advice or assistance from the CO, Commissioner or anyone else with respect to matters which form or might form the basis of such an assertion.
3 *Other*
  (a) Refusing to comply with a penalty arising out of an act for which discipline has been ruled unjustifiable either in relation to that person or some other person.
  (b) Proposing to do anything listed above (that is, 1, 2 and 3(a)).
  (c) Preparing or doing anything incidental to engaging in anything listed above (that is, 1, 2 and 3 (a)).

Discipline against a member for working through a strike, crossing a picket line or working normally when partial sanctions are being applied (that is, partial performance of duties) will be unjustifiable under the terms of the Act. So too will be discipline for speaking out against industrial action and refusing to pay a strike levy.

Asserting breaches of rule and so on will include the bringing of any proceedings. Making an assertion will not amount to unjustifiable discipline, however, if the individual making it, or helping another to make it, knows it is false or otherwise acts in bad faith. Nor will discipline be unjustifiable if it would have occurred irrespective of it being listed in the Act, for example discipline for disruptive behaviour in a meeting when alleging breach of a rule.

The procedure for a complainant in these cases is to apply to an industrial tribunal. Figure 10.3 summarizes the sequence. Cases can be transferred between EAT and tribunals (and vice versa) if they are in the wrong forum. Complainants must mitigate their losses, and compensation can be reduced if there is contributory fault. The procedure differs somewhat from the similar provisions on expulsions and exclusions in closed shops:

- There are appeals on points of law only, from the declaration.
- The basis of compensation is different at an industrial tribunal.
- The amounts of compensation are different at the EAT.

Ballots prior to industrial action

While the Trade Union Act 1984 had removed trades union immunity in the absence of a successful ballot, the union member had no statutory right to insist that a ballot be held.[30] The Employment Act 1988 remedied this matter.[31] It provides that there is a right to apply to court for an order to restrain a union from industrial action. The application can be made by any member induced or likely to be induced to take part regardless of whether they will be induced. If the court is satisfied that the union is responsible for the action it will make an order.[32] Assistance from the Commissioner may be available. The ballot must be conducted in accordance with the legal requirements (see above pp. 240–3). A ballot not so conducted would leave it open to members to seek restraining orders.

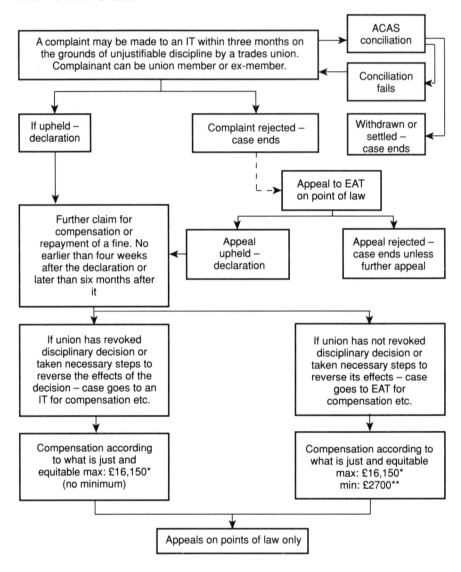

* The sum of the basic and compensatory awards for unfair dismissal
  (see above, pp. 186–8).
** The equivalent of the minimum basic award where dismissal is for reasons of
  trades union membership or activity or non-membership
  (see above, p. 188)

Figure 10.3 Claims against trades unions for remedies for unjustifiable discipline

Access to the courts

Hitherto, courts could refuse to hear a case if a union member had not fully used the union's internal procedures in connection with any grievance. As a result of the Employment Act 1988 it is not now possible for courts to dismiss or adjourn cases for this reason provided a valid application has been made to a trades union and six months have elapsed since that application.[33] The kinds of cases to which this provision relates are those which the union's rules require or allow to be submitted to the union for resolution or conciliation, and for which the courts have jurisdiction. These are essentially issues arising under the common law contract of membership, but are restricted to points of law (such as interpretation or breach of rules) or breaches of natural justice (see above, p. 251).

Deduction of union subscriptions from wages[34]

This will be allowable providing the requirements of the Wages Act 1986 are met (see above, pp. 61–3). The Employment Act 1988 makes provision for situations where the employee terminates their union membership.[35] If the employee notifies the following in writing to their employer, the employer must stop deducting union subscriptions as from the specified date:

● that union membership has ended or will end on a specified date of which the union is aware; or
● that notice of resignation has expired or will expire on a specified date.

If the employer does not stop deducting subscriptions on the relevant date (or as soon as is reasonably practicable thereafter), the employee may apply to an industrial tribunal (within three months of the deduction) under the Wages Act 1986. If the deduction contravenes the provisions of the Employment Act, as above, it will be an unlawful deduction under the Wages Act and a tribunal will make a declaration to that effect and order repayment of amounts deducted.

Union funds, property and accounts

Access to union accounting records
The Employment Act 1988 requires trades unions to keep their accounting records open for inspection and gives union members the right of inspection, including the right to be accompanied by an

accountant if they wish.[36] Accounting records are a requirement of TULRA 1974 (see p. 250 above) and relate to a union or a branch or section of that union. They must be kept available for inspection for six years. This requirement relates to records for any period commencing on or after 1 January 1987. The inspection right for any period is given to someone who was a member for at least part of that period.

A union must give a member access within 28 days of the request. Normally, access will be at the place where the records are kept and at a reasonable hour. Copies of accounts may be taken. If the union notifies the member in advance, a reasonable charge may be made for complying with the inspection request. The principles on which a charge is made must be indicated in advance and it must not exceed reasonable administrative expenses. Where an accountant accompanies a member, that accountant may be asked to protect the confidentiality of the records. A refusal to do so will allow the union to prevent the accountant accompanying the member.

A person who has a request refused may ask the court to order that:

- They be allowed to inspect the records.
- They are allowed to be accompanied by an accountant.
- They are allowed to have copies of the accounts.

The Commissioner may give assistance with cases taken under these provisions. If a union refuses or wilfully neglects the duties under these provisions it commits an offence punishable by a fine. The same applies if a person falsifies documents.

Indemnifying unlawful conduct

As a result of the Employment Act 1988 it is unlawful for a union to indemnify anyone in respect of a penalty imposed on them for contempt of court or for a criminal offence.[37] A union has power under the Act to recover such sums, and any member can apply to a court if the union fails to bring or continue proceedings for such recovery. Courts may make an order allowing the individual member to bring or continue proceedings on the union's behalf and at its expense. The assistance of the Commissioner might be available to the member under such circumstances.

Unlawful use of property by trustees

Union trustees cannot lawfully use union property, or allow it to be used, for unlawful purposes; nor can they lawfully comply with any unlawful direction given to them under the rules of the union.[38] A member may apply to the courts if the trustees have done any of these things or propose to do any of them. If the act has occurred, the member complaining must have been a union member at the time of the act. The Commissioner may provide assistance.

A court may require the trustees to take specified steps to protect or recover the union's property. It also has the power to appoint a receiver of the union's property who will stay in control of the union's funds until the court is satisfied that they can be returned to the trustees. It may remove one or more of the trustees. Where actions are proposed or taken in contempt of court all of the union's trustees will be removed except for any who can convince the court that they should remain. In contempt, trustees will be liable as individuals for any penalties for contempt and it would be unlawful for the union to indemnify them (see above, p. 264).

Inspection of the union's membership register

The Trade Union Act 1984 requires unions to compile, and keep up to date, a register of the names and addresses of its members.[39] The 1988 Act allows any member to check whether they are included on the register and to obtain a copy of their register entry which should be provided free of charge or for a reasonable fee, as soon as is reasonably practicable after the request is made.[40] A member must give reasonable notice of wishing to check the register, which they can do free of charge at a reasonable time. A complaint under these provisions may be made to the Certification Officer or to the High Court. Both may make declarations, but only the latter can make an order for enforcement. Assistance from the Commissioner may be available.

Union mergers[41]

The Trade Union (Amalgamations etc.) Act 1964, lays down various rules for trades union mergers.[42] The Act also covers unincorporated employers' associations. Of prime importance is the fact that mergers are of two types: amalgamations and transfers of engagements. Under a transfer of engagements the transferor loses its legal identity and the transferee continues with its legal identity unchanged. An amalgamation produces a new organization replacing the amalgamating bodies, which then cease to exist. In the latter case, therefore, there has to be a new rule book and a new name for the union. Unions wishing to merge must prepare an instrument setting out the proposed terms and an explanatory notice to members. These documents have to be approved by the Certification Officer before balloting on the instrument can go ahead. In a transfer of engagements only the members of the transferring organization need to vote on whether to accept the instrument. In an amalgamation, each amalgamating organization must have a ballot.

Where a majority of those voting are in favour, the union(s) can apply to the Certification Officer to have the instrument registered. An interval of six weeks is allowed for any member of a transferor union or amalgamating union to make a complaint that one or more of the statutory requirements for the ballot has not been met. The Certification Officer will investigate and make a decision on any complaint, which may include laying down conditions to be met before registration will be allowed. There is a right of appeal to EAT on a point of law. The Certification Officer also has a responsibility to deal with changes of name of listed unions and employers' associations, and to approve changes as long as the new name is not the same as, or very similar to, any other listed organization.[43]

Race and sex discrimination

In their capacity as employers of staff, trades unions are governed by discrimination law in the same ways as other employers. However, trades unions are also subject to legislation covering the relationships they have with their members, that is, as providers of benefits and services. Trades unions must not discriminate as regards the terms of membership, or by refusing admission, or in access to any benefits facilities or services. Nor must they deprive people of membership on any of the prohibited grounds, nor subject people to any other detriment. An exception is made here (as regards sex discrimination) for death or retirement provisions, but this exception was narrowed substantially by the Sex Discrimination Act 1986. The exception still applies but not in relation to retirement provisions affecting promotion, demotion, dismissal, training and transfer. More recently, the decision of the European Court in *Barber* v. *Guardian Royal Exchange Assurance Group* seems to signal the end of discrimination of this sort being considered lawful. Unions may need to be careful if they are involved in an employer's recruitment process. Where a union provides all of the candidates for recruitment, there could be unlawful discrimination if the union membership is all male, for example, or all white. (If a non-member was refused, this might be an unlawful refusal of employment under EA 1990, see above, p. 42).

Unions may lawfully engage in a certain amount of positive discrimination. Seats on their national executive committees may be reserved for women. Election to such seats, however, must not be restricted to women members. Training can also be provided for those groups who are under-represented in respect of union positions. Thus, there may be women-only courses or courses for black people. Unions are advised by codes of practice to become involved with the introduction of equal opportunities policies and their monitoring.[44]

Facilities for Ballots

Right to hold a ballot on the employer's premises

In firms with over 20 employees an independent, recognized union has a right to hold one of the various ballots which attract public funding (on industrial action, NEC elections, amending rules, amalgamations and so on) on the employer's premises. The employer must comply if it is reasonably practicable to do so. A trades union has three months in which to complain of a refusal. If a tribunal upholds the complaint it will make a declaration, and may award any compensation which is 'just and equitable' taking into account the expenses incurred by the union and the infringement of rights.

Time off

The EP(C)A gives a right to reasonable time off for union activity, but does not require the employer to pay. The code on time off cites voting in union elections as an example of such activity.[45]

Public funds for trades union ballots

The Certification Officer is responsible for administering this scheme under the Employment Act 1980.[46] He is empowered to refund certain costs incurred by independent trades unions in holding secret postal ballots for specified purposes. The purposes are listed below.

1 Calling or ending industrial action.

2 Union elections:
  (a) statutory elections for principal executive committees and so on;
  (b) elections under union rules including principal executive committee members, president, chairman, secretary, treasurer of the union or any elected employee of the union.
3 Amending union rules.
4 Merger ballots.
5 Political fund review ballots (that is, excluding ballots to set up a new political fund).
6 Ballots on offers made by employers relating to terms and conditions of employment.

The ballot must be secret, postal and be held for one of more of the above reasons. Detailed requirements laid down in a set of regulations must also be met.[47] In the case of ballots under (1) and (6) above the papers may be distributed at the workplace and be returned by post. Applications must be made within six months of the end of the voting period.

The costs which are refundable are as follows.

Stationery and printing expenditure:
● voting papers;
● envelopes used for voting papers;
● literature enclosed which explains the subject to be voted upon and the procedure for voting, including election addresses.

Postal costs:
● Second class postal costs of sending out and returning voting papers, unless it is reasonable to use first class post.

The following are examples of what is *not* covered.

● Expenses of sorting and insertion of voting papers.
● Capital depreciation of machinery.
● Expenses arising out of the use of a returning officer or scrutineer.
● Election addresses not enclosed with voting papers.
● Nomination costs.
● Transport costs.

Notes

1 TULRA 1974, s. 28
2 TULRA, s. 2.
3 TULRA, s. 8.

4 The 1991 Green Paper proposes (pp. 30–32) an extension of unions' duties in this area and an increase in the powers of the Certification Officer. It is also proposed that individuals found guilty of breaches of certain duties would be debarred from standing for or holding specified national union positions.

5 TULRA, s. 10.

6 TULRA, s. 11.

7 EPA 1975, s. 8.

8 TULRA, s. 30 and EP(C)A, s. 153.

9 EPA, s. 8.

10 The 1991 Green Paper proposes (p. 24) that nobody should be excluded from a trades union because they were previously a member of another union or because of inter-union arrangements giving sole recruitment rights to another union.

11 TULRA 1974, s. 11(4).

12 TULRA, s. 7.

13 The legal status of the closed shop is dealt with on pp. 230–1.

14 EA 1980, Ss. 4–5.

15 *Closed Shop Agreements and Arrangements*, DE Code of Practice, London: DE, 1983. This was revoked in 1991.

16 The 1991 Green Paper (pp. 19–20) makes the following proposals.

• Union members should be given a right to inspect the membership register as a whole (rather than just their own entry, as now). This proposal has now been dropped for security reasons.

• The above right should also be given to candidates in the election.

• Independent scrutineers should have access to the membership register and should be required to retain a copy for one year.

• Unions should be required to state in their annual returns the number of members listed on their registers for whom there is no address.

• Independent scrutineers should be required to state the number of voting papers distributed and returned in respect of the smallest practicable administrative unit (rather than for the union as a whole, as now).

17 TU Act 1984, Ss. 1–9 as amended by EA 88, Ss. 12–15.

18 EA 88, Schedule 3, para 5(2).

19 EA 88, s. 13.

20 The 1991 Green Paper proposes (p. 21) that there should be a duty not to discriminate between candidates as regards campaign facilities more generally.

21 EA 88, s. 15.

22 EA 90, s. 5.

23 Trade Union Ballots and Elections (Independent Scrutineer Qualifications) Order, SI 1988/2117 as amended by SI 1989/31 and operative from 1 February 1989.

24 EA 1982, s. 17.

25 TU Act 1913, s. 3(2).

26 TUA 1984 as amended by the EAs of 1988 and 1990.

27 TU Act 1984, s. 17.

28 EA 1988, Schedule 3, para 6.

29 EA 1988, s. 3.

30 TU Act 1984, Ss. 10–11.

31 EA 1988, s. 1.

32 The tests are laid down in EA 1982, s.15 (as amended by EA 1990, s. 6).

33 EA 88, s. 2.

34. The 1991 Green Paper proposes (p. 26) that an annual, written authorization to deduct should be required for any deduction to be lawful. Moreover, the paper canvasses the possibility of written authorization being required before any increase in subscriptions can be lawfully deducted. The proposal for annual authorization has now been amended. Authorization would be required every three years.

35 EA 88, s. 7.

36 EA 88, s. 6.

37 EA 88, s. 8.

38 EA 88, s. 9.

39 TU Act 1984, s. 4.

40 EA 88, s. 33 and Schedule 3, para 5(3).

41 The 1991 Green Paper proposes (p. 27) a requirement that ballots in respect of union mergers should be secret, postal and subject to independent scrutiny.

42 See also, Trades Unions and Employers' Associations (Amalgamations etc.) Regulations 1975, as amended.

43 Trades Unions (Amalgamations etc.) Act 1964, s. 6.

44 *CRE Code of Practice for the Elimination of Racial Discrimination etc.*, pp. 23–27, London: CRE, 1984.

45 ACAS Code of Practice 3, *Time off for Trade Union Duties and Activities*, para 21 (p. 11) London: HMSO, 1991.

46 EA 1980, s. 1.

47 The Funds for Trade Union Ballots Regulations, SI 1984/1654. Revised by SI 1988/1123 and 1988/2116.

11

Managing the Human Resource

Instruction, Supervision and Appraisal

Instruction and supervision

An issue here which may have important legal consequences is health and safety. There may be negligence and/or a breach of statutory duty if a worker is not instructed properly on what to do or is not supervised adequately. A failure in this area can lead to claims for damages at civil law and/or to prosecution for criminal offences. The HSWA lays down a requirement for instruction and supervision as is necessary and the COSHH regulations (issued under HSWA) require necessary instruction.[1]

As regards unfair dismissal law, inadequate instruction or lack of supervision may undermine an employer's case where dismissal is for incompetence. Moreover, where there is misconduct, a case can be weakened if the employee has not been properly instructed in the employer's rules. Inadequate supervision may allow practices or behaviour to develop which management should have known about. This again may weaken a case. In relation to race and sex discrimination, an instruction to discriminate is an unlawful act in itself, as is putting pressure upon others in order to persuade them to discriminate. Any instruction to carry out criminal activity will of course itself be illegal.

Apart from the above, there is the question of whether an instruction is lawful within the terms of the employee's contract of employment. Determining this will involve examining the various sources in order to identify the contract terms (see chapter 2).

Management should not only ensure that instructions are lawful, but also that they are conveyed clearly to employees.

Appraisal

Appraisal schemes may assist in improving performance, establishing training and development needs and indicating potential for future promotion as well as providing a basis for merit awards and other performance-related pay. Such schemes and the data they produce may also be of assistance to employers in selecting employees for redundancy and avoiding findings of unfair dismissal for redundancy, see above p. 216. The employee is likely to provide information, both on paper and orally, about what their job involves, their strengths and weaknesses, and their future activities. If this information is computerized it will be subject to the requirements of the Data Protection Act (DPA) 1984 (see below). Moreover, the assessment criteria used in the appraisal will need to be non-discriminatory.

In addition, appraisal can give rise to other issues which may have legal implications. For example, if there is to be any kind of fine or deduction for substandard work, it will need to comply with the requirements of the Wages Act 1986 (see chapter 3). Second, what if appraisal information is used for disciplinary purposes? If the appraisal scheme encourages employees to be honest about their shortcomings (in order to identify training needs for instance) what is the position if the employee finds themselves dismissed rather than given more training, albeit, perhaps, after having received counselling? Could this be breach of the term of trust? Much may depend on the terms of the scheme itself, especially if it has been agreed by a trades union on behalf of its members on the basis of acceptance of particular terms. Third, what is the status of the agreed targets which are the objectives of an appraisal interview? Are these targets of a different status from actual standards required? Are they, instead, things to be aimed at, with no punishment for failure – motivational devices rather than standards where failure might lead to discipline?

The appraisal and other aspects of probation are discussed in chapter 7.

Training, Development and Promotion

Training and development

Statutory duty to train or provide facilities for training
There is no general statutory requirement to train employees but there is a statutory requirement to provide training, instruction etc under

HSWA and under the COSHH regulations. Thus, section 2(1)(c) of HSWA states that an employer must provide such information, instruction, training and supervision as is necessary to ensure, so far as is reasonably practicable, the health and safety at work of their employees (see chapter 4). There are also training requirements under specific regulations, such as those for young people working on dangerous machines. Regulation 12 of COSHH, and the approved code of practice, also lay down training requirements.

Employers dismissing for incompetence may find their cases undermined if there has not been adequate training (see chapter 7).

Another statutory training requirement relates to union officials. An employer is under a duty to allow such officials a reasonable amount of paid time off for training for their duties.[2] Safety representatives are included in this but in any case would have such a right under the Safety Representatives and Safety Committees (SRSC) regulations.[3]

An employer may be under a duty to ensure that persons who are *not* their employees are trained. This derives from the duty of care towards people other than employees. (See also the *Swan Hunter* case at p. 93 above.) Again, HSWA and the COSHH regulations are important. Thus, an employer must conduct their business to ensure, so far as is reasonably practicable, that persons other than their employees are not exposed to risks to their health or safety.[4]

Some employers have duties under the Companies Act 1985 to include details of the recruitment, training, promotion and career development of disabled persons in their Annual Report (see above, p. 29). The white paper, *People, Jobs and Opportunity*, introduces the idea of requiring employers to provide employees with training policy statements more generally.

Codes of practice

Where an employer has an equal opportunities policy, the race relations and sex discrimination codes of practice state that managers and other staff should be trained in its requirements. In addition, various codes of practice issued under HSWA have training require-ments, for instance the approved code of practice on COSHH.

Common law duty to train or to provide facilities for training

An employer has a duty under the contract of employment to take reasonable care in relation to an employee. Depending upon the circumstances, this could mean that some training would be needed on safety grounds and that failure to provide it could amount to negligence. Moreover, training to enable the employee to fulfil the duties required of them may be seen as an implied term of the contract – part of the responsibilities stemming from the duty of mutual trust and confidence. A failure here might allow an employee to sue for breach of contract or resign and claim unfair constructive dismissal. Particular care needs to be taken with: probationers and trainees (especially if very young), those newly promoted and those who are experiencing major changes in their work.

As with statute, the employer may have common law duties to people other than employees, and these may make necessary some training of the employee (see above p. 111). If it is reasonably foreseeable that other people can be affected by the acts or omissions of the employee, and that the employee requires training in order to competently perform their duties, a failure to train adequately could amount to negligence.

The status of trainees
There is no general legislation which determines the form of relationship governing the employment of trainees. Contractual matters are likely to be the main consideration, although contracts may not necessarily be contracts of employment. An existing employee undergoing part-time or full-time training will normally remain an employee under a contract of employment. If that training involves a secondment to some other organisation (for example as part of the employee's individual development programme) much will depend on the terms agreed but clearly continuity will need to be preserved for the purposes of accrued benefits.

The position is least clear where the individual is taken on as trainee. Here, the possibilities are that the trainee:

- is an employee of the company providing the training, in which case a contract of employment (or contract of apprenticeship) will exist;
- is not an employee of the firm but may have a contract for training with the firm or with a training agency. (The firm and the training agency would almost certainly have a contract of some kind with each other.)
- may have neither a contract of employment nor a contract for training. He or she may have a contract of its own kind or no contract at all (see above, p. 55).

Much will depend on the details of what was agreed.

For there to be a contract of any sort there will need to have been an intention to create legal relations. In the absence of a clear statement to the contrary, the courts will assume that there is no contract of employment and no contract for training (*Daley* v. *Allied Suppliers*

Ltd). Where there is a contract, the label put on it by the parties will not necessarily be conclusive evidence of its real nature (*Young and Woods Ltd* v. *West*). The test developed is that of discovering the underlying purpose of the contract. If it is to create the standard employment relationship it will be a contract of employment; if it is to provide general training and work experience it will be a contract for training; if it is a contract to teach a specific trade it will be a contract of apprenticeship (*Wiltshire Police Authority* v. *Wynn*). The Secretary of State may make an order specifying the status of people undergoing government-funded training. The order can state that they are to be treated as employees, trainees or 'in such other manner as may be specified'.[5]

The status of the apprentice is quite clear. An apprentice should have a written, signed contract of apprenticeship under which the employer agrees to teach them the trade. In return, the apprentice agrees to serve and learn. For the purpose of employment legislation the contract is treated as if it were a contract of employment for a fixed term. Because the apprentice starts as a minor, the contract as a whole must be beneficial if it is to be enforceable. The parties have only limited rights to end the contract during its term, although the position will be influenced by the contractual terms themselves (such as provision for termination by notice and provision for summary dismissal for gross misconduct). An apprentice may agree in writing to waive unfair dismissal and redundancy payments rights. The employer is obliged to provide written confirmation that the apprentice has satisfactorily completed his or her training, if this is the case. (The dismissal of apprentices and the failure to offer jobs after expiry of apprenticeship are matters dealt with in chapter 7).

Work experience
This is permitted by the Education (Work Experience) Act 1973,[6] which prohibits any child from doing anything on a work experience placement which is prohibited for a young person to do under health and safety legislation. School students on such placements are neither trainees nor employees and are unlikely to be under any sort of contract with the organization in which they are placed. However, the normal rules of the law of torts will apply. The placing body will have a duty of reasonable care as will the host organization because the student will be on the organization's premises. Moreover, the requirements of section 3 of HSWA will need to be met since these apply to people other than employees. Race and sex discrimination

may be outlawed under the education rather than the employment provisions of the respective Acts, with complaints going to the county courts rather than to industrial tribunals.

As a result of the Employment Act 1990[7] work experience can now take place during the last term of the penultimate year of compulsory schooling, as well as during the final year. Regulations have been made which require students undergoing work experience to be treated as employees for health and safety purposes.[8]

Rights of trainees

Recent amendments to the Sex Discrimination Act 1975 and Race Relations Act 1976 mean that trainees are fully covered by these Acts whatever their status.[9] Therefore, to refuse to offer training opportunities on grounds of race or sex would be unlawful, as would offering the opportunities but on less favourable terms. Care needs to be taken here to avoid the indirect discrimination trap referred to in chapter 2. For example, there may be a rule that training for promotion to higher grades of work is not provided for certain occupations because they are not seen as including people of potential. If the occupations in question tend to be made up largely of one sex, such a rule could amount to indirect sex discrimination. The same concept applies in the field of race discrimination. As far as union membership or non-membership is concerned, any discrimination (apart from dismissal itself) may amount to action short of dismissal and open up the possibility of a claim to a tribunal. Dismissal would be subject to the law of unfair dismissal (see chapter 7). Unlike sex and race discrimination, only employees are covered – the trainee who is not an employee would not be covered. The concept of indirect discrimination is limited to race and sex (including marriage) and does not apply to the question of union discrimination.

Positive discrimination in training on grounds of sex or race is allowed if an employer or training body feels that a particular sex or race has been under-represented in that kind of work in the last 12 months either in Great Britain as a whole, or in an area within Great Britain.[10] Positive discrimination in recruitment remains unlawful. Discrimination in favour of lone parents when on training specified in a ministerial order is exempt from being unlawful marital discrimination under the Sex Discrimination Act 1975.[11]

Whatever the status of the trainee, there are regulations which require those receiving training (or work experience, as already noted) from an employer in a workplace to be treated as employees for health and safety purposes. The regulations do not apply to educational bodies (with the exception of Training Agency establishments) nor to training under a contract of employment but do apply to the work-based parts of sandwich courses. Work is defined to include training and trainees are to be regarded as employees.[12]

Where trainees are employees all the normal employment rights apply subject, where relevant, to the employee having sufficient continuous employment. Training under a contract of employment counts towards that period of continuous employment providing the hours requirements are met. Where an employee has a fixed-term contract its expiry will constitute dismissal. The most likely argument that can be put forward is that it is for some other substantial reason (SOSR – see chapter 7).

The costs of training

Where training needs are substantial and training is costly, a question which arises is whether the employee can be asked to share in its cost. First, can the employee be required to contribute while in employment? Second, can the employee be required to pay back some of the training costs if they leave before a specified period has expired and the employer has not sufficiently recouped the benefits from the investment in training?

The former is primarily a contractual matter and depends on the willingness of the employee to agree to such terms. However, courts might well restrict the operation of terms of this sort if disputed if there has been duress or the employee has been taken advantage of in some way. Moreover, if the employee is providing their own training, the employer may not be fulfilling his or her duties in providing training. Clearly, however, where training is expensive, a reasonable contribution might be expected. This is especially the case if the training is not employer-specific and will give the employee substantial future benefits in other employment; benefits which the employer in question will not be sharing.

Where an agreement is made for the employee to repay training costs if he or she leaves before the expiry of a specific period, the issues are the same but there is one additional point of importance: is such an agreement in restraint of trade by preventing free movement of labour between firms? *In Strathclyde Regional Council* v. *Neil* it was held that such a term, where the repayment was genuinely related to the employer's loss, was enforceable as part of the contract. In *Electronic Data Systems Ltd* v. *Hubble*, the employee had agreed, as part of the contract of employment, to repay some part of his training costs if he left before a certain date. He did so leave and the company sought their money. The High Court ordered payment but the Court of Appeal granted an injunction stopping the enforcement of payment. The issue was whether the agreement was valid, or unlawful for being in restraint of trade. The case was settled and it is understood that the employee did make some payment to his former employer. (See *People, Jobs and Opportunity*, pp. 17–18, on this subject).

Promotion

Statutory provisions

The provisions of discrimination law apply to promotion as they do to any aspect of employment. There must be no discrimination in the way a person is treated in relation to promotion. This requirement has given rise to a number of (often lengthy, and often bitter) cases in industrial tribunals in relation to both sex and race. Moreover, it should be noted that the statutory requirements cannot be avoided by dispensing with open competition. Succession planning and subsequent appointments without competition may be discriminatory if the policy is to groom only those of a particular sex or race, even if indirectly (for example by drawing upon those in a small number of selected positions where those in the selected positions were all males).

Indirect sex discrimination in relation to promotion may occur if part-time and full-time staff are treated differently. In *Nimz* v. *Freie und Hansestadt Hamburg* there was automatic progression to the next, higher grade after six years, providing that the employee had worked at least three-quarter time. Ninety per cent of those working less than three-quarter time were women. Therefore, the time requirement amounted to indirect sex discrimination unless the employer could objectively justify how experience of performing the longer hours related to the nature of the duties performed. In the absence of national law giving proper effect to the requirements of article 119 of the Treaty of Rome, the provisions operating were void and the arrangements should be applied to part-time and full-time staff alike (see pp. 33–5 above on indirect sex discrimination).

If account is to be taken of union membership or non-membership the provisions on action short of dismissal apply (see above pp. 226–7).

The intentions of employers do not fall within the scope of the Data Protection Act 1984 (see below). Computerized data comprising intention to promote would not therefore have to be disclosed to the data subject.

Common law requirements

Outside discrimination law, one of the main legal implications of promotion relates to contractual arrangements. The newly-promoted person will need to have the required standard of performance defined and the likely effects of not meeting it made clear. Any probationary terms will need to be spelled out. A final factor is whether the promotion of an unsuitable person could amount to negligence and be subject to legal action if someone suffered a loss through the promoted person's acts or omissions. Can there be negligent promotion in the same way that there can be negligent recruitment? There seems to be no reason why not, but clearly there would have to be some gross failure to give training and/or a serious and perhaps obvious case of the person promoted not being suitable.

Can there be a contractual right to be promoted conditional upon sufficient progress being made by the employee? Certainly a formal condition (for example, promotion to a higher grade on passing professional examinations) could be contractual, as could a promise to promote subject to the achievement of certain sales or other measureable targets. The less specific the words, the less likely that the matter is contractual. Thus, advising someone that there are good promotion prospects if they work hard is unlikely to constitute a promise or anything contractual.

Promotion procedures

Where the promotion procedure is flawed, for instance by a failure to adhere to laid-down procedures or by a breach of the principles of natural justice, challenge might be possible under the terms of a contract or of a statute. In the public sector, there might be the possibility of a challenge by means of application for judicial review. Thus, where one or more members of a selection panel in local government knew and showed favouritism towards one of the candidates, this might be challenged as a breach of the principles of natural justice warranting judicial review.

Employee Communication and Involvement

Employee communication

There is very little law in this area, whether concerning the communicating of information to employees or the obtaining of information from employees. The latter, of course, will be governed by data protection requirements if it is computerized (see below) unless it is in one of the excepted categories (payroll information, data for business accounts and so on). Computerized personnel records will fall within the DPA's requirements. As far as any requirement to provide employees with information is concerned there are a number of areas. These are:

- health and safety;
- pensions (see chapter 6);
- written particulars of main terms (see chapter 2);
- details of computerized data held by employers (on request);
- written reasons for dismissal (on request; see chapter 7).

The race relations and sex discrimination codes state that an employer's EO policy should be communicated to all employees.

The Access to Medical Reports Act 1988 is relevant where an employer requests a medical report from a medical practitioner in respect of an employee or prospective employee. The individual's consent is needed and the individual can, with exeptions, have access to the report. He or she may veto it, secure amendments to it or have it qualified by an attached statement. The legislation applies where the report is prepared by a medical practitioner responsible for the clinical care of the individual. This will normally be the employee's own GP or specialist. Therefore, it seems unlikely that the Act will apply to reports made by a company's own medical advisers or to a report commissioned by the company from an outside specialist. Actions lie in the county court.

The Access to Health Records Act 1990 came into force on 1 November 1991. It applies to health records held by 'health professionals', which is likely to include company doctors, and gives individuals a right of access, with exceptions, and a right to have records corrected. The legislation applies to health records which are not subject to the provisions of the Data Protection Act 1984.

On the health and safety front employees must have the following:

- Instruction, training and information.[13]
- Information, instruction and training for persons who may be exposed to substances hazardous to health. This would cover details of the risks created by exposure and the precautions to be taken, including the results of any monitoring of exposure and the collective results of any health surveillance.[14]
- Information from a factory inspector where necessary to keep employees or their representatives informed about matters affecting their health, safety or welfare.[15]

Employees will be entitled to various information under statute when they 'wear other hats' for example, when they are pension fund trustees, union officials or shareholders. Moreover, employees also have information rights, indirectly, through their trades union officials. This applies to redundancies, transfers of undertakings, pensions, collective bargaining and health and safety.[16]

Employee involvement

Companies must make a statement in their Annual Reports about employee involvement.[17] However, there is no requirement to actually involve employees. Whether it is collective bargaining, joint consultation, works councils, quality circles, team briefings, employee surveys or employees on the board – all of these are ultimately a matter for the company. In no case is there any legal requirement to involve employees in the running of the organization, although, as already noted, there are indirect requirements via union officials.

What if employee involvement leads to an employee performing a task in connection with their involvement which causes injury or loss to someone else? Is the responsibility the employer's because the employee's legitimate work activity has been widened? Presumably yes. Where safety representatives are involved (for example, in conducting safety surveys), they are expressly excluded from being personally liable if, for instance, they carried out a negligent survey.

Data Protection

Introduction

The processes of recruitment and subsequent employment will have generated a substantial amount of paper, much of it containing personal details of individuals. Two main areas of law operate here. First, the Data Protection Act 1984 covers computerised data, which must be registered. Second, the terms of the contract could probably be used if there was an abuse of personal material held by the organization. Inadequate security of personal data could possibly amount to a breach of the term of mutual trust and confidence (see chapter 2). Special considerations apply to former offenders covered by the Rehabilitation of Offenders Act 1974 and medical reports used during the recruitment process may be subject to the Access to Medical Reports Act 1988.

The Data Protection Act 1984 applies to the 'use of automatically processed information relating to individuals'. The personal data covered include opinions but not intentions. The Act introduces the concepts of data user and data subject. The former is a person who holds data, the latter a person who is the subject of personal data. A data user is within the scope of the Act if:

- the data is part of a collection to be processed by or on behalf of the user;
- he or she controls the content or use of the data;
- data is in a form suitable for processing or reprocessing.

Data users must register under the Act, abide by the Act's principles and ensure that the data held are accurate.

Notwithstanding the above, there are some exemptions. Preparation of the text of documents (such as standard letters) is not within the definition of processing, so names and addresses held for this purpose are exempt. Payroll information need not be registered providing it is the minimum necessary for calculating pay and pensions. The exemption would not extend to personnel data (including absenteeism and disciplinary record). There is also an exemption for accounts or records of transactions providing the information is for payment or management forecasting purposes. Information kept for domestic or personal uses (for example, on a home computer) is also exempt as is information held where there is an overriding question of national security.

Unincorporated members' clubs are exempt providing the members do not object to information being held. Mailing lists are exempt as long as the information does not exceed the minimum necessary and subject to some non-disclosure rules. Statutory information available to the public (for instance industrial tribunal decisions if computerized) are also exempt. Subject access is restricted where access might hamper crime prevention or tax collection. Some relaxation of the limits on disclosure is possible in certain cases, for example, if urgently required for the health and safety of any person; in relation to health and social work activities. Finally, subject access to examination marks will be 40 days or five months from the date of request (whichever is earlier) where the request is made prior to the announcement of the results. Otherwise the normal 40 days applies. The definition of examinations may be wide enough to cover some of the tests used by employers in recruitment and promotion procedures.

Data protection principles

There is a set of data protection principles and the Act gives some guidance on their interpretation: The principles are:

' 1 The information to be contained in personal data shall be obtained, and personal data shall be processed, fairly and lawfully.
2 Personal data shall be held only for one or more specified and lawful purposes.
3 Personal data held for any purpose or purposes shall not be used or disclosed in any manner incompatible with that purpose or those purposes.
4 Personal data held for any purpose or purposes shall be adequate, relevant and not excessive in relation to that purpose or those purposes.
5 Personal data shall be accurate and, where necessary, kept up to date.
6 Personal data held for any purpose or purposes shall not be kept for longer than is necessary for those purposes.
7 An individual shall be entitled:
  (a) at reasonable intervals and without undue delay or expense:
    (i) to be informed by any data user whether he holds personal data of which that individual is the subject; and
    (ii) to access to any such data held by a data user; and
  (b) where appropriate, to have such data corrected or erased.
8 Appropriate security measures shall be taken against unauthorized access to, or alteration, disclosure or destruction of, personal data and against accidental loss or destruction of personal data'.

The last principle applies to computer bureaux as well as to data users. In as much as computer bureaux are also data users, all the principles will apply to them. Principles (1) and (6) will not be breached just because data are held for historical, statistical or research purposes providing that they are not used in ways which cause (or are likely to cause) damage or distress to any data subject.

The Home Secretary may, by statutory instrument to be approved by Parliament, modify the principles to give additional safeguards in respect of the holding of sensitive information such as racial origin, political or religious beliefs, health or sexual life.

Operation of the Act

There is a Data Protection Registrar (DPR) who is responsible for overseeing the legislation, and a Data Protection Tribunal (DP tribunal). DP tribunals comprise a legally-qualified chairman, a representative of data users and a representative of data subjects. They hear appeals by data users from decisions of the DP Registrar.

Data users must register with the Registrar by providing the following details:

- Their name and address.
- A description of the data.
- The purpose (s) for which data are to be held or used.
- A description of the sources of the data.
- A description of any person to whom they may wish to disclose the data.
- The names of any places outside the UK to which the data may be transferred, directly or indirectly.
- One or more addresses for the receipt of requests from data subjects for access to the data.

It is a criminal offence to hold data without being registered or to hold or use data in ways which are not covered by the register entry. Entries may be altered upon application to the Registrar, and additional entries made. The register is available for inspection by members of the public free of charge. A copy may be obtained for a small charge.

The Registrar's role involves a general supervision of the legislation – that is, ensuring its terms are complied with – as well as the handling of specific complaints. He has substantial powers of entry, search and seizure, subject to judicial authorization. In pursuance of his supervisory role, he may issue enforcement, de-registration and transfer prohibition notices as well as initiating criminal prosecutions.

Data users may appeal to a DP tribunal against the Registrar's decision to refuse registration or against any enforcement, de-registration or transfer prohibition notice. An appeal will succeed if the Registrar's decision is not in accordance with the law or, where the Registrar's discretion was exercised, if it should have been exercised differently.

The more serious offences such as holding data when unregistered, or knowing or reckless contravention of any of the particulars contained in a register entry, are subject to proceedings in either magistrates' or Crown courts. In the latter case, fines are unlimited. Other offences, for example failure of a registered person to notify a change of address, are to be heard only in the magistrates' courts (current maximum fine, £2,000), but the new maximum provided for by the Criminal Justice Act 1991 is £5,000 (see above p. 26). Liability may be individual as well as corporate. The former will apply if the offence was committed with the consent or connivance of any director, manager or secretary or was attributable to any neglect on their part.

The Registrar may consider any complaint involving a breach of the Act and must consider any complaint which raises a matter of substance and which is reported to him without undue delay by a person directly affected.

Once registration has been achieved the main effect of the legislation upon employers is likely to derive from requests for access to information by data subjects. The access rights are triggered by a request in writing to the data user, and payment of the appropriate fee, which has a statutory limit. Proof of identity needs to be given. Information must be supplied within 40 days of receipt of request, or within 40 days of proof of identity if later. The information must be accurate and up to date. Data subjects may only have access to data relating to themselves. The data should be intelligible and not identify any third parties without their consent.

A complaint can be made to the Data Protection Registrar or to the civil courts – the county court or High Court – about any contravention of the Act. Such complaints include:

- refusal of request for access;
- the holding of inaccurate information;
- loss of data or unauthorized disclosure.

Orders for access may be given, and compensation for damage suffered as a result of inaccurate information may have to be paid. Inaccuracy applies only to factual data (rather than opinion). Orders for rectification or erasure of data may be made.

Organizational Security

Competition and other work

Where an employee is in competition with their employer they are likely to be in breach of their contractual duty of fidelity and good faith. This duty requires faithful, loyal and honest service on the part of the employee. Being in competition is likely to be a failure to carry out such a duty as would be the making of secret profits out of the employment and the divulging of the employer's confidential information. In addition to the implied duty of fidelity there may be express terms which provide additional protection for the employer. However, if these terms are too widely drawn they may be unenforceable because they are in restraint of trade and therefore contrary to public policy.

Any work done other than for the employer during working hours is likely to be a breach of contract regardless of whether or not it is done in competition with the employer. This would be a breach of the implied term of fidelity. The situation is quite different, however, for jobs done outside working hours. In the absence of an express term to the contrary, an employee is free to do what they like with their spare time providing that the activities do not cause signifiicant harm to the employer (*Hivac Ltd* v. *Park Royal Scientific Instruments Ltd*). They might cause such harm if they materially aided a competitor or adversely affected the employee's own work. It is this question of harm caused to the employer which will determine (in the absence of express restrictions) whether there has been a breach of contract. Soliciting the employer's customers for their own or some third party's benefit is likely to be a breach of the term of fidelity by the employee and dismissal for such activity may be fair.

Express terms may be used to prevent an employee:

- from working for competitors during their employment;
- from conducting preparatory business activities during employment leading to them setting up in competition after termination of their employment;
- from working elsewhere without permission,

although the last of these runs the risk of being unenforceable because it is so widely drawn. However, this would depend on the circumstances of the case. Adding a restrictive term after the commencement of employment without the employee's agreement will probably be a unilateral variation of terms and may amount to a breach of contract. A combination of express terms, of the type mentioned above, and what is known as 'garden leave', may prevent competition until the employment ends. Garden leave is the use of long notice periods where the employee is not required to be at work. (An express term allowing lay-off with pay during the notice period may be of use here.) The employment contract continues and therefore the restrictive express term operates throughout. A similar effect can be achieved by insisting on a fixed-term contract continuing until expiry. Courts may grant injunctions preventing the employee breaching the contract, as in *Evening Standard Co. Ltd* v. *Henderson*, but will award damages instead if they think that the intended restriction upon the employee is less important (see *Provident Financial Group plc* v. *Hayward*). The courts may also refuse to grant injunctions where the employee needs to perform their duties in order to prevent their skills deteriorating.

The danger of employees being in competition may continue after employment. Employers may tackle this problem through restrictive covenants – contract clauses which govern behaviour after employment. In general, such clauses will be in restraint of trade and contrary to public policy unless they can be shown to be reasonable. This means demonstrating that they:

- offer adequate protection, but no more;
- serve the legitimate interests of the employer (*Nordenfelt* v. *Maxim Nordenfelt Guns and Ammunition Co.*).

Legitimate interests means trade secrets or trade connections.
Restrictive covenants may contain the following:

1 Non-competition clauses – restrictions on the ex-employee working for competing businesses including any business the ex-employee may set up themselves. These are designed to protect trade secrets and trade connections.
2 Non-solicitation or non-dealing clauses – these restrain the ex-employee from soliciting or dealing with the company's customers.

It may be possible to have a clause restricting the poaching of employees by a former employee. Such poaching may in any case be tortious if it induces employees to break their contracts of employment, for example, because they have non-competition clauses.

A reasonableness test will be applied to restrictive covenant. This involves judging:

- subject matter coverage;
- geographical area;
- duration.

Non-competition clauses are clearly the most restrictive and employees might argue that a lesser restriction (such as a non-dealing clause) would suffice. Generally, the reasonableness test is to be applied to the facts at the time the clause was introduced. The burden of proof of reasonableness is upon the employer. In drafting such clauses, it should be remembered that contract terms must be certain and unambiguous if they are to be enforceable. However, where there is more than one restrictive clause, and only one clause is too wide to be enforced, the courts may sever the offending clause and enforce the others rather than refuse to enforce the whole. Much depends on whether it is possible in practice, that is, on whether each clause can stand on its own. A restrictive covenant can be part of the contract of employment or a separate, new contract to take effect when employment ends.

Sensitive information

The employee has an implied contractual duty not to disclose to third parties their employer's trade secrets and confidential information. This is part of the duty of fidelity and good faith (*Faccenda Chicken Ltd* v. *Fowler and ors*). Much will depend upon the person's employment, the nature of the information, whether it has been made clear that the information is confidential and whether the information can be easily separated from more generally available information. Information which is part of the employee's know-how or stock-in-trade is unlikely to be regarded as confidential. Express confidentiality clauses are possible and are especially useful in showing what the employer regards as confidential. They may not add much in practice to the implied contractual terms, but may have a deterrent effect. Information which it is in the public interest to disclose will not be confidential even if it damages the employer (for example, tax fiddling) (*Initial Services Ltd* v. *Putterill*).

The implied duty of fidelity applies beyond the termination of employment in relation to trade secrets, but not generally to otherwise confidential information. Thus, ex-employees who retain trade secrets for ulterior purposes can be sued for breach of contract (*Robb* v. *Green*). Where confidential information other than trade secrets has been obtained as a result of a breach of the term of fidelity during employment this may also be subject to protection afterwards. There could be an express clause to deal with release of information after employment. To be enforceable this would need to be restricted to trade secrets and connections.

Company property – unauthorized access; removal; wilful damage

Unauthorized access to, removal of or wilful damage to company property will probably constitute a breach of disciplinary rules as well as a breach of the term of fidelity and good faith in the employment contract. Whether a dismissal for such acts will be fair will depend upon the decision passing the normal unfair dismissal tests of fair reason and reasonableness (see chapter 7). If a case is serious it may well amount to gross misconduct. Rules should state explicitly that access is restricted (for example, to computers or parts of the site) and that property must not be removed, and should indicate if such breaches might constitute gross misconduct or warrant dismissal. All this needs to be communicated clearly to employees. Actions of these sorts by employees may in any case be criminal, so that employers might need to decide whether the police should be notified.

Rules in this area will need to be reasonable as will any other security measures taken to prevent unauthorized access or removal of property. The rules may be strengthened by being laid down at the outset as a condition of employment, so securing consent by the employee. Searches of car boots or other receptacles raise no particular difficulty although they could amount to trespass to goods if damage is caused. Personal searches (for instance by security staff) could constitute battery unless consented to by the employee. Where personal search is established as a condition of employment and a dismissal for non-compliance follows a major question will be whether the rule was reasonable. A relevant issue will be whether such a requirement was a lawful and enforceable term of the contract. In apprehending someone who it is believed has committed or is committing an offence, a security (or any other) person must use force only if resisted and even then only an amount reasonable in the circumstances.

Inventions and intellectual property

Inventions

Prior to the Patents Act 1977 (which relates to employee inventions made on or after 1 June 1978) this area was covered only by common law.

The statutory patents system gives an exclusive right to exploit an invention for a period of up to 20 years. Patents are granted, however, only if the invention:

- is new;
- involves an inventive step;
- is capable of industrial application;
- does not fall into one of the excluded categories (such as scientific theories and computer programmes) which are usually covered by copyright law – see below).

The Patents Act 1977 lays down that an invention will belong to the employer only if:

- it was made in the course of the employee's normal duties or some specially assigned duties; and either
- it might reasonably be expected to result from the carrying out of such duties; or
- the employee had a special obligation to further the employer's interests. (This will be influenced strongly by the employee's status.)

Compensation is payable to employees if the employer benefits from the invention in the ways indicated below. First, if the invention is owned by the *employer*, the employee will be entitled to compensation if they can show that:

- it has been patented;
- it is of outstanding benefit to the employer;
- it is just that they should be compensated.

Where the invention is owned by the *employee*, compensation will be payable if they can show that:

- the invention has been patented;
- they have assigned or exclusively licensed the rights to their employer;
- the benefit to the employee is inadequate when compared with the benefit derived by the employer;
- it is just that compensation be paid over and above the amount agreed for the licence or assignment.

The amount of compensation will be that which will secure a fair share of the benefits having regard to all the circumstances. Contractual arrangements cannot be used to overrule the employee's rights contained in the Act, but an employee is free to grant their employer rights subsequent to the making of the invention.

Intellectual property
This area is subject to the Copyright, Designs and Patents Act 1988 as well as to any contractual arrangements between the parties. The Act covers the following categories:

- Literary work, that is, work which is written, spoken or sung. This includes tables and computer programmes.
- Artistic work, such as graphical work, photographs and sculpture.
- Musical work.
- Dramatic work, such as mime and dance.

Sound recordings, films and broadcasts are included. The general rule is that ownership lies with the employer if the employee creates the work in the course of their employment, that is, it is part of the employee's job to create the work. This rule would not apply, however, where there was a contractual term to the contrary. Such a term might be expressed or implied, including through custom and practice.

Screening and records

Employers in areas exempted from the Rehabilitation of Offenders Act 1974 may seek information about job applicants from the police, courts or government departments. Procedures for such checks are generally regulated by the Home Office or other departments of government. There should be no disclosure of information by any of these bodies (or indeed by private agencies) unless the employer is exempted and makes this clear.

Where employers require job applicants to make a subject access application to police computer records and present the results to them this is likely to be seen as an abuse of the subject access provisions of the DPA 1984. (The law may be changed to prohibit this.) Moreover, police computer records do not, apparently, distinguish between spent and unspent convictions, so the information may be inaccurate or out of date, and so challengeable under the DPA. The information may also not be comprehensive so that its value to an employer might be in doubt. According to the Data Protection Registrar, this whole matter is under review.[18]

Where a company is using a private vetting agency it would be as well to check that if the agency's information is computerized it has been registered with the DP Registrar. The individual subject will have access rights and all the other DP principles will also apply. The individual may claim compensation from the agency for losses and distress if, for example the information is inaccurate, and the DPR may enforce criminal sanctions.

As far as a company's own records are concerned there is no justification for them to include spent convictions unless the employment is excepted from the 1974 Act. Unspent convictions should be regarded as confidential information and employer and employee should make clear who has access. The contractual term of mutual trust and confidence might be invoked where there are breaches.

The criminal law will have a stronger application where an employee has access to official records as part of their job. This would apply to certain people employed in the courts, police service, some government departments and local authorities. Disclosing information about spent convictions to another person except in the course of official duties is a criminal offence. Obtaining such information by means of fraud, dishonesty or bribe is also a criminal offence. In addition, an employee disclosing confidential information may be in breach of fidelity and/or discipline. An employer might be vicariously liable for the actions of the employee who has disclosed the information if the subject of the disclosed information pursues legal action. Important considerations would be the extent to which the employer has properly instructed the employee about confidentiality and generally done all that they can reasonably do to achieve security.

Actions and remedies

As already indicated, restrictive covenants are a useful means of protecting the security of the company against competition, release of confidential information and so on. Ideally, these would be part of terms and conditions from the outset of employment. In some cases, however, it may be necessary to alter the terms of existing staff to include restrictions, and the question of refusal to accept the changed terms might arise. The various matters already considered in respect of changes in terms and conditions of employment (see above, pp. 76–85) would then be relevant. If there is a dismissal, it might be for some other substantial reason. A tribunal would want to know whether the restriction was for a reasonable period, territory and set of activities. Whether other employees had agreed to it might have a bearing on reasonableness as might the existence of past and/or present problems (*R. S. Components Ltd* v. *Irwin*).

Another possibility is to transfer the employee to a part of the organization where he or she does not have access to sensitive information. Again there is a risk of breach of contract through unilateral variation of terms if the transfer is not agreed, but again a fair dismissal might be possible if the transfer is reasonable.

Dismissal is also likely to be seen as a fair response if there is a clear breach of fidelity or of an express restrictive term. Indeed, the actions of the employee might amount to gross misconduct. Where the employee is moonlighting and his work performance deteriorates there may be a possibility of dismissing fairly on grounds of capability. In all cases of dismissal, however, there needs to be proper procedure and overall reasonableness on the part of the employer. Moreover, the employer must make sure that the dismissal itself is not wrongful – that is – in breach of contract. A failure to give due notice or to go through a contractual disciplinary procedure would be wrongful. The importance of this is that where an employer dismisses wrongfully they will not be able to rely on any restrictive covenant. This is because of the general rule of law which prevents a person who breaches a contract from subsequently relying on any of the terms to their own advantage. The payment of wages in lieu of notice may present a problem here since following the Court of Appeal's decision in *Delaney* v. *Staples*, payment in lieu is confirmed as damages for wrongful dismissal. Thus it can be inferred from payment in lieu that dismissal has been wrongful, therefore any restrictive covenant might not apply. It may be possible to overcome this problem by drafting contracts to allow for termination by notice or payment in lieu of notice.

A major question arises where the ex-employee will not be bound by the term of a restrictive covenant. The ex-employer may seek an injunction or damages (or both if the injunction is an interlocutory (that is, interim) one). In deciding whether to grant an interim injunction the courts will apply the balance of convenience test (see above, p. 83) except in extreme cases where the interlocutory hearing effectively disposes of the issue. In such instances the relative merits of the cases will be assessed. The courts will not however order specific performance if it involves compelling an employee to work for an employer, and this is in any case prevented by TULRA.[19] If a restrictive covenant turns out to be unenforceable, there may be a claim on the basis of negligence against any solicitor who drafted it, provided that the six-year time limit for such cases has not expired.

Where the ex-employee is known to have important information and there is a real possibility that they will destroy it before any application for a hearing between the parties can be made, an Anton Piller order might be sought (*Anton Piller KG* v. *Manufacturing Processes Ltd*). This order is granted as a result of an ex parte application and confers a right to enter premises to search for and seize documents or property. To obtain an order it will be necessary to show that:

- there is a very strong prima facie case;
- the potential or actual damage must be very serious;
- the defendants are known to have the information or objects in their possession;
- there is a real possibility that they will destroy them before any application *inter partes*.

There must be proportionality between the perceived threat to the plaintiff's rights and the remedy itself. Orders to allow copies of documents to be taken or to preserve or deliver-up documents are more likely to be granted than an Anton Piller order.

Finally there is the possibility of taking action against third parties. First, anyone inducing a breach of contract commits a tort, so there is the possibility of action in tort against anyone who induces existing employees to break their contracts. This includes the possibility of an injunction to stop the inducement. Second, anyone knowingly receiving information disclosed in breach of contract will be committing a tort and can be proceeded against.

Notes

1 Health and Safety at Work etc. Act, 1974, s. 2(2)(c); COSHH Regulations, SI 1988/1657 (under s. 15 of the Health and Safety at Work etc. Act 1974), Regulation 12.

2 EP(C)A 1978, s. 27.

3 Safety Representatives and Safety Committees Regulations, Regulation 4(2).

4 HSWA, s. 3. See also COSHH, Regulation 3.

5 EA 1988, s. 26. The Social Security (Employment Training: Payments) Order, SI 1988/1409 has been made under this section.
6 Education (Work Experience) Act, 1973 *c.23*.
7 EA 1990, s. 14.
8 Health and Safety (Training for Employment) Regulations, SI 1990/1380.
9 EA 1989, s. 7.
10 SDA 1975, s. 47 as amended by SDA, 1986, s. 4; RRA, 1976, s. 37 as amended by EA 1989, s. 7.
11 EA 1989, s. 8.
12 SI 1990/1380, *op cit.*
13 HSWA, s. 2(2) (c).
14 COSHH, Regulation 12.
15 HSWA, s. 23(8).
16 For example, safety representatives are entitled to information from their employers under Regulation 7 of the SRSC Regulations.
17 Companies Act 1985, s. 234(4) and Schedule 7, as amended by the Companies Act 1989.
18 *Annual Report of the Data Protection Registrar*, London: HMSO, 1989.
19 TULRA 1974, s. 16.

12

Handling an Industrial Tribunal Case

The Industrial Tribunals

Industrial tribunals are statutory judicial bodies. They were first established under the Industrial Training Act of 1964 to hear employers' appeals against levies made by the various training boards that were set up under the Act. Since then the tribunals have been given the task of deciding many other types of disputes, typically those between individual employees and their employers. Unfair dismissal complaints account for the majority of the tribunals' cases. In addition tribunals deal with disputes about whether an employee is receiving the amount of redundancy pay to which they are entitled, claims for equal pay between men and women, time off for union representatives, allegations of race and sex discrimination in the employment field and other issues put within their jurisdiction by various statutes (see chapter 1 for a full list of jurisdictions). Provision was made in 1978 for tribunals to deal with claims for damages for breach of contract in certain cases, but no order has yet been made to activitate this jurisdiction.[1] Since most industrial tribunal cases are complaints of unfair dismissal, this chapter is written as if an unfair dismissal case was being dealt with. Special provisions apply to certain other types of case (such as claims for equal pay for work of equal value and appeals against health and safety notices), and in this respect the questions procedure in race and sex discrimination cases is described briefly.

Tribunals currently operate as a result of the Employment Protection (Consolidation) Act 1978, with most of the procedural detail set out in regulations issued under that Act.[2] Except in rare cases tribunals comprise three people – one from a panel nominated by unions, one from a panel nominated by employers and a legally-qualified chairman. The chairman is appointed by the Lord Chancellor,

(Lord President in Scotland) while the two other members are appointed by the Secretary of State for Employment. Most of the chairmen and all of the lay members are part-time. The purpose of having a combination of lay members and a lawyer is to get a blend of legal knowledge and industrial experience. A majority decision suffices, but in all except a handful of cases the decision is unanimous.

From the parties' point of view, industrial tribunals have a number of advantages over the mainstream courts. Firstly, they are cheaper, since legal representation is not compulsory and so legal fees can be avoided. Furthermore, costs are not normally awarded. Secondly, tribunals are quicker than the courts. About three months is the average time between application and hearing, and most hearings last only a day. Thirdly, the tribunals are easier to use – the paperwork involved in pursuing or defending a case is relatively straightforward. Finally, although legal procedure is used, and there is a degree of formality, the setting and proceedings are less formal than would be experienced in a courtroom. There are for instance, no wigs or gowns, the chairman is not addressed as 'm'lud' or 'your honour' and the parties are not hidden behind bundles tied up with pink ribbons. Nevertheless the parties may find tribunals slow and legalistic when compared with procedures in their own organizations. Moreover, unlike arbitration by ACAS, industrial tribunals' terms of reference do not extend to considering the wider industrial relations aspects of the case.

Procedure Prior to the Main Hearing

Actions prior to a tribunal application

Written statement of reasons for dismissal
An employee has a legal right to request and obtain from their former employer a written statement of the reasons for their dismissal. This right is given to those who had two years' or more continuous employment with their employer prior to termination. The claim for compensation for refusal to give written reasons is usually put on the same application form as the unfair dismissal claim itself, and must be at the Central Office of Industrial Tribunals within three months. The respondent employer has 14 days in which to reply to a request for written reasons. Where there is an unreasonable refusal to comply, or where the particulars of reasons were inadequate or untrue, a tribunal

will make a penalty award of two weeks' pay. The week's pay is gross, and since the right to have written reasons is separate from the right not to be unfairly dismissed there is no percentage deduction for any contributory fault. The award will usually be made at the end of the hearing of the substantive unfair dismissal claim.

The questions procedure in race and sex discrimination cases
These procedures are intended to help a person who thinks that they have been discriminated against obtain information in order to:

- decide whether or not to bring legal proceedings; and
- if legal proceedings are brought, to present the complaint in the most effective way.

There are prescribed forms for this purpose, comprising a question-naire to be completed by the complainant and a form on which the respondent can reply.

The respondent cannot be compelled to reply but a failure to reply within a reasonable period, or an evasive or equivocal reply, allows the tribunal to draw any such inference as is just and equitable, including an inference that the person questioned has discriminated unlawfully. An employer would need to have a reasonable excuse if they are to avoid a tribunal drawing adverse inferences.

If the questionnaire is to be admissible in tribunal proceedings it must be served either before an industrial tribunal application is made or within 21 days of one being received by the industrial tribunal. The time limit may be extended by leave of the industrial tribunal.

The questions procedure applies only to race and sex discrimination cases. Moreover, the use of interrogatories – formal questions put by one party to the other before the hearing, in order to obtain evidence – is not provided for in tribunal procedure.

Application to an industrial tribunal and employer defence

The tribunal process is triggered off by an individual who thinks they have been unfairly dismissed completing an originating application form – known as an IT.1 – and sending it to the Central Office of the Industrial Tribunals (COIT) within three months of the effective date of termination. An application may arrive later than this if it was not reasonably practicable to apply within three months but in practice tribunals enforce the three-months rule quite strictly. For example, an application will not be accepted if the reason for its lateness was a mistake by a professional representative (for example, a solicitor or union official); the denied applicant's remedy would be to sue the representative. The time is measured from the effective date of termination (see chapter 7) and is expressed in calendar months. Thus, if termination is on 30 November, the three months for unfair dismissal claims expires on 28 February, except in leap years when it would expire on 29 February. The date on which an application is received is the date on which it is delivered to COIT (or the Regional Office, ROIT) even if this is not a working day. Absence or illness may mean that it is not reasonably practicable to submit an application within three months, but ignorance of the law will not of itself be justification. More than one application may be made on a single IT.1 form, for instance a complaint of unfair dismissal, a complaint of sex discrimination and so on.

Regardless of whether a request for a written statement of reasons has been made the respondent employer will need to reply to the originating application. A copy of the IT.1 will be sent to them, and a form IT.3 on which the reply can be made. The IT.3 – known as the notice of appearance – should be returned to the specified regional office within 14 days, although in practice the period is often extended. This act secures for the respondent the right to take part in any hearing which might ensue. A copy of the IT.3 is sent to the applicant. The regional office of the industrial tribunals then sets in train the arrangements for a hearing. A brief questionnaire is sent to the parties asking about representation at the hearing, and about the number of witnesses they will be bringing. Finally, the regional office will fix a date for a hearing and notify the parties.

The above description constitutes the minimum of what might happen. There may be more. Firstly, COIT will notify an applicant if it looks as though the case is not within the tribunals' jurisdiction, and indicate that the case may be struck out unless the applicant confirms in writing that they are determined to go ahead. Secondly, the regional chairman may decide that a full hearing of the case should not go ahead until there has been a pre-hearing assessment (PHA). Thirdly, there may be a preliminary matter to determine. An application may be struck out if it not pursued. Also, the tribunals can strike out applications and notices of appearance if they are 'scandalous, frivolous or vexatious'.

ACAS conciliation

The stages of procedure up to the full hearing are summarized in figure 12.1. It can be seen that there is an important role for ACAS. Copies of the papers – the IT.1 and the IT.3 – are sent to the regional office of ACAS. The purpose of this is to allow ACAS to perform its statutory duty, which is to conciliate. The duty is 'to endeavour to promote a settlement of the complaint without its being determined by an industrial tribunal'.[3] The duty to conciliate applies if ACAS is requested to do it by the parties, or in the absence of such a request, if the conciliation officer considers that there is 'a reasonable prospect of success.' Where it is sought by the applicant, and where it is 'practicable', the conciliation officer must try to promote re-employment rather than a cash settlement. ACAS defines conciliation in the way that the process is commonly understood. The essential features are that the outcome (that is, the agreement) is a joint decision of the two parties, the employee and the employer, and that the conciliator does not impose nor even recommend what the particular outcome should be. Nearly all the settlements achieved are in the form of cash compensation rather than re-employment. Because of this it is useful to have some idea of what a tribunal might award (see pp. 316–18 below). It may be more difficult for the respondent to do this calculation, since only the applicant will know the detail of their own losses, and in any case future loss is something of an imponderable. Nevertheless, a rough estimate will inform the bargaining process. If a hearing looks likely any party unfamiliar with tribunals should seek advice on how to proceed.

The tribunal may promulgate the agreed decision (that is, publish it and send it to the parties). Any information conveyed to a conciliation officer is privileged – it cannot be admitted in evidence at the hearing without the permission of the person who communicated it. Moreover, it should be noted that once ACAS has conciliated and an agreed settlement has been reached, the right to pursue the case through to a tribunal hearing is lost. The same is not true if the settlement is agreed without ACAS. The ACAS role can continue until all questions of liability and remedy have been decided (*Courage Take Home Trade Ltd* v. *Keys*). This means that ACAS could be used to conciliate over

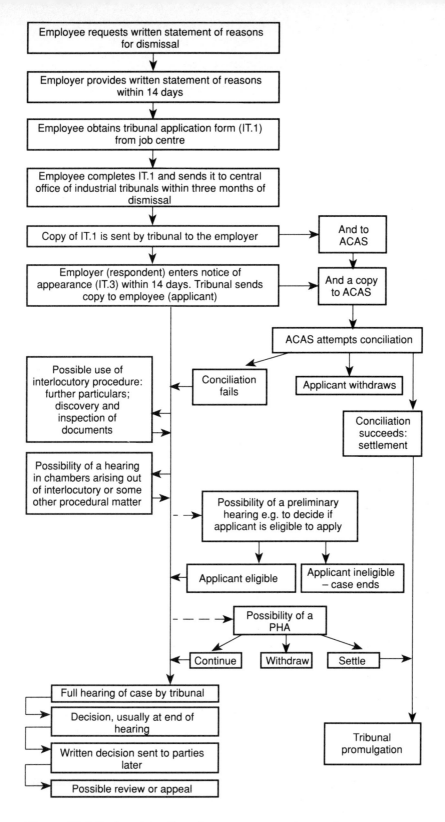

Figure 12.1 Industrial tribunal cases – stages of procedure

compensation if the tribunal decides unfair dismissal but leaves it to the parties to settle compensation.

A settlement (as distinct from a tribunal order of compensation) is not subject to the recoupment regulations,[4] so the applicant does not have to repay any State benefits that they have received (see pp. 316–17). Thus, where State benefits amount to a substantial sum, the potential for agreeing a settlement is increased. A settlement can be made by withdrawal of the application on the agreed terms or by the tribunal recording the agreement and adjourning the case indefinitely. Reporting the settlement to ACAS for them to record is probably the safest way of guaranteeing no further proceedings on the one hand and the honouring of the terms of the agreement on the other. (ACAS may be reluctant to record the settlement (on form COT3) unless they have been involved in settling the case.)

Interlocutory procedure

If there is no PHA and there is no preliminary matter to decide, the parties will not meet the tribunal until the full hearing. They might, however, meet the chairman if there are any procedural difficulties. Such difficulties might arise if the parties choose to implement the interlocutory procedure. This procedure allows the parties to deal with each other, requesting and providing information, and exchanging documents. Ultimately there may be an agreed bundle of documents. In the event of a refusal to co-operate by one of the parties, a tribunal order may be sought by the other. The tribunal regulations allow orders for discovery and inspection of documents, and for further particulars of the grounds of the case. Discovery means finding out what documents the other side is relying upon, while inspection is the right to see one or more of those documents. If the other party refuses, it will be necessary to make out a case to the regional chairman, and a hearing in chambers (the chairman's room) will be held at which his or her decision will be given. The chairman may order discovery and/ or disclosure – it is particularly likely that disclosure will be ordered in sex and race discrimination cases (see p. 39 above). The other members of the tribunal are not present. An industrial tribunal may, of its own volition, ask for further particulars. A failure to supply them may result in the IT.1 or IT.3 being struck out. Otherwise, it is up to the parties to seek further particulars. It will be justifiable only if the other side's grounds are rather sketchy.

The tribunal may also compel witnesses to attend. Application for witness orders is made to the chairman. If the orders are granted they will be sent to the party requesting them and that party will serve them on the witnesses. (The tribunal serves them in Scotland). Failure to abide by tribunal orders is a criminal offence punishable by fine.

Pre-hearing assessment

This device was introduced in order to prevent meritless cases being pursued. It can be requested by either party, or ordered by the chairman of his or her own volition. A PHA involves the full tribunal in a brief, perhaps 30-minute hearing, at which the arguments are put, but little or no evidence is given. The hearing is held in private. The regulations say that the tribunal may consider the IT.1, the IT.3, any representations in writing and any oral argument. If the tribunal considers that a party's case has 'no reasonable prospect of success', it may warn that party of the possibility of costs being awarded against it if it continues. The outcome of a PHA therefore is either a 'costs warning' or no such warning. If the case proceeds, it will be heard by a different tribunal and the PHA outcome will be kept secret until the final decision is made. Costs warnings at PHAs have a powerful effect on withdrawal rate. Nevertheless, the Employment Act 1989 makes provision for regulations which will replace PHAs with pre-hearing reviews with the possibility of a chairman instead of a full tribunal and a requirement for a cash deposit to continue instead of a costs warning. No regulations have yet been issued.

Preliminary hearings

Irrespective of whether or not the case involves a PHA there may be a preliminary matter to settle before a full hearing of the case is considered. Such matters usually concern eligibility:

- Is the applicant an employee?
- Was the IT.1 received in time?
- Has the employee the requisite length of qualifying employment?
- Is the applicant under normal retiring age?

A preliminary hearing, therefore, is held to establish whether or not the case can proceed. If the answer is yes, the substantive hearing will then take place, although usually on a different date.

Preparing the Case

General points

Anyone handling an unfair dismissal case at a tribunal will need the following:

- A knowledge of the statutory provisions on unfair dismissal.
- An understanding of the concept of the contract of employment and knowledge of the contract of employment of the applicant.
- A familiarity with industrial tribunal procedure.
- An awareness of some of the principles established through case law.

Higher courts lay down the rules of approach for the local tribunals through the system of judicial precedent. That may seem a far cry from the original idea of tribunals as a place where the 'ordinary' person could handle their own case. Indeed it is. However, human resource managers are not 'ordinary' persons, so they need not necessarily be put off by the above requirements. For one thing a degree of familiarity with some or all of the requirements is quite likely, either through day-to-day experience or through training. Moreover, gaps can be quickly filled in as the case begins to loom, either by expert advice or by do-it-yourself means. For example case law is the subject of a detailed indexing system that directs a person to the issues relevant to the particular type of case, and there are also summaries of established case law on all the important issues.

Firstly, however, the manager has to make the difficult transition from the world of personnel management to the world of the lawyer. Managers will not be accustomed to a third party, that is, the tribunal, controlling the proceedings and dictating what can be said and when. More importantly perhaps, they will find it difficult to adjust to the fact that evidence (that is, proof) rather than argument or bargaining power is going to decide the case. In preparation, therefore, a party must ask itself:

- Have I got a case? (not on humanitarian or equitable grounds, but in terms of the statute).
- Have I got the evidence, or can I get the evidence, to establish that case? As noted earlier, the test of proof is the balance of probabilities, not 'beyond all reasonable doubt' as in the criminal courts.

The answer needs to be yes in both cases.

A point to be checked even earlier, however, is whether the case falls within the jurisdiction of the industrial tribunals: is the issue in dispute one which industrial tribunals are empowered to decide? If it is, the next thing to check is whether there is any bar to the applicant pursuing their case, for example, insufficient continuous employment. The onus of proof on preliminary matters of eligibilty will lie with the applicant. A case may not proceed, therefore, simply because the applicant cannot prove their eligibility.

It would be unwise for a respondent employer to depend exclusively on the failure of the applicant to establish their eligibility. Thus in a complaint of unfair dismissal an employer should have arguments and evidence to show that any dismissal was fair, even if the preliminary question of eligibility has to be determined first. Indeed, as a generality, it is permissible (and often desirable) to plead in the alternative. Essentially, this means having your cake and eating it. For example: 'Our case is that the applicant was not dismissed – rather, he walked out, thus resigning. However if it was a dismissal, it was fair because of the applicant's misconduct.'

Representation

This is the next issue to be decided. The parties may represent themselves or be represented by a person of their own choosing. Because legal representation is not compulsory, legal fees can be avoided. Legal advice is available under the Legal Aid and Advice Scheme, but legal aid (including representation) is not. In a large company there may be clear procedures with the case being handled by in-house solicitors. It may be that outside solicitors are used, or that one of the industrial relations staff will handle the case. In small firms there will not be an in-house specialist, so it will fall to a proprietor or general manager, unless an outside solicitor is preferred. The applicant has a ready-made advocate if he is a union member because many full-time officers, and some lay officials, are experienced in handling tribunal cases. The non-unionist will perhaps use a law centre, or the local Citizens' Advice Bureau, or may even hire a private solicitor. Free legal advice and assistance in completing the IT.1 may be available depending on income, but legal aid is not, so representation at the hearing is not covered (but see p. 25 above in relation to race and sex discrimination cases).

The preparation of a case is extremely time-consuming. The advantage of a solicitor is that they not only save you preparation time, but also, if that solicitor is familiar with employment law and tribunals, you have an experienced representative. On the other hand the cost is high, especially when compared with the likely level of compensation that the respondent might have to pay. If a representative is named on the IT.1 or IT.3 all the documents (including the notice of hearing) will go to the representative, and not to anyone else (that is, not to the applicant or respondent).

Evidence

The filling of the forms – the IT.1 and the IT.3 – requires some care, since these are in effect part of the evidence. An employer has to set out the grounds of their defence. Too vague an answer here might attract a request for further particulars from the other party under the interlocutory procedure mentioned earlier. On the other hand too much information may help the other party prepare their case. Completion of the forms and the writing of any letters should be handled by the representative, who should also insist on having the ACAS conciliator deal with them rather than with the respondent in person.

It falls on the representative to consider in detail what evidence can be marshalled. The evidence will comprise witnesses on oath or affirmation, and documents. A witness can read a prepared statement on oath. The written signed statement of a witness not present will count for less because they are not under oath, and cannot be cross-examined. The representative needs to ask themselves:

- What facts do I need to establish?
- Which documents and witnesses do I need to establish them?

The representative should be clear as to the role of each witness, including the respondent, or document. What am I expecting this person to prove? What does this document prove? The fact needs to be considered that when witnesses are under cross-examination they are at the mercy of the other party. Any witness who might not stand up to hostile treatment may be better omitted. So too might any witness who will clearly not come across as credible. The credibility of witnesses is important, especially where there is a conflict of evidence.

Witnesses will need to be interviewed by the representative in advance so that the main lines of their evidence can be agreed. Choice of witnesses and the sequence in which they appear is a matter for each party. However, because reasonableness has to be decided with reference to what was known (or should have been known) at the time of dismissal, the person who carried out the dismissal will be a key witness, and the tribunal may prefer to hear his or her evidence at an early stage. Witness orders may be obtained as described earlier. Often they are used by applicants if their witnesses are still in the employment of the respondent. Witnesses may stay throughout the proceedings in England and Wales (but not in Scotland), although a party may ask for a witness to be excluded until they give their evidence.

The best type of evidence is that provided directly by a witness under oath or affirmation. Where documentary evidence is provided, the original (as well as copies) should be available and the author of the document should be there to confirm its legitimacy and his or her authorship. A set of documents should be provided for the other party, for the witness stand and for the tribunal (that is, five copies). The best practice is to exchange sets beforehand, or better still to agree a common, properly paginated bundle. In most cases, however, the paperwork is minimal. Where documents are hand-written (for instance the notes of a meeting) a typed transcript should be provided in addition to the original.

Video and audio tapes are not automatically inadmissible. This is a matter of discretion for the tribunal. There would have to be a transcript for an audio tape and the tribunal might need expert evidence to show that the tape had not been interfered with. Any expert witness fees would have to be paid by the party engaging the witness. The other party would need to hear any tape and have the transcript prior to the hearing.

The flowchart (figure 12.2) poses the questions that representatives need to ask themselves. It can be seen that a constructive dismissal follows a different route from the normal two-stage process. Here the test is breach of contract. A constructive dismissal is not necessarily unfair however. There may have been compelling reasons (such as the state of the business) for the employer being in breach. Thus refusal to be flexible and carry out tasks not within the contract may nevertheless constitute a fair dismissal if the business has its back to the wall.

Sources of information

As already noted, a representative will need knowledge of the law of unfair dismissal, an understanding of the contract of employment and

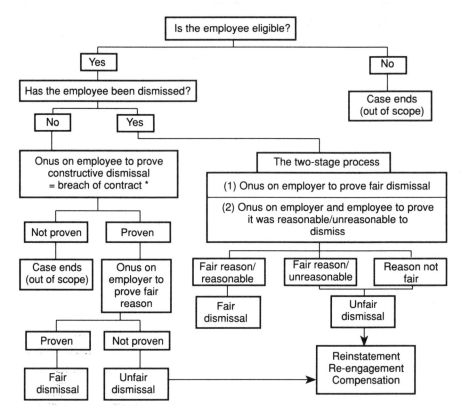

* *Western Excavating (ECC) Ltd* v. *Sharp* [1978] IRLR 27.

Figure 12.2 Unfair dismissal cases before industrial tribunals

some familiarity with tribunal procedure and the principles established by case law. As far as the legislation is concerned it is probably unnecessary to go to the primary source, the Employment Protection (Consolidation) Act 1978, and busy practitioners may find secondary sources both easier and quicker to use. Employment law books have a chapter or more on unfair dismissal, and the book by Anderman is devoted entirely to the subject.[5] For those who want the statute itself it can be purchased through HMSO or found in a bound volume of 1978 Acts of Parliament (chapter 44) in a central library. It should be noted, however, that the copy purchased, or inspected in the library, will be the statute as originally enacted. In the case of the law on unfair dismissal the fair reasons in section 57(1) and (2) have remained unaltered, but the test of reasonableness in section 57(3) and various other parts of the legislation have been amended. Hence it will be necessary to look at an up-to-date secondary source, or at one of the employment law encyclopaedias containing updated statutes.

The main sources which will help the practitioner understand the concept of the contract of employment will be secondary. Employment law books deal at length with the subject. In preparing the case however, it is also necessary to look at the primary materials. Representatives should always ask themselves, and try to answer, the following question.

● What were the terms of the dismissed employee's contract?

This is especially important if the dismissal has been in any way to do with a refusal to obey instructions or accept changes. The following are some of the primary materials which may throw light on the terms of contract:

● Any advertisement for the post.
● Any particulars sent to would-be applicants on enquiry.
● Any letters, for example, appointment, and acceptance.
● Any conditions laid down on an application form.
● Any written particulars issued under section 1 of the EP(C)A 1978.
● Any works or office rules. These may be issued in the form of handbooks, memos or even notices attached to walls, boards or clocks.
● Any job description.
● Collective agreements.

It is important to consider whether the operation of any rules has been overtaken by custom and practice, and what evidence can be adduced on this point.

The busy practitioner might find it diffficult to take time off in order to sit-in at a tribunal hearing. If they can do this, however, they will be rewarded, since they will get an idea of the procedure, and an indication of the atmosphere. Tribunals, like courts, are open to members of the public, and prior arrangement with the tribunal office is not necessary. In practice, however, a phone call to check that there is a hearing scheduled for that day is sensible. The tribunals are listed under 'Tribunals, Industrial' in local telephone directories. The booklet ITL.1 is compulsory if not compulsive reading. Applicants should be given one when they are handed their IT.1, and respondents should receive one through the post with their IT.3. This is as much detail as is necessary, although employment law books are also a source, and in addition there are books specifically about tribunal procedure.[6] The primary source of procedure is the Industrial Tribunal Regulations, a statutory instrument issued in 1985.[7] This can be purchased from HMSO, or found in the bound volumes of statutory instruments in central libraries.

For case law it is probably best to use one or both of the Industrial Relations Legal Information Bulletin (IRLIB) or Incomes Data Services (IDS) Brief. These are fully indexed by name of case and subject and are available on a subscription basis or in central libraries. Both are issued twice a month. In addition to giving brief reports on major cases they also cover any changes in the statutes, and provide useful summaries of case law on key issues. Where necessary the fuller law reports may be used. A principal series is the Industrial Relations Law Reports (IRLR) which is monthly, and can be subscribed to or found in central libraries. Pages are numbered continuously throughout each calendar year, and references are written [1986] IRLR 148 to mean page 148 of the 1986 reports. Other series are the Industrial Cases Reports (ICR) and the more general Weekly Law Reports (WLR) and All England Reports (All ER).

Presenting the Case

Procedure

Legal procedure is used. This means that the representative will proceed by examining witnesses (asking them questions). Each witness is examined firstly by the representative of the party for whom they, the witness, are appearing. Then they will be examined by the representative of the other 'side' (that is, cross-examined). At this stage the tribunal may well ask some questions. Finally, the witness may be re-examined by the representative of their own side. Tribunals have some discretion about procedure, but the typical hearing tends to follow a well-established pattern:

1 Brief introduction by chairman. This will state the parties, and any representatives, the burden of proof and the relevant legislation.
2 The respondent's case (if dismissal is not disputed – if it is, the applicant's case will come first):
  (a) short opening statement – this is not a legal right following changes in the regulations in 1980 and may be discouraged;
  (b) the calling of witnesses. Each witness undergoes:
    (i) examination-in-chief – from the respondent's representative;

    (ii) cross-examination – from the applicant's representative;
    (iii) re-examination – by the respondent's representative.
3 The applicant's case. As above. The applicant is likely to be a witness.
4 Closing addresses:
   ● applicant's representative;
   ● respondent's representative.
5 Tribunal adjourns.
6 Tribunal announces its decision.

After cross-examination the tribunal may ask questions, although technically the responsibility for bringing out the facts and arguments lies with the parties. The purpose of re-examination is to enable the representative to deal with points arising out of the cross-examination. It is not an opportunity to introduce new evidence or arguments. Such attempts will either be blocked by the chairman or result in the other side being given another chance of cross-examination. More generally it will be difficult to spring new arguments at the tribunal hearing without someone raising the question of why they were not put in the original claim or original defence. Any significant documents sprung on the other party at the hearing are likely to cause objections. If there is a resulting adjournment costs could be awarded. Tribunals will expect documents to have been exchanged beforehand, and to be put in as evidence with sufficient copies (see p. 307 above).

The essential features of the law of unfair dismissal were described in chapter 7 and the two-stage process emphasized. Now it must be noted, however, that the hearing does not follow this pattern. Instead, each witness is examined on all matters to bring out the evidence in its entirety. The only exception is likely to be the question of remedies. A chairman should indicate at the start of the hearing whether he wants to hear evidence on remedies, or whether this will be heard separately, and only if the finding is one of unfair dismissal (*Smith* v. *Clarke*). Evidence on any contributory fault is taken with the main stream of evidence. Parties should take their evidence on remedies (for example, the applicant's attempts at mitigating loss, local unemployment, pay in any new employment or the respondent's ability to reinstate) to the first tribunal hearing in case the issue is dealt with at that hearing.

As already noted, certain types of cases are governed by different procedures. Equal value claims, for example, are subject to a procedure which may involve a job evaluation expert preparing a report for the tribunal. Appeals by employers against improvement and prohibition notices (under the HSWA), against non-discrimination notices issued by the EOC and CRE, and against training levies, also have different procedures. In health and safety notice appeals the employer is the appellant and the inspector the respondent. In appeals against discrimination notices, the CRE or EOC is the respondent.

Normally hearings are held in public, that is, members of the public may observe and listen to the proceedings without any requirement to seek permission or give notice of attending. Hearings may be held in private, for example where the interests of national security dictate, or if a public hearing might damage the respondent's business other than by the adverse publicity of being involved in an industrial tribunal case.

Marshalling the evidence and arguments

Functioning effectively at the hearing requires the representative to be highly-organized. A useful device is to have paper with the pages divided in half vertically. Questions for each witness can be entered in the left half, and answers in the right half. For one's own witnesses most of the questions can be written in advance, as can some of the questions for the opposition, especially if it is known in advance who their witnesses will be. The structure of the questions and answers should follow the tribunal's procedure for each witness *viz*: evidence-in-chief, cross-examination, tribunal questions and re-examination.

Giving evidence includes the right to present and read a signed, written statement. Written evidence (documents) in addition to any witness statement may also be admitted. Evidence submitted by the respondent is marked R1, R2, R3, and so on, and by the applicant A1, A2, A3 and so on. Such documents should include any that set out the terms and conditions of employment, details of pay and other benefits, including pension, in the job from which the applicant was dismissed, and any subsequent job(s), and evidence of State benefits paid during any unemployment following dismissal. The applicant will need to give evidence of job search and should take copies of job applications and replies. Details of the costs of searching for a new job, or moving to a new job will be needed. When the respondent's last witness has been examined the applicant's case is put, and follows the same procedure. Finally, the parties have a right to sum up. The respondent, having the onus of proof, goes last. Summing up means succinctly putting the essential legal arguments and an evaluation of the evidence upon which those arguments rest, as well as trying to play down the significance of the other party's arguments and evidence. The tribunal will appreciate any attempts at clarifying the issues and evidence on the key points of the case. Finally, the tribunal should be asked to find in your favour.

It is common for parties who are represented to cite authorities, that is, cases judged by the higher courts which decide principles and approaches as well as the facts of the particular case. The purpose is to persuade a tribunal that higher authorities have decided on an approach which you consider will help your case. Tribunals are a little defensive about criticism that they are unduly legalistic. Some chairmen may positively discourage the citing of cases as the EAT President did in *Anandarajah* v. *Lord Chancellor's Department*, and the Court of Appeal did in *British Gas Corporation* v. *Woodroffe*. None will encourage it unless it is genuinely helpful and all will get irritated by a long closing statement punctuated by numerous case references. Against this background, having photocopies of the reports of cases, in order to save the tribunal the trouble of looking them up in the law reports, may be politic.

It should be noted that a failure to challenge the evidence of an opposition witness during cross-examination will mean that that evidence is established. Thus, a good representative will ensure that all points of disagreement are brought out during cross-examination. Moreover, all allegations need to be put in cross-examination. This may occasionally mean that the representative's own witness can 'adopt' the previous cross-examination if it covers all of the evidence which has to be put. This reduces the time spent on evidence-in-chief which would otherwise be highly repetitive. Another time-saving device is for a witness to be 'tendered', that is, offered up for cross-examination without giving evidence-in-chief. This might be done where the evidence of the witness would merely be repeating that already put by someone else. The right to re-examine remains. One witness may also simply confirm the testimony of another.

Costs

The normal legal rule under which the loser pays the victor's costs does not apply. Costs will be awarded only if a party acts frivolously (pursues a hopeless case), vexatiously (pursues a case in order to inconvenience the other party) or behaves unreasonably in some other way. The last-mentioned may include unreasonably causing postponements or adjournments. It is usual for tribunals to themselves determine the amount of any award of costs rather than referring the matter to the county court for taxation, which would be slower and less responsive to the ability to pay of the party. Appeals can be made against the award of costs but an appeal solely against the amount would be unlikely to succeed.

After the Hearing

The decision

The tribunal will adjourn to make its decision. In most cases it will return to announce the decision and its reasons later the same day. Sometimes, if a lot of evidence has been given, or if there are complex legal issues, the decision might be reserved (that is, not announced). In both types of situation a written decision will be sent to the parties later. As a result of the 1985 tribunal regulations decisions may be 'in summary form' except in certain types of case (such as discrimination), although the parties still have a right to request full reasons. Such a request can be made orally at the hearing or in writing within 21 days of the date on the tribunal's written summary decision. In the decision, the two-stage process mentioned earlier (that is fair reason, reasonableness) will be discernible.

Reviews

A tribunal may review its decision if there is a written request for a review within 14 days of the date of the tribunal's written decision, and the request is accompanied by reasons. The circumstances in which a tribunal may conduct a review are:

- if an error on the part of the tribunal staff caused a wrong decision;
- if a party did not receive notice of hearing;
- if a person entitled to attend did not attend;
- if new, unforeseen evidence has become available;
- if the interests of justice require it.

Where a chairman believes a review has no reasonable prospect of success they may refuse the application for review. The decision to conduct a review, however, is made by the EAT.

Appeals

By contrast appeals are to a higher body – the Employment Appeal Tribunal – and in most types of case must be on a point of law. (See above, p. 254 for details of one type of case where an appeal can be on fact or law.) Once an industrial tribunal has decided a fact, that fact can no longer be disputed. A point of law means in essence that the tribunal's approach to some matter was wrong. For example, it may not have followed higher authority on some point, or it came to a conclusion which was perverse in the sense that no reasonable tribunal could have arrived at it on the evidence available. 'Perverse' means that the decision made by the tribunal was not a permissible option because:

- it was based upon a finding of fact unsupported by any evidence; or
- the tribunal clearly mis-directed itself in law.
  (*Piggott Bros and Co. Ltd* v. *Jackson and ors*).

The chairman's handwritten notes are typed and forwarded to the EAT when there is an appeal. Where an appeal is being launched on the basis that no reasonable tribunal could have come to such a decision on the evidence before it an appellant will need to request notes of evidence. An appeal must be made within 42 days of the date of the tribunal's decision with full reasons. Thus it is necessary to obtain full rather than summary reasons from the tribunal, and forward them to EAT.

Employer appeals against decisions in respect of health and safety notices lie with the 'divisional court' of the Queen's Bench Division (See above, pp. 12–13).

Enforcement

In the typical case the industrial tribunal decision marks the end of the legal process. For a few applicants, however, the process will be extended by action necessary to ensure the respondent complies with the tribunal's compensation award. The tribunals cannot enforce their own awards, so it is necessary to apply to the county court for an order, and ultimately the court will take steps to obtain settlement as with any normal debt.

Interest on industrial tribunal awards

An order which became operative on 1 April 1990 lays down rules for the payment of interest on industrial tribunal awards.[8] Interest is payable when awards remain unpaid 42 or more days after the tribunal decision is promulgated. Costs, expenses, recouped amounts, national insurance and tax are excluded from the calculations for interest purposes. Interest also applies to the awards made by higher courts, for example, the Employment Appeal Tribunal, Court of Appeal and so on. In the case of an appeal or review the commencement date for the calculation of interest is unaffected. The same is true where the amount of the award is varied on appeal. Where an appeal body decision is the first award made, the 42 days applies from the time of that decision. Interest is calculated on a simple and day-to-day basis at the current Bank of England base rate. Awards made before 1 April 1990 but unpaid by that date will be treated as if they were made on that date.

Worked Example of Unfair Dismissal Compensation

Details

1 Gross weekly earnings – £210
2 Net weekly earnings – £150
3 Time between dismissal and hearing – 30 weeks of which:
   (a) the first 20 weeks unemployed, receiving £50 per week in State benefits;
   (b) the following 10 weeks employed with net earnings of £140 per week.
4 The applicant's age is 55 years.
5 Length of continuous employment prior to dismissal is six full years.
6 There is no claim for any additional or special award.

Basic award

There is 1½ weeks' pay for each year of employment in the age category 41 years and over, so the basic award will be $6 \times 1\frac{1}{2} = 9$ weeks' pay. Gross earnings, excluding non-contractual overtime, are taken, but there is a statutory maximum, currently £205. The calculation, therefore, is $9 \times £205 = £1,845$.

Compensatory award

This is in addition to the basic award.

1 Net earnings were £150 per week.
2 In the 30 weeks upto the hearing the applicant would have earned $30 \times £150 = £4,500$.

3 Against this has to be set net earnings of £140 per week for the 10 weeks in which the applicant was in a new job = £1,400.

Any wages in lieu of notice in respect of the former job would have to be added to this (*Babcock FATA Ltd* v. *Addison*).

4 Net loss of earnings = £4,500 – £1,400 = £3,100.

5 Add to this £150 for loss of statutory rights, for example the loss of a right to claim a statutory redundancy payment in the next two years. (The most recent EAT decision on this was £100 in 1986: *S. H. Muffett Ltd* v. *Head*).

6 Add any expenses in looking for or travelling to new work (assume £50).

7 Add any future losses that the tribunal accepts (say, 20 weeks×£10 = £200: the applicant is £10 per week worse off in his or her current job).

The compensatory award is therefore £3,500.

From this, the State will recoup benefits paid for 20 weeks×£50 = £1,000, leaving a net payment of £2,500.

Format of tribunal decision on compensation

1 *Monetary award*
£3,500 plus the basic award of £1,845 = £5,345.

2 *Prescribed element*
This will exclude the basic award and those parts of the compensatory award not relating to the period of the prescribed element, that is, items (5) and (7) above and £100 (10 weeks × (£150 – £140)) from item (4) = £3,050.

3 *Period of the prescribed element*
This is the period of 20 weeks between termination and the start of new employment that is, the period during which State benefits were received.

4 *The excess of (1) over (2)*
Thus £2,295 will be payable immediately while £3,050 must be withheld until the State has recouped £1,000 from it. Had the parties settled the compensatory award between themselves in the range £2,500–£3,500 they would have both benefited at the State's expense. As it is, the respondent has to pay the full compensatory award of £3,500, while the applicant receives only £2,500.

Reduction of the compensatory award

Tribunals should reduce the compensatory award if they find that the dismissal was to any extent caused or contributed to by any action of the complainant. This may be a factor in misconduct and capability cases but will rarely apply to ill-health dismissals. The amount of the reduction should be what the tribunal considers just and equitable. An employer can rely only on information held by them at the time of the dismissal. However, there is a more general provision for the compensatory award to be what the tribunal considers just and equitable in all the circumstances, having regard to the loss sustained by the applicant as a result of the dismissal. This would allow for a reduction for conduct discovered, or even taking place, after the dismissal, as well as for a failure to mitigate losses.

Pension loss

A formula for calculating this is set out in a document produced by the industrial tribunal chairmen in consultation with the Government Actuary's Department.[9] It has no statutory force but provides useful guidance.

Notes

1 EP(C)A, s. 131. The government has announced that new legislation will be introduced. (See *People, Jobs and Opportunity*, p. 17).
2 Industrial Tribunals (Rules of Procedure) Regulations, SI 1985/16.
3 EP(C)A, s. 134(1).
4 Employment Protection (Recoupment of Unemployment Benefit and Supplementary Benefit) Regulations, SI 1977/674, as amended by SI 1980/1608 and 1988/419.
5 Anderman, S., *The Law of Unfair Dismissal*, 2nd edition, Butterworths, 1985.
6 For example, Goodman, M., *Industrial Tribunals: Practice and Procedure*, Sweet & Maxwell, 4th edition, 1987.
7 Industrial Tribunals (Rules of Procedure) Regulations, SI 1985/16.
8 Industrial Tribunals (Interest) Order, SI 1990/479.
9 *Industrial Tribunals : Compensation for Loss of Pension Rights*, London : HMSO, 1990.

Index

Index prepared by Patricia Baker